Praise for *Elements of Christian Thought*

"Rarely does a theologian blend deep scholarship with accessible, engaging, and relatable language in a way that communicates the nuance and depth of theology while also demonstrating the relevance and importance of age-old questions for contemporary life. Rogers does this with humor, authenticity and skill. His love for not only his subject, but his students illuminates this book. I look forward to using this resource in my local church context, for small group classes, leader training and personal study."
    —Jill Duffield, senior pastor, First Presbyterian Church, Greensboro, NC

"No one has made Christian theology as exciting for me (a lapsed Catholic who identifies as an atheist) as Gene Rogers has. In his supple hands, what so often seems to be merely lame and authoritarian dogma becomes a living tradition; its debates become as fascinating and urgent as matters of US Supreme Court jurisprudence. *Elements of Christian Thought* presents itself as a vocabulary lesson in 'Christianese,' and it is that. But it also teaches its readers the essential skill of distinguishing better theology from worse theology, and readers from all backgrounds will profit from his efforts in this book to minimize the anti-Jewish, sexist, and racist strains in Christian thinking."
    —Martin Kavka, Florida State University

"Concise, fresh, and very smart, Gene Roger's textbook lets beginning students in on what is too often a carefully guarded secret: Christian theology is one of the most fascinating subjects anyone can study."
    —R. Kendall Soulen, professor of systematic theology, Emory University;
    and author of *The Divine Name(s) and the Holy Trinity*

"Many teachers are good at conveying content and describing what other people think. Few have the gift of inviting students to think alongside the teacher him- or herself. Eugene Rogers belongs to this second group. His *Elements of Christian Thought* shows its readers how they may better 'speak Christian' and enter the church's centuries-long conversation over the gospel."
    —Joseph Mangina, professor of theology, Wycliffe College, Toronto

"Could one wish for a more provocative and generative introduction to and outline of Christian theology? In these pages, you are in the hands of one of Christianity's most creative living theologians and one of our best teachers. Here, Rogers is characteristically analytical and grammatical, yet he also writes as a lover of language and thought, a lover committed to depicting the Christian grammar not as a suffocating unified mode of speech but as space within which passionate, illuminating disagreement can occur. Rogers writes, too, as a reader—his well-stocked and omnivorous mind is on full display, as he draws on a delightfully variegated range of Christian and

Jewish sources, from Michael Wyschogrod to Thomas Aquinas to Thomas Jefferson. If you are a Christian, this splendid book will help you better speak as one—and if you are not a Christian, it will, since knowing how those who occupy a mode of life speak is a crucial means of understanding them, help you know Christians better."
—Lauren F. Winner, Duke Divinity School

"I have waited for this book for twenty years, since I sat in the introductory course upon which it is based, and yet the book managed to surprise me in the same way that Eugene Rogers insists the well-traveled doctrines of the Christian faith still can. Rogers artfully transports his reader into a classroom in which one is given at least three answers to any question, an approach to teaching tradition that empowers imagination for new ways of speaking the Christianity that Rogers insists is a language. Whether used as an exemplary approach to teaching Christian theology for doctoral students, the very backbone of a course for undergraduates, or as a reminder that Christian theology (and its pedagogy) can be a delight, *Elements of Christian Thought* is a gift that will change the way you think, speak, and live. Start reading it now."
—Rev. Sarah Jobe, prison chaplain, Interfaith Prison Ministry for Women; prison educator, Duke University Divinity School; and author of *Creating with God: The Holy, Confusing Blessedness of Pregnancy*

"These lectures have been legendary among undergraduates for decades and here they are, finally, for the public. For insiders and outsiders alike, this book offers a unique, elegant, and deeply learned path into understanding the Christian tradition."
—Willis Jenkins, Hollingsworth Professor of Ethics, University of Virginia; chair of the department of religious studies; and co-director of the Coastal Futures Conservatory

"Rogers is one of the true masters of the craft of teaching theology. Here, in his inimitable style, he guides us into the rich texture of 'a language in which to disagree.' This is the book we didn't even realize we were waiting for. But we were."
—Anthony Baker, professor of systematic theology, Seminary of the Southwest in Austin, Texas; and author of *Shakespeare, Theology, and the Unstaged God*

"*Elements of Christian Thought* not only teaches readers how to 'speak Christian' but how to *think* in Christian terms as well. Through reflection upon the central intellectual puzzles of the Christian tradition, Rogers' deeply incarnational theology speaks to the myriad dimensions of our full humanity. This engaging and inspiring book is a vital resource for both Christian theologians and non-Christian readers alike, helping all of us to think and live in more faithful, hopeful, and loving ways with one another."
—Willie Young, professor of religion and philosophy, Endicott College

"With extraordinary acuity, considerable humor, and remarkable grace, Gene Rogers takes us through the most central teachings of historic Christianity in a way quite different from what we are used to hearing from academic theologians. His book is refreshing (though part of that is that it should make each of us squirm a little), and I can't wait to try teaching with it."

—Rev. Dr. R. Guy Erwin, president, United Lutheran Seminary; and former bishop, Evangelical Lutheran Church in America

"If you are looking for a serious but accessible introduction to Christian Theology, look no further. Rogers dives deep into the waters of theology and surfaces with questions and topics that are timeless and timely. A great book for ecclesial group-reading and classroom teaching as well as for individual edification!"

—Serene Jones, president, Union Theological Seminary

"The idea of Christianese is a compelling way to introduce students to the words and frames of thought which have shaped the Christian faith across centuries. In this work, Rogers gets to the heart of the matter that people tell you what they believe and those words create fields of vision often more vast than simple attention to doctrines. In these time in which religious belief is so often reduced to performance, it is refreshing to be reminded that language can offer paths of understanding which set the religious imagination free."

—Stephen G. Ray Jr., president, Chicago Theological Seminary

"All of us who teach theology are always looking for a single book that introduces students not only to Christian thought but also to the ways Christians think their faith. Our search can pause for now here at Eugene Roger's wonderful text. I know of no book that displays a cultural linguistic approach to teaching doctrine more creatively and beautifully than what this brilliant and rightly celebrated theologian has given us. I and my students will be thanking him for many years to come."

—Willie James Jennings, Yale University

"Perhaps you are a Christian, perhaps not. Either way, you must have been puzzled by some of the strange things Christians say—about faith and reason, love and justice, divine and human freedom, a Triune God, evil, sin, and salvation, death and resurrection. If you haven't been puzzled, perhaps you should have been. Christians have been debating the meaning of their central commitments for many centuries while also exercising massive power in the world. Eugene Rogers knows this language as well as anyone and his new book lays it out with maximal clarity and grace."

—Jeffrey Stout, author of *Democracy and Tradition*

"In *Elements of Christian Thought*, Gene Rogers teaches his students a language, 'Christianese,' so that he can draw them into a conversation. What makes this book extraordinary is that Rogers doesn't merely tell the reader what such a conversation is like. He shows them. And the conversation that unfolds—living and lively, suffused with a winsome theological vision—actually empowers his students to respond."

—Sean Larsen, visiting professor, Marquette University;
and managing editor, *Syndicate*

17-41

OCT 9/10 — 109-119

Elements of Christian Thought

Elements of Christian Thought

A Basic Course in Christianese

Eugene F. Rogers Jr.

FORTRESS PRESS

MINNEAPOLIS

For Derek,
bel compagno in quarantine and in life,
who understands the dangers of Christian-speak better than I

Contents

Why You Should Read This Book   xi

Why You Should Not Read This Book   xiii

What Theologians Talk About   xv

Preface   xvii

Acknowledgments   xix

Christianity Is a Language in Which to Disagree

1. Jefferson and Lewis Disagree on the Elements of Christian Thought   3

2. The Study of Religion Is like the Study of a Language   9

Christians Talk about Election, or How God Chooses

3. Wyschogrod Talks about God Choosing the People Israel   17

4. Calvin Talks about God Choosing Individuals for God's Purpose   23

5. Barth Talks about God Choosing Humanity in Jesus   31

Christians Talk about Incarnation, or God Chooses Humanity

6. Athanasius Talks about a God Who Becomes a Human Being   45

7. Tanner Refuses to Talk about Human and Divine as Rivals   49

Christians Talk about Atonement, or God Chooses the Lost

8. Athanasius Talks about God Becoming Human to Make Humans Divine   57

9. Anselm Talks about Christ Paying a Debt of Honor   63

10. Abelard Talks about Christ Teaching Love by Word and Example   69

11. Excursus: Protestants Talk about Anselm and Abelard to Debate Punishment   73

12. Ray Talks about the Community around a Dead Body   83

13. Julian of Norwich Talks about Sin as a Wound   87

14. Balthasar Talks about Christ Emptying Hell   95

Christians Talk about the Trinity, or Love Stronger Than Death

15. Christians Ought to Talk about the Trinity Joining Them to Itself   109

Christians Talk about God Enabling Difference in Creation and Freedom

16. Barth Talks about the Trinity Enabling Creation   123

17. Augustine Talks about God's Freedom Empowering
    Human Freedom   127

Christians Talk about God's Body Absorbing Evil

18. Chesterton Talks about God Drinking a Cup of Suffering   143

19. Trible Almost Talks about God in the Victim of Sin   149

Christians Talk about God's Body in Resurrection and Eucharist

20. Williams Talks about Your Victim as Your Hope   155

21. Christians Talk as if Breaking the Wafer Opens the Trinity   161

Christians Talk about Human Bodies in Sex and Slavery

22. Williams Talks about God Desiring Humans as If They Were God   167

23. Stringfellow Talking about Slavery Shows How Not to Interpret
    the Bible   173

Christians Talk about Salvation in Many Ways

24. Harvey and Tillich: Body or Soul?   181

25. Barth and Chrysostom: Faith or Works?   187

26. Cone and Schmemann: Heaven or Earth?   191

    Appendix: Objections to the Cultural-Linguistic Approach   195

A Syllabus in Theses with Readings   203

General Index   213

Scripture Index   219

Why You Should Read This Book

1. You want to know how Christians can talk about God as three, different ways they talk about how Jesus saves, how they talk about God permitting evil, how they talk about what God does about it, how they talk about God and death, how they talk about God and sex, or what they mean when they say "salvation," anyway.
2. You think of Christianity as being like a language that you'd like to understand or maybe speak better.
3. It's a good first book about Christian thought, designed to be informative to those who know little.
4. It's a good advanced book about Christian thought, designed to be interesting and even surprising to those who know a lot.
5. It's designed for students of Christian thought both inside and outside Christianity, since both insiders and outsiders want to study how Christian language works.
6. The interlocutors are great! We engage with the greatest hits in Christian thought.
7. You want to engage with classic old stuff, like Augustine and Calvin.
8. You want to engage with the latest new stuff, published in July.
9. It's part of the liberal education envisioned by Thomas Jefferson that citizens should know about religion, as we can see from his letters.
10. Students in the underlying course sometimes ranked it as the best class they took in college.
11. Instructors will find that the twenty-six sections divide well into a twelve- to fourteen-week semester, whereas the ten parts divide well into a ten-week trimester.
12. The language analogy allows the book to work both in secular departments of religious studies and in seminaries or divinity schools—or for independent readers who want to understand what Christians are on about, whether they believe it or not.
13. The lack of textbook paraphernalia makes the book friendly to independent readers.

Why You Should Not Read This Book

1. You think of it as Sunday school.
2. You know it all already because you or your friends went to church.
3. You're not interested in sex, death, or evil.
4. You're afraid thinking is incompatible with Christianity.
5. You like sermons or devotions better than reasoning and arguments.
6. You don't like surprises.
7. You don't like questions and puzzles.
8. You prefer a historical rather than a topical approach.
9. You don't want to read medium-length extracts from the greatest hits of Christian thought, people like Athanasius, Augustine, Anselm, Abelard, Aquinas, Julian of Norwich, Calvin, and Barth—or from twentieth- and twenty-first-century thinkers like Paul Tillich, Kathryn (Kathy) Tanner, Phyllis Trible, or Stephen Ray.

What Theologians Talk About

You will never be tested on these, but we will talk about them for the whole book.

Mock *True or False*

1. If the human being had not sinned, Jesus would not have come.
2. Jesus could have come as a woman.
3. God should have become incarnate at the beginning.
4. The God of the Christians intends other religions.
5. O happy fault, that merited so great a Redeemer!
6. The ability not to sin is freer than the ability to sin.
7. God has died.

Mock *Multiple Choice*

1. How does God's freedom relate to ours?
    - a. The freer God is, the less free I am.
    - b. The freer God is, the freer I am.
2. The word of God is
    - a. the sermon,
    - b. Jesus, or
    - c. the Bible.
3. Jesus saves because
    - a. he pays the debt for sin,
    - b. he teaches humans how to love,
    - c. he defeats death,
    - d. he tricks the devil at his own game,
    - e. the Spirit gathers others around his body, or
    - f. he releases the prisoners of hell.
4. The "debt for sin" is owed to
    - a. the devil,
    - b. God the Father, or
    - c. your neighbor.
5. Salvation is
    - a. freedom from sin,
    - b. joining the Trinity,
    - c. perfect community, or
    - d. resurrection of the body.

6. Does God have a body?
    a. No, silly, God doesn't have a body.
    b. God has a body in Jesus.
    c. God has a body in the church.
    d. God has a body in the bread.

Preface

This book began as a one-semester undergraduate course almost thirty years ago. Because it was only one semester and intended for undergraduates, I thought of it privately as my baby systematics course. I have only taught it in the secular religious studies departments of public universities. It began and matured at the University of Virginia (1993–2005), where I took over the name Elements of Christian Thought from Julian Hartt, and continued with simplifications and greater breadth of shorter readings at the University of North Carolina at Greensboro (2005-), where I usually teach it twice in the fall semester, and sometimes both fall and spring. In those contexts, I taught it like a language course: Christianese is a language you can learn, whether you believe it or not—one in which Christians have developed the ability to test their views and disagree with one another—one in which, they believe, the face of Jesus becomes legible over time and in the course of controversy. Even with the frequent leaves with which both universities have blessed me, I have taught it some forty times. If you have ever heard the analogies and anecdotes that fall out of teachers' mouths when students' eyes glaze over, that should be warning enough; to such emergency instruction, I have nurtured other faults from one semester to the next and perfected them by repetition.[1]

In the spring of 2020, the coronavirus pandemic (COVID-19) forced classes online shortly after the halfway mark. Because students were scattering to situations in which they would have much less control of their time—changing jobs, handling childcare, caring for the illness of others, and, as it happened, at least two students from that class recovering from the virus—I thought I would write up the lectures as closely as possible to the way I would have delivered them aloud. My husband observed (as he has before) that I was writing a book. At the end of the semester, not knowing how many future semesters the virus would disrupt, I thought it wise to use my momentum, return to the beginning, and keep transcribing the lectures that I ran in my head. I call it my minimum opus.

Although the book would work well in a class—the twenty-six sections track a twice-a-week series of lectures for a fourteen-week semester with time for two tests—I never taught the class with a textbook but with a sourcebook of readings from primary texts: Athanasius, Chrysostom, Augustine, Anselm, Aquinas, Abelard, Julian of Norwich, Calvin, Thomas Jefferson, Chesterton, Barth, Tillich, Schmemann, Michael Wyschogrod, Phyllis Trible, James Cone, Jeffrey Stout, Susan Harvey, Kathy Tanner, Stephen Ray, and others. (At the back, "A Syllabus in Theses with Readings" ties those sources to the chapters and provides a template for

---

1 I riff on Stanley Hauerwas, *Character and the Christian Life* (San Antonio: Trinity University Press, 1975), vii.

independent, distanced, or face-to-face students.) The book conducts disputes among primary sources from Jewish, Catholic, Orthodox, and Protestant traditions, usually in dialogue with others, so that there are three views of election, six views of atonement, six views of salvation, and so on. In a single-semester course without a sequel, I favored diversity of views over breadth of topics. For that reason, some topics may seem to be missing—but you can find them. The discussion of election implies views about the church; Tillich on salvation covers justification. Most of the readings have stood the test of time; they are not popular religion but texts that belong to the expanding canon taught in universities and in seminaries with close ties to universities. In some cases, the dialogue remains implicit because I avoid views that may be familiar from Sunday school. As I told students who complained for that very reason, if you heard it in Sunday school—with the single exception of Anselm—it probably isn't on the syllabus.

Many students had fled the universities with little sense of how the semester would unfold and even (unaccountably!) without their books, as well as with less easy access to shared household computers over dodgy internet. So I turned the readings into interlocutors that they—and you—could encounter either within these pages alone or, if you like, by reading the primary texts for yourselves. Each section is meant to be self-contained enough to make sense on its own, and there are none (I hope!) of what I think of as the boring encumbrances of the textbook genre: no study guides, no teacher's manual, no exhaustive coverage, few to no carefully parsed statements designed to offend and satisfy no one. Rather, I was typing as quickly as possible, trying to resist looking things up, because I discovered it took about four times as long to write up a lecture as it did to speak it—not least because I had no eyes to look into and see if the light had dawned. I hope that readers will find the spontaneity and relative absence of ass covering an advantage.

It was in trying to make section titles parallel that I experienced the greatest conflict of genre. I feel as a teacher that the best titles are complete sentences, and I crave as a student of theology to proceed *thesenhaft*, in theses. But I entertain the title theses with varying degrees of commitment. Some are my own view, and some are the views of others that I use to set up a view that I prefer. I hope that the exposition will show what a title, even in a complete sentence, is too short to reveal. A classroom allows for greater slippage and variety of tone. The table of contents also conveys a lot of "talk." The practices of Christianity do of course go far beyond talk. But a lot of talk is what you would hope for in a language class. Finally, I am aware that when the chapter titles speak of "Christians," they might as well speak of "theologians." My comparison of theologians to highly practiced native informants is seriously meant, but it's a bit of a conceit, like Aquinas's use of Aristotle. Sometimes you catch a twinkle in his eye.

I have hundreds if not thousands of students to thank for the inventiveness their questions inspired, and for the failures of that inventiveness, I have to thank only myself.

Acknowledgments

Among those students, I wish to thank in particular Sarah Jobe, Joseph Naron, Raquel Dawkins, and Joseph Duffield, as well as those who prompted better explanations because they failed to understand, and even those who provoked explanations because they failed to read. I wish to thank my editor at Fortress Press, Will Bergkamp, who said that my reply to his query of eight years earlier was the latest he had ever received. It wasn't: I had answered at the time to say no. I wish to thank also the readers for Fortress Press who had faith that something so informal could make a book, as well as Kendall Soulen and Joe Mangina, who read the whole manuscript.

Eugene F. Rogers Jr., "Theology in the Curriculum of a Secular Religious Studies Department," *CrossCurrents* 56 (2006): 364–74, which is now the appendix, is used with permission.

Spencer, Stanley (1891-1959) © ARS, NY. *The Resurrection, Cookham.* 1924-27. Oil paint on canvas, 2743 x 5486 mm. Acquisition Presented by Lord Duveen 1927. Artist's © Copyright Tate.

Christianity Is a Language in Which to Disagree

1 Jefferson and Lewis Disagree on the Elements of Christian Thought

Two thinkers beloved of laypeople and students of religion—Thomas Jefferson and C. S. Lewis—disagree on what the elements of Christianese might be. We will be investigating, as a cultural anthropologist might, the reasons many Christians consider central the very beliefs Jefferson found dispensable. Our native informants are called theologians.[1]

Thomas Jefferson (1743–1826) wrote to one William Short from Monticello, April 13, 1820:

> Dear Sir
>
> Your favor of Mar. 27. is received, and my granddaughter Ellen has undertaken to copy the Syllabus, which will therefore be inclosed. It was originally written to Dr. Rush. On his death, fearing that the inquisition of the public might get hold of it, I asked the return of it from the family, which they kindly complied with. At the request of another friend, I had given him a copy. He lent it to his friend to read, who copied it, and in a few months it appeared in the theological magazine of London. Happily that repository is scarcely known in this country; and the Syllabus therefore is still a secret, and in your hands I am sure it will continue so.
>
>   But while this Syllabus is meant to place the character of Jesus in it's [sic] true and high light, as no imposter himself, but a great Reformer of the Hebrew code of religion, it is not to be understood that I am with him in all his doctrines. I am a Materialist. . . .[2]

Now, "syllabus" doesn't mean that Jefferson is teaching a course. He uses it in a broader, eighteenth-century meaning of a list of topics, especially a list of religious theses, like the theses that make up the table of contents of this book.

---

1 Clifford Geertz, "Thick Description," "Religion as a Cultural System," and "Ethos and Worldview," in *The Interpretation of Cultures* (New York: Basic Books, 1973), 3–30, 87–141. Note esp. 14n1 and 15n2, where theology can be regarded as a higher-order native model. For more, see the appendix.
2 The reading for the course was Thomas Jefferson, *Jefferson's Extracts from the Gospels: "The Philosophy of Jesus" and "The Life and Morals of Jesus,"* ed. Dickinson W. Adams and Ruth W. Lester, The Papers of Thomas Jefferson (Princeton, NJ: Princeton University Press, 1983), 401–2, 405–6, 391n3; here, 391. Further references during the discussion of Jefferson will be by page number in the text. To see all the interlocutory texts aligned with their chapters, consult the syllabus at the back.

He also wrote to Jared Sparks on November 4, 1820:

> Sir
>
> Your favor of Sep. 18. is just received, with the book accompanying it. . . . Being just setting out on a journey I have time only to look over the summary of contents. In this I see nothing in which I am likely to differ materially from you. I hold the precepts of Jesus, as delivered from himself, to be the most pure, benevolent, and sublime which have ever been preached to man. I adhere to the principles of the first age; and consider all subsequent innovations as corruptions of his religion, having no foundation in what came from him. The metaphisical [sic] insanities of Athanasius, of Loyola, and of Calvin, are to my understanding mere relapses into polytheism, differing from paganism only by being more unintelligible. The religion of Jesus is founded on the Unity of God, and this principle chiefly, gave it triumph over the rabble of heathen gods then acknowledged. . . . If the freedom of religion, guaranteed to us by law *in theory*, can ever rise *in practice* from under the overbearing inquisition of public opinion, truth will prevail over fanaticism, and the genuine doctrines of Jesus, so long perverted by his pseudopriests, will again be restored in their original purity. This reformation will advance with the other improvements of the human mind but too late for me to witness it. (401–2)

Finally, he wrote to Benjamin Waterhouse on June 26, 1822:

> I have received and read with thankfulness and pleasure your denunciation of the abuses of tobacco and wine. Yet however sound in it's [sic] principles, I expect it will be but a sermon to the wind. You will find it as difficult to inculcate these sanative precepts on the sensualists of the present day, as to convince an Athanasian that there is but one God. I wish success to both attempts, and am happy to learn from you that the latter, at least, is making progress, and the more rapidly in proportion as our Platonising Christians make more stir and noise about it. [What follows is, I take it, Jefferson's secret "syllabus."]
>   The doctrines of Jesus are simple, and tend all to the happiness of man.
>
> 1. that there is one God, and he all-perfect:
> 2. that there is a future state of rewards and punishments:
> 3. that to love God with all thy heart, and thy neighbor as thyself, is the sum of religion.
>
>   These are the great points on which he endeavored to reform the religion of the Jews. But compare with them the demoralising dogmas of Calvin.

1. that there are three Gods:
2. that good works, or the love of our neighbor are nothing:
3. that Faith is every thing; and the more incomprehensible the proposition, the more merit in it's [sic] faith:
4. that Reason in religion is of unlawful use:
5. that God, from the beginning, elected certain individuals to be saved, and certain others to be damned; and that no crimes of the former can damn them, no virtues of the latter save.

Now which of these is the true and charitable Christian? He who believes and acts on the simple doctrines of Jesus? or the impious dogmatists of Athanasius and Calvin? Verily, I say, these are the false shepherds, foretold as to enter, not by the door into the sheep-fold, but to climb up some other way [John 10:1]. They are mere Usurpers of the Christian name, teaching a Counter-religion, made up of the deliria of crazy imaginations, as foreign from Christianity as is that of Mahomet. Their blasphemies have driven thinking men into infidelity, who have too hastily rejected the supposed Author himself with the horrors so falsely imputed to him. Had the doctrines of Jesus been preached always as purely as they came from his lips, the whole civilized world would now have been Christian. I rejoice that in this blessed country of free enquiry and belief, which has surrendered it's [sic] creed and conscience to neither kings nor priests, the genuine doctrine of one only God is reviving, and I trust that a young man now living in the US. [sic] who will not die an Unitarian. (405–6)

That then is the "syllabus," in the sense of a list of propositions or elements, framing Christian thought, according to Thomas Jefferson, author of the Declaration of the Independence of the United States, founder of the University of Virginia, and author of the Virginia Statute for Religious Freedom. His syllabus and its elements differ markedly from those of another student of Christian thought, C. S. Lewis, who wrote instead,

What are we to make of Jesus Christ? . . . On the one hand you have got the almost generally admitted depth and sanity of his moral teaching, which is not very seriously questioned, even by those who are opposed to Christianity. In fact, I find when I am arguing with very anti-God people that they rather make a point of saying, "I am entirely in favor of the moral teaching of Christianity"—and there seems to be a general agreement that in the teaching of this Man and of His immediate followers, moral truth is exhibited at its purest and best. It is not sloppy idealism, it is full of wisdom and shrewdness. The whole thing is realistic, fresh to the highest degree, the product of a sane mind. That is one phenomenon.

The other phenomenon is the quite appalling nature of this Man's theological remarks. You all know what I mean, and I want to stress the point that the appalling claim which this Man seems to be making is not merely made at one moment of his career. There is of course, the one moment which led to his execution. . . . [Lewis, speaking extemporaneously on the radio, here puts words on the lips of Jesus that do not appear in the Gospels.] What on earth would you say if someone had done *you* out of £5 and I said, "That is all right, I forgive him"? . . .

Well, that is the other side. On the one side, clear, definite moral teaching. On the other, claims which, if not true, are those of a megalomaniac. . . . If you had gone to Mohammed and asked, "Are you Allah?" he would first have rent his clothes and then cut your head off. If you had asked Confucius, "Are you Heaven?" I think he would probably have replied, "Remarks which are not in accordance with nature are in bad taste." The idea of a great moral teacher saying what Christ said [better: what the theological tradition has made of the Gospels] is out of the question. In my opinion, the only person who can say that sort of thing is either God or a complete lunatic suffering from that form of delusion which undermines the whole mind of man. If you think you are a poached egg when you are looking for a piece of toast to suit you, you may be sane, but if you think you are God, there is no chance for you.

We may note in passing that He was never regarded as a mere moral teacher. He did not produce that effect on any of the people who actually met Him. He produced mainly three effects—Hatred—Terror—Adoration. There was no trace of people expressing mild approval.[3]

Now, Jefferson could never have read Lewis, and it's unlikely that Lewis ever read Jefferson's letters. But the clash between them is remarkable. It's clear that Jefferson would regard Lewis as one of those "false shepherds" and "pseudopriests." And it's equally clear that Lewis would regard Jefferson as one of those "very anti-God people." Students of Christianity disagree on what the elements of Christian thought might be.

We are going to read the very figures that Jefferson derides as thieves, heretics, usurpers, blasphemers, and impostors, including Calvin and Athanasius. The elements of Christian thought are topics on which to disagree, and Christianity is a language in which to conduct that series of disputes. Christians such as Rowan Williams treat the Holy Spirit as the conductor of such disputes, in which the hidden face of Christ may slowly come to be revealed.

---

3 The reading for the course was C. S. Lewis, "What Are We to Make of Jesus Christ?," in *The Joyful Christian: 127 Readings from C. S. Lewis* (New York: Macmillan, 1977), 72–74. Subsequent references to Lewis by page number in the text.

They disagree, and yet they disagree within a common language, which we may call "Christian-speak" or "Christianese." If they did *not* have a common language, it would be difficult to tell that they were actually disagreeing rather than just careening past one another. How is it that a book about the elements of Christian thought emerges from someone who has always been educated in departments of religious studies and has almost always taught in public, secular universities? It happens because . . .

2 The Study of Religion Is like the Study of a Language

Native speakers can speak it badly, and nonnative speakers can speak it well. In this book, we will be considering well-formed samples of Christian-speak. The insights of both "insiders" and "outsiders" are necessary to teach us what's going on. The late twentieth and early twenty-first centuries offer five ways of relating Christian-speak to common language.

Approaches to Studying Religion

Religious studies departments began to appear in the United States in 1948. Since then, two views have dominated their teaching of religious thought (as opposed to its history). Especially in Catholic, evangelical, and traditionally denominational colleges, religious studies departments first tried to reproduce the disciplines represented in seminaries and divinity schools. This led to a "propositionalist" approach, which treated various sentences as true, corresponding to reality. It did well in teaching doctrinal Christian theology, but except in a few cases it did poorly in representing other religions. Examples include Catholic manual theology before Vatican II, evangelical apologetics on the model of science textbooks, and Tibetan Buddhist philosophy at the University of Virginia. By the 1960s, the propositionalist approach was largely in retreat because other religions fit poorly within the Christian theological model—and it was unpopular with students.

Its successor was what George Lindbeck called the "experiential-expressivist" approach.[1] Always popular, that approach assumed religious expression arose out of religious experience. There were two branches depending on your view of the underlying religious experience. The more popular branch held that all religious experience was underlyingly the same and only came to different expressions. Another sectarian approach held that you had to have a particular sectarian experience in order to have the proper religious expression. The trouble was that both views did a disservice to non-Christian religions. That was obvious in the sectarian case: unless you had had a particular Christian experience of being born again or of Catholic Mass, you would never be able to understand the expressions

---

1 An appropriate reading would be George Lindbeck, *Nature of Doctrine* (London: SPCK, 1984), 30–42, 73–88.

of that experience. Therefore, religion without the experience was unteachable, and university classes were pointless. Better to go away and join a cult in order to get some experience.

But the opposite assumption—the nonsectarian assumption that all experience was underlyingly alike—developed a similar problem. If all religious experience was alike, then all religious expression was reducible, and religious differences were finally unimportant. And all religions were reducible to (of course) Christianity. Real scholars of Judaism, Buddhism, Hinduism, and Islam bridled at the notion that quietly Christian categories could explain the experience of their adherents. Students sometimes began to suspect that they would like to learn about real differences instead of iterations of the same. By the twenty-first century, intersections with race and gender studies suggested that in experiential-expressivism, the universal religious experience worked like the universal "man": it *washed out* real differences among Muslims and Buddhists, as it made them crypto- or even failed Christians, just as the universal "man" washed out women, queer people, and people of color as secret or even failed men. In that way, experiential-expressivism turned out once again to render different religious experiences unteachable and university classes pointless. As Hegel might have diagnosed it, it was the night in which all cows are black.

The solution, according to Lindbeck, was to teach religion as a cultural-linguistic system—that is, like a natural language. You can learn a language without becoming an adherent of a national group. It can take years, but people do it all the time. It helps to go to France to learn French, but you don't have to become a French citizen. It's not a betrayal of your English to learn Russian; you don't have to become a Russian spy. And learning a language is all about appreciating differences. Religion, like language, is eminently teachable. You don't have to join it to get it.

And in learning the language, you benefit from both native and nonnative interlocutors. Native speakers, obviously, have native competence, but we all know that some native speakers can speak a language badly, and some nonnative speakers can speak it well. We all know that some native speakers are hopeless teachers, and some nonnative speakers excel. Joseph Conrad, the famous novelist, grew up speaking Polish but wrote in Nobel-worthy English. The best English grammar was written by Otto Jespersen, a Dane. I'm a native speaker of English, but I was stumped when someone buttonholed me on a corner in Cairo to explain the difference between a "road" and a "street." This was before smartphones, so I couldn't just google it. I agreed there was a difference—we weren't standing on a road; we were standing on a street. But then why was it *called* Something Road? When, weeks later, I got back to the *Oxford English Dictionary*, I looked up the words you would have thought I knew. It turned out that a "street" is defined by its edges—usually buildings. And a "road" is defined by its end points, often towns. In Greensboro, North Carolina, High Point Road leads to High Point, North Carolina. And in High Point, Greensboro Road leads to Greensboro. They are the same road, and at some point between the two towns, the name switches over. For much of its length, High Point Road is bordered by buildings and certainly counts as a street. A native speaker wouldn't notice that. It takes a nonnative speaker to raise the question.

In this book, we study samples of excellent Christian-speak to gain skill in understanding or deploying Christian language.

Now, *excellent* is a loaded word. When the headings and the table of contents repeat the phrase "How Christians Talk about X," I'm not describing the whole population of the baptized. Nor do I mean Christians in Sunday school. I mean professionally trained teachers of Christian thought in departments of religious studies and theology departments of university divinity schools and of seminaries that share students or libraries with universities. So "How Christians Talk about X" includes plenty of variety and lots of disagreement, but it means disagreement in the academy, not in the pews. Not that you couldn't disagree in those ways in the pews or in the public square. I'd like to see such reasoned disagreement spread.

Skill is a loaded word too. I help myself to the trope of grammatical "correctness." That's appropriate because Christianity has always been a religion that inculcates certain mental as well as physical practices, practices that amount to "Say it like this." I don't mean to reduce Christian theology to questions of rules or grammar. "Grammar" is a useful trope for certain purposes, like identifying heresy or teaching learners, and it works well in religious studies departments, secular colleges, and public universities, as well as churches, seminaries, and divinity schools. But almost everyone who speaks "Christianese" learns it without a "grammatical" approach, and my other theological books proceed in first-order Christianese and use the trope of grammar rarely if at all.

Skill in Christianese matters also because fragments of Christianese underwrite political and other public arguments in society, whether you agree with those bits of Christian speech or not. Even with churchgoing in decline, there is scarcely any issue on which (fortunately or unfortunately) baptized voters could not prevail if only they agreed among themselves. More immediately, as I said, the study of Christianity needs both native and nonnative speakers to work well.

For objections to this approach, see the appendix.

Types of Christianese

Hans Frei (1922–88) identified five types of Christian theology in the modern period (that is, since Kant). Jeffrey Stout (b. 1950) recasts Frei's five types as five "languages."[2] Consider them five dialects of Christianese. All language textbooks focus on a particular dialect of their language: Modern Standard Arabic, Levantine

---

2 The reading for the course was Jeffrey Stout, "Five Types of Christian Theology," a section in "Hans Frei and Anselmian Theology," in *Ten Year Commemoration to Hans Frei*, ed. Giorgy Olegovich (New York: Semenenko Foundation, 1999), 30–32.

Arabic, Egyptian Arabic; when I was in Jerusalem, I studied the local Levantine Arabic. Which dialect of Christianese comes to the fore here?

All dialects of Christianese seek to do justice to a predecessor language, the language of the Bible (as if it were one thing); Christianity is a strange offshoot of Judaism, in which its speakers claim to speak of "one God" even as they say that God is three, "Father," "Son," and "Holy Spirit." Christianese has also received influences from Greek, Latin, and German philosophy. Stout charts its dialects by the ways in which they manage the encounter of "biblical language" with "common language."

One approach Stout calls "Esperanto." It seeks to be universal. An example would be *Religion within the Bounds of Reason Alone* by Immanuel Kant (1743–1826). You chuck out of Christianese anything that does not accord with "reason," and you ignore the fact that what counts as reason might change over time or according to human difference.

A second approach Stout calls "Presentese." It attempts to make Christianity relevant to the "present." An example would be Gordon Kaufmann (1925–2011), who taught at Harvard for over thirty years. You admit that what counts as reasonable changes over time, and you chuck out what no longer fits now.

A third approach Stout calls "dialogical." It tries to let culture ask questions and Christianity provide answers, and sometimes the other way around. An example would be Paul Tillich (1886–1965). You don't set the priority in advance, but you seek the best fit.

The fourth approach Stout calls "Anselmian." He takes its name from the dictum of Anselm of Canterbury (1033/34–1109) that theology is "faith seeking understanding." Examples include not only Anselm but Karl Barth (1886–1968). So you start with "biblical language" *and its internal problems and conflicts,* and you attempt to solve those problems with whatever works, taking in "outside" categories not systematically but ad hoc, like a mechanic in Cuba keeping a beautiful old car in the best possible condition by using whatever comes to hand. But because the goal is *understanding,* or *logos,* which involves conformity to God's Logos, or Reason, these pages show a consistent bias toward reason formed by love.

The fifth approach Stout calls "segregationist." Like experiential-expressivism of the sectarian sort, this approach seeks to immerse the outsider in Christian language *alone,* cutting it off from other ways of speaking without recourse. The usual example—often disputed—is the "vulgar Wittgensteinian" D. Z. Phillips (1934–2006).

The approach adopted in this book is the fourth, the Anselmian approach. It mirrors the development of a natural language. Except for Esperanto, which has no native speakers, languages do not reform themselves by reason, purge themselves in the present, subject themselves to prolonged bilingual dialogues, or segregate themselves from others. They are constantly taking what they need to keep themselves in the best running condition.

This does not mean the Anselmian approach is apologetic in the sense of trying to bring the outsider onto the insider's ground. Rather, it assumes, with Barth's book on Anselm,[3] that the insider and the outsider have a desire, the same desire: they seek to understand. They therefore occupy the same ground and pursue the same quest. The Anselmian approach does not seek to convert in the sense of modern apologetics. It seeks rather the joy of understanding. Whether the joy of understanding is also *attractive* depends on the nature of its Object, which lies beyond all human language.

This approach, which owes much to George Lindbeck (1923–2018) and Kathy Tanner (b. 1957), is not *merely* descriptive linguistics but also able to distinguish better uses of language by also describing the language's "grammar." Because Christianity polices its mental and linguistic practices and puts forth approved religious speech in the form of creeds, liturgies, hymns, and the biblical and theological texts to which it appeals in teaching and dispute, it is possible to distinguish "better" and "worse" examples of Christianese in terms of "grammar," somewhat as in teaching natural languages. Grammar matters in teaching a language whether you teach it by paradigm or by example, whether your linguistic approach is prescriptive or descriptive. Here are some examples of bad grammar widespread in Christianity that the best texts nevertheless seek to avoid, dispute, and root out: referring to Jews as "superseded," referring to the natures of Christ or the persons of the Trinity as "parts," referring to grace and freedom as rivals, accounting for evil as something with a reality of its own, or talking about atonement in a way that makes it hard to distinguish between God and the devil.

---

3 Karl Barth, *Fides Quaerens Intellectum: Anselm's Proof for the Existence of God in the Context of His Theological Scheme* (London: SCM, 1960).

Christians Talk about Election, or How God Chooses

3 Wyschogrod Talks about God Choosing the People Israel

The "language" that Christians speak (as well as the language of the rabbis) developed out of one first spoken by Jews. Central to this Jewish "language" is the concept of chosenness, or election. Christians (and Jews and Muslims) speak of a God who makes particular choices. This is a case in which it is useful for a learner to hear speakers of a related language.

Jews and Christians both speak of a character in their Scriptures who exists beyond the world and yet acts within it, whom they call God. The hallmark of these languages is that they posit a character, God, who acts differently from creatures. This character is different in two ways. First, God is different from each human being in that God is not under our control, certainly not our pet, or even trained pet, who responds to polite requests in prayer, like "Fetch!" In that way of being different, God is a bit like other people. But this character is also different from other people. Because God created the world, God can work on the world from the inside, bringing each creature to do its own thing, working most intimately to do what is most its own. With humans, we[1] speak of this internal activity of God as moving the heart. When God moves the heart of things and brings them to do their ownmost, their most individual thing, we say that God is founding the freedom of that thing. Other humans can't do that for one another, except rarely in deep love: in that case, the Spirit would be using them as channels for grace. To break the habit of thinking that "God" is the name of a servant, I open with the perhaps offensive notion that both Jews and Christians speak of God as "choosing" or "electing"[2] people for specific service or witness. In the Hebrew Bible (which Christians call the Old Testament and Jews call Tanakh), Israel is God's "chosen people" and God "calls" the prophets; in the New Testament, Jesus "calls" or chooses his disciples, and the Greek word for the church, *ekklesia*, is a word for those called out of a larger group. Whatever you think of this notion, it's a massive feature of the texts.

Furthermore, it's useful, at the beginning of a book on Christianity, to start with a version of election that *decenters* Christian expectations of their own chosenness and centrality. Michael Wyschogrod (1928–2015) was an Orthodox Jewish student of

---

1 I try to be careful with "we" language. Here I use "we" language not to indicate Christian hegemony but to teach a language, like the "we" in "For 'how are you?' we say, '¿Cómo está Usted?'"

2 The word *election* in this context does not refer to voting. *Election* just means "choice." The one whom God elects is the prophet, nation, or king that God chooses. In the Holy Roman Empire, the emperor was chosen by noblemen called "electors," and in the United States, the president is officially chosen not by popular vote but by the "electors," for whom the people vote in each state.

Christianity. He wrote a dissertation on Kierkegaard and for years led the National Association of Christians and Jews. (He was also the husband of the philosopher Edith Wyschogrod.) His article "Israel, the Church, and Election" is an exercise in Jewish, not Christian, theology: a Jewish author is explaining to Jewish readers what it means for them that the Catholic Church, at Vatican II, has renounced the idea that Christians "replace" or "supersede" Jews. So he's not writing *for* Christians or *to* Christians; he's writing *about* Christians for Jews.[3] Because he's talking *about* Christians, many Christian readers assume he's writing *to* them; because he has studied Christianity and speaks accurately about its history and about Paul, they assume that he *is* Christian, and therefore those readers get mad because they expect him to have a Christian view about election, and of course he doesn't. Many readers object, in short, that Wyschogrod is being a bad Christian. He's not trying to be a Christian at all. He's trying to be a good Jew. Starting this way is a *Verfremdungseffekt*, an alienation device. This interlocutor is the first in my evil plan to surprise readers and make them think.

Writing as a Jew for Jews, Wyschogrod also expects that some Christians will read what he publishes. He is, after all, professionally engaged in interreligious dialogue. He knows that what he says will be overheard. He knows that Christians will eavesdrop on an internal, family conversation. We know he knows this also because he identifies himself and his audience as *themselves* eavesdroppers on the intra-Catholic conversation in Vatican II. And so, while he does not address the Christian audience, he does write with the eavesdroppers in mind. It may be that most readers of this book are such eavesdroppers.

Wyschogrod simply points out what scholars of the Hebrew Bible and of the New Testament all know—that in the Bible, there are two kinds of people: Jews and Gentiles. In the Bible, *Gentiles* means "non-Jews." In the Gospels and Paul, the word *Christian* does not yet exist. Even when Paul is talking about Christ-followers, they come in two flavors, Jews and non-Jews. Jews are "chosen"; non-Jews are . . . have different jobs. In New Testament terms, most of the readers of this book will be Gentiles, and that is what the great majority of Christians has become also: Gentiles. When I first read Wyschogrod's *The Body of Faith*[4] in grad school, it was the best thing I read (among the greatest hits of Christian thought) in the entire year surrounding it, and what it taught me was simple: I was a Gentile. I wasn't central. I was extra. Many readers of this book would benefit by learning that too. It would improve their readings of Paul as well as their thinking about Jews.

---

3 The reading for the course was Michael Wyschogrod, "Israel, the Church, and Election," in *Brothers in Hope*, ed. John M. Oesterreicher (New York: Herder and Herder, 1970), 79–87. Further references to Wyschogrod will be by page number in the text.

4 Michael Wyschogrod, *The Body of Faith: Judaism as Corporeal Election* (New York: Seabury, 1983), also with different subtitles from different presses: the text is always the same.

Paul's question is, Why are the *Gentiles*, who have ethnic gods of their own, coming to worship the God of *Israel*?[5] Even if the God of Israel is, as Paul believes, the one true God, it still seems unnatural and surprising that Gentiles should come to worship that God. It is unnatural in the etymological sense that it contrasts with their birth, ethnic, or natal gods. In the Roman Empire, an ethnic group worshiped its own gods. Romans worshiped Jupiter and Juno. Greeks worshiped Zeus and Hera. Egyptians worshipped Osiris and Ra. Germans worshiped Thor and Wotan. Jews worship the God of Abraham and Isaac. But Gentile Christ-followers are weird. They worship a god *not their own*, somebody else's god, the God of Israel.

Paul has a context for this state of affairs.[6] It belongs, like the Messiah, to the end of the world. To put it crudely, Paul has two possibilities for the end, and he thinks he sees empirical evidence that one of them is coming true. In plan A, the Messiah comes, the Gentiles acknowledge the God of Israel as the one true God, and they become Jews by getting circumcised and keeping kosher. In plan B, the Messiah comes, the Gentiles acknowledge the God of Israel as the one true God, and (although they acknowledge the God of Israel) they do not convert in the sense that they do not get circumcised or keep kosher. Paul's hearers are Gentiles who are coming to worship the God of Israel (this is controversial but textual: Rom 1:13; 9:3–5; 10:1–2; 11:13; 11:23, 28, 31; 15:15; 16:4).[7] Therefore, Paul's hearers are *Jesus-following Gentiles insecure about their socioreligious status and anxious about their relation to Jews*. Something of that ancient anxiety seems to bother Christians even now.

Now, when two groups speak similar languages, the possibility of misunderstanding can go *up*. That is, you *assume* that people who speak similarly use words as you do. It's well known, for example, that in Britain, to "knock someone up" means to wake them by tapping or pounding on the door of their room, whereas in the United States, it means to get them pregnant. Similarly, when Wyschogrod uses the word "election" or "the chosen people," Christian readers tend to assume that since Gentiles are . . . have different jobs, that means most Christians are rejected, damned. Note this carefully: *Wyschogrod never says anything like that*. It is *Christians* who assume, on the basis of *their* theology, that the opposite of chosenness is "rejection" or damnation. It's very important to see what's missing in Wyschogrod. His article is not about "salvation," a word that hardly or never appears. There is no talk of damnation or hell, and Wyschogrod insists that "nonelection does not equal rejection" (86).

The binary "salvation/damnation" (and particularly damnation) is a peculiarly *Christian* preoccupation. Wyschogrod doesn't share it. It is as if Christian and Jewish

---

5 This paragraph and the next derive from material first published in Eugene F. Rogers Jr., "Romans on the Gender of Gentiles," *Soundings: An Interdisciplinary Journal* 94 (2011): 359–74; here, 361–62.
6 Paula Fredriksen, "Torah-Observance and Christianity: The Perspective of Roman Antiquity," *Modern Theology* 11 (1995): 195–204.
7 Stanley Stowers, *A Rereading of Romans* (New Haven, CT: Yale University Press, 1997), 29–33 passim.

theologies generate different psychologies. It's as if Jews have the confidence, the sense of security of "natural" children—that is, children who trust that their parents love them whether they are good or not. (The metaphor of "natural" children arises from the metaphor of descent from Abraham, the use of genealogy as a figure for community cohesion.) Christians, on the other hand, do not use metaphors of being "natural" children of God. Baptism, for example, is sometimes a matter of choice and always a rite of adoption. It arises, in part, from the Jewish ritual for adopting a Gentile child into a Jewish household, which requires not only circumcision for uncircumcised boys but submersion in a mikvah, or ritual bath, for Gentile boys and girls. One of the things that baptism washes away is the Gentile lack of family relation to the God of Israel.[8] So many Christians seem to have the insecure psychology attributed to adopted children, by which they trust less that their parents love them and worry more about rejection. That may be (as a psychological analogy, not a historical argument) why rejection is a Christian preoccupation: not because they really think others are worthy of rejection but because they secretly fear that they themselves are.

So the first surprising feature of Wyschogrod's account of election is that it does not have rejection as its opposite. Rather, nonelection is a calling for something else. The nonelect are second children, siblings of the elect. Wyschogrod says, "The non-election of God is never a finality, only one way of being touched by the finger of God." "In the non-election of the nations there is also the father's love for all of his children," says Wyschogrod. He continues: "Ishmael and Esau, the sons of non-election, are suffused in the divine word with a compassion in some respects more powerful than the love of the sons of election" (86–87).

Wyschogrod has a much more positive view of Christianity than you might suppose. Among the nonelect, the church may not have a sheerly different, unrelated, or even rival role. Rather, its role is a supporting one. Wyschogrod says, "To be envious of the election of Israel, the Church must seek the God of Israel, the Church must love the God of Israel. . . . The nations, as represented by the Church, seek the God of Abraham. . . . There is a portion of the gentile world into which the word of the God of Abraham has penetrated" (85). Wyschogrod realizes, with Maimonides and with Paul, that Gentiles seeking to acknowledge the God of Israel—a God not their own, somebody else's God—as the one true God, creator of heaven and earth, are fulfilling a prediction of Jewish eschatology. Wyschogrod says, "Maimonides pointed out that Christianity and Islam 'served to clear the way for King Messiah to prepare the whole world with one accord,' since through them 'the messianic hope, the Torah, and the commandments have become familiar topics . . . of the far isles and many peoples, uncircumcised of heart and flesh'" (83).

The second surprising feature is that election in Wyschogrod is not for goodies and favor and heaven. It is for "service" (80) and "witness"—"a living witness

---

8 I owe this formulation to Kendall Soulen.

that the God who chose it is the Lord of history and that His purpose will be achieved" (82). As in the story of Joseph and his brothers, being the favorite of the father comes with "great dangers," and the "mission laid upon it" (79) or the "role assigned by God . . . is a difficult one" (80). Referring to the Gentile—in this context, Christian—persecution of Jews, Wyschogrod twice uses phrases like "the crucifixion of Israel's body" (80) or "[Gentiles] crucifying it whenever an opportunity presents itself" (81–82) to show the people Israel as the suffering servant. He can use such phrases because he's Jewish; it would be frightening for Christians to copy them. Election is dangerous with Gentiles around; therefore it is to be accepted "in humility, in fear and trembling" (84).

Wyschogrod also describes this dangerous turn in terms of the firstborn son, the one of whom more is expected. If any readers are firstborn children with younger siblings, they will be familiar with the syndrome in which the firstborn are loved with higher expectations and the latter-born with greater indulgence. The Bible, Wyschogrod points out, deploys that metaphor to describe the election of Israel. It is also firstborn animals who are sacrificed and the firstborn of Egypt who are slain by the Angel of Death. In Christianity, the elect One is Jesus, and we know how he dies. All of these considerations change the picture of election so that it is double-edged and not straightforwardly a good thing to be specially loved by God. Not that pie-in-the-sky, heavenly glory that Christians often imagine.

The third surprising thing is that Wyschogrod's account of election is not individual; it's communal. The object of God's election is "Israel"—a group. Note that "Israel" in his article never means the *country* of Israel, founded in 1948. It is always "the *people* Israel," whether in the Bible or in the present—that is, Jews and their ancestors to Abraham or Adam. That means that relationship to God is a group thing, apart from your individuality.

We may summarize these surprises in this chart:

Author	Identity of the electing God	Identity of the elect	Identity of the nonelect	Nature of election	Nature of nonelection
Wyschogrod	God of Israel; God of Abraham, Isaac, and Jacob; God of the Covenant	The people Israel	Gentiles	Service, witness	Different job, younger brother

4 Calvin Talks about God Choosing Individuals for God's Purpose

> Against Calvin's intention, succeeding generations came to regard his
> God as a giant sorting mechanism.

Perhaps Wyschogrod made you uncomfortable because you discovered you're a Gentile and don't belong at the center of God's dealings with the world. Perhaps you'll like Calvin better. His view is in many ways more familiar to Christians. It's starkly binary. *Election* means salvation, glory in heaven, and its opposite is rejection, reprobation, damnation. It's about individuals, in a way: God decides about *you*, even if it's God who decides.

On the one hand, everything you've heard about Calvin is true: God "does not indiscriminately adopt all into the hope of salvation but gives to some what he denies to others." Calvin continues: "For all are not created in equal condition: rather, eternal life is foreordained to some, eternal damnation for others. Therefore, as any man has been created to one or the other of these ends, we speak of him as predestined to life or to death."[1] Calvin quotes Romans 9:13 and Ephesians 1:4: "Jacob I have loved, Esau I have hated"; they were "elect before the creation of the world" (III.xxii.4, 936; III.xxii.2, 934).

Indeed, it's worse than that. Calvin's God does not predestine because God foreknows: Calvin's God foreknows because God has predestined (III.xxi.5, 926; III.xxii.2, 934).[2] Shakespeare does not write the part because he knows what the characters will do: Shakespeare knows what the characters will do *because he wrote the part*. Of course, Shakespeare knows what the characters will do, but that's not the *reason* they do it. The reason they do it, in this way of thinking, is that Shakespeare wrote it that way.

---

1 The reading for the course was John Calvin, *Institutes of the Christian Religion*, trans. Ford Lewis Battles (Philadelphia: Westminster Press, 1960), 2: 920–36, 970–71 (III.xxi–xxii.3, xxiv.5). Here the reference is to III.xxi.1, 921; III.xxi.5, 926. Further references to Calvin in this section will be by the book, chapter, and section numbers in the *Institutes* with page numbers to that edition.

    For further reading, the most charitable interpretation of Calvin's doctrine of election (which makes him sound like Barth) is Wilhelm Niesel, *The Theology of Calvin*, trans. Harold Knight (Philadelphia: Westminster Press, 1956), 159–81.

2 By the way, if you go to read these passages for yourself, Calvin—like most of the theologians in this book—is not writing a textbook. Like most of the theologians in this book, he is writing *in the midst of an argument*. He will frequently and without explicit warning rehearse the views of his opponents—views that he does not hold, views he is against—in order to refute them. You can't take any sentence out of context and assume it's Calvin's view; you have to listen for tone and for telltale words like "we" (Calvin's group) and "they" (his opponents). If you are reading an opinion piece in a newspaper about contemporary politics, you quickly catch on who "we" and "they" are, and you can follow the arguments for each side even without labels. You will need to develop that sense—the sense of tone—for reading theologians too.

You may disagree with this view. But it's Calvin's view. He thinks it's reasonable, and he even thinks it allows free will, because after all, the plot of a play not only allows but depends on free will. In an example Calvin does not use, Macbeth might be able to defend himself against the charge of murder by claiming, "My wife made me do it. She's very manipulative." You could write an English paper about that. Or you could, on a different level, write about how Shakespeare constructs the characters of Macbeth and his Lady Macbeth and how cleverly Shakespeare has them interact. But the English paper you cannot write is the one in which Macbeth defends himself by saying, "It's not my fault! Shakespeare made me do it."

You are allowed to hate on Calvin. But let me explain the context and audience for Calvin's doctrine—because we are not in Calvin's context; we are not Calvin's audience; and, unlike Wyschogrod, Calvin is not writing for us to overhear.

First, consider where the predestination[3] section stands in the whole work, the *Institutes of the Christian Religion*. What are the page numbers? They start at 920. The whole work is printed in two volumes, with continuous pagination, and runs to 1521 pages before bibliographies and indexes. That's two or more Harry Potter volumes. What comes in the first 920 pages? And who would read that far? Certainly not just anyone. Only members of Calvin's own group and professional polemicists whose job it is to dispute him in books or in public. Ordinary people, wondering whether they're saved, will never reach this section. It's deeply unfair to Calvin for me to present to you this late, arcane, and distant section, the section on predestination, without referring to the previous 920 pages.

Who are the members of Calvin's own group? Calvin (1509–64) lived a quarter century after Martin Luther (1483–1546). Although in English we say his name in the English way, he was born in France: you can also pronounce his name in the French way, Jean Calvin, like *vin*, the French word for wine. By 1540, Calvin had converted to Protestantism, and France, after alternating between toleration and persecution of Protestants, had issued the Edict of Fontainebleau (1540), which declared Protestantism "high treason against God and humanity," punishable by torture and death. At the time, the means of execution for heresy was burning alive.

Calvin and other Protestants fled into Switzerland, and his congregations in Basel and Geneva felt that they were figuratively brands snatched from the burning (Amos 4:11; Zech 3:2). Like survivors of other catastrophes—earthquakes, tidal waves, viruses—they felt no worthier than those who had died. Their sisters who sold Bibles or their brothers who preached in secret had been burned at the stake, and who was to say that those martyrs were not more precious to God than they?

---

3 "Predestination" is not the same as "election." *Election* means chosenness. *Predestination* means both chosenness *and* rejection. Some authors will distinguish between "single predestination" (election alone) and "double predestination" (election and reprobation together). In the next section, Karl Barth will speak almost exclusively of "election" and almost never of "predestination," which he uses for the view of others.

It was not because they were better that they had lived. They could only give glory for God's unaccountable mercy, who gave life to some and martyrdom to others: it must be that God had some purpose for them, some purpose beyond human understanding. As it was in this life, so it was in the next: God's ways were past finding out, and yet they felt certain, because of their survival, that God was merciful.

Unlike their descendants, the first generation of Calvinists knew in their guts that "God not only offers salvation but so assigns it that the certainty of its effect is not in suspense or doubt" (III.xxi.7, 930). "We teach nothing," Calvin wrote, "not borne out by experience: that God has always been free to bestow his grace on whom he wills" (931). Like infamous biblical sinners—Moses the murderer, David the adulterer, Peter the denier—they also knew that it was no previous or future merit that saved them: "Let them answer why they [were created] men rather than oxen or asses" (931). Rather, God delighted in turning the tables so that election brought rather than followed merit, as the orchardist plants the tree not *because* it has produced good fruit but *in order that* it will produce good fruit. God even grafts branches onto trees with *other* roots, so far is God from doing the foreseeable (Rom 11:23–24).

The first generation of Calvinists, safe in Switzerland, are prominent in the text whenever Calvin uses "we" language. Take a look at the running head on the recto (the right-hand side) of every page: "The Way in Which *We* Receive the Grace of Christ." It is the title of book 3. It's about Calvin's own group. It's about what they have *received*. What they have received is *grace*. And their question is, Why us? Why did *we* receive the grace of Christ? Was it because we were worthy? No, it was because God was gracious. It was as if they all bought the T-shirt that said, "I survived the tsunami." I don't know why the palm tree I climbed survived the flood and my neighbor's did not. But I certainly feel that God is with me.

Their question was *not* the one that arose later, perhaps as early as the first generation after him: "What has God decided about me?" Sociologically, Calvin's own generation felt the answer to that question in their gut.

Now, Calvinists are quick to point out that Calvin uses experience only to buttress and not to found his argument. He founds his argument on Scripture. That gives him grounds to argue that *the mercy of God is also just*—because Calvin does not argue what you probably assume: that in Christianity, people would start from goodness or neutrality and find their own way to heaven or hell. No, because of the fall, Calvin assumes that *all people start from deep sinfulness*, so sinful that God would be just to damn them all. Fortunately, God shows God's mercy by saving some. According to Calvin, the doctrine of predestination, so far from showing injustice, shows both justice and mercy.

Because Calvin understands predestination to show justice *and* mercy, and because the first Calvinists experienced their escape from persecution as profound and unaccountable grace, Calvin can write that his doctrine brings peace, humility, and thanksgiving. If you don't understand that, you don't understand

Calvin. Everything belongs in this context: experience bears out what Scripture teaches, that God is merciful to us unworthy ones. (Wyschogrod says something similar about the worthiness of the people Israel.) When "we" (Calvin's group) ask why we were snatched from the burning, the answer can only be, God had mercy. Therefore, when, 920 pages in, Calvin poses the question, "Why did *we* receive the grace of Christ?" the only possible answer is, God had mercy. If others are damned, that is only what we, too, deserved. Therefore, Calvin can write, "We shall never be clearly persuaded, as we ought to be, that our salvation flows from the wellspring of God's free mercy until we come to know his eternal election, which illumines God's grace by this contrast: that he does not indiscriminately adopt all into the hope of salvation but gives to some what he denies to others" (III.xxi.1, 921).

We can sum up Calvin's doctrine in the same chart as chapter 3:

Author	Identity of the electing God	Identity of the elect	Identity of the nonelect	Nature of election	Nature of nonelection
Wyschogrod	God of Israel; God of Abraham, Isaac, and Jacob; God of the Covenant	The people Israel	Gentiles	Service, witness	Different job, younger brother
Calvin	God, who is just and merciful to different individuals, plucking some from the burning	At least Calvin's Christians in Geneva	Although we don't know the extent of God's mercy, Calvin acts as if Catholics, non-Christians, and critics of the Trinity like Michael Servetus are damned	Salvation to show God's mercy	Damnation to show God's justice

• • •

Perhaps you still have misgivings about Calvin. Let me make them worse. The peaceful trust in God's mercy did not outlast the first generation. The second generation of Calvinists, under Calvin's successor Theodore (1519–1605), already began to ask a more modern question, one Calvin had advised against: How do I know whether I am one of the saved or the damned? Beza codified this quest into a famous flow chart that he named the *Summa Totius Christianismi*, "the sum of all Christianity" (1555; see figure 4.1).[4]

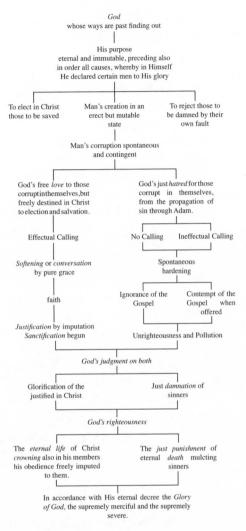

Figure 4.1. Theodore Beza, the predestination flow chart from *Summa Totius Christianismi* (1555). Almost all of the phrases are biblical, but the problem is the order. At the beginning, Beza places God, whose "ways [are] past finding out" (Rom 11:33 KJV), substituting a mystery for the revelation in Christ, whom John 1:1 places with God "in the beginning."

---

4   Translated in Heinrich Heppe, *Reformed Dogmatics Set Out and Illustrated from the Sources*, trans. G. T. Thomson (Grand Rapids, MI: Baker, 1978), 147–48.

God, "whose ways are past finding out," serves here as a giant, unknowable sorting mechanism. Signs of election can be misleading: calling may be "ineffectual," and hardening can happen "spontaneously." Although Calvin himself advised those in doubt to look to Christ as the "mirror" of their election "so that we who are among the members may not be troubled about it" (III.xxii.1, 933; III.xxiv.4–11, 968–78), the member of the Trinity to whom Calvinists appropriated the choosing and electing sounds more like the Father—especially in a chart like Beza's.

If you were a Calvinist in doubt, you might have looked, a hundred years later, to a whole theological topic that developed in Beza's wake: "the question of assurance." How could you find assurance in your anxiety about predestination? The Westminster Confession (1648) offered an answer. A surprisingly unstable answer. Read this aloud, noting the change of tone in every paragraph, as different hands cobble together an assurance written by committee. It shows switchbacks of hope and despair that—if you are unconcerned—you can enjoy like the plot of a horror movie.

Of the Assurance of Grace and Salvation

1. Although hypocrites, and other unregenerate men, may vainly deceive themselves with false hopes and carnal presumptions: of being in the favor of God and estate of salvation; which hope of theirs shall perish: yet such as truly believe in the Lord Jesus, and love him in sincerity, endeavoring to walk in all good conscience before him, may in this life be certainly assured that they are in a state of grace, and may rejoice in the hope of the glory of God: which hope shall never make them ashamed.

2. This certainty is not a bare conjectural and probable persuasion, grounded upon a fallible hope; but an infallible assurance of faith, founded upon the divine truth of the promises of salvation, the inward evidence of those graces unto which these promises are made, the testimony of the Spirit of adoption witnessing with our spirits that we are the children of God; which Spirit is the earnest of our inheritance, whereby we are sealed to the day of redemption.

3. This infallible assurance doth not so belong to the essence of faith but that a true believer may wait long and conflict with many difficulties before he be partaker of it: yet, being enabled by the Spirit to know the things which are freely given him to God, he may, without extraordinary revelation, in the right use of ordinary means, attain thereunto. And therefore it is the duty of everyone to give all diligence to make his calling and election sure; that thereby his heart may be enlarged in peace and joy in the Holy Ghost, in love and thankfulness to God, and in strength and cheerfulness in the duties of obedience, the proper fruits of this assurance: so far is it from inclining men to looseness.

4. True believers may have the assurance of their salvation divers ways shaken, diminished, and intermitted; as, by negligence in preserving of

it; by falling into some special sin, which woundeth the conscience, and grieveth the Spirit; by some sudden or vehement temptation; by God's withdrawing the light of his countenance and suffering even such as fear him to walk in darkness and to have no light: yet are they never utterly destitute of that seed of God, and life of faith, that love of Christ and the brethren, that sincerity of heart and conscience of duty, out of which, by the operation of the Spirit, this assurance may in due time be revived, and by the which, in the meantime, they are supported from utter despair.[5]

What kind of assurance is this, that can be "shaken, diminished, and intermitted," that begins with hypocrisy and unregeneracy and ends with "utter despair"? The switchbacks display what Calvin denies: that the God of this faith is arbitrary and capricious.

---

5 Paragraphs 6.097–6.100 from "The Westminster Confession of Faith," ccel.org, accessed November 25, 2020, https://tinyurl.com/y6cctmdq.

5 Barth Talks about God Choosing Humanity in Jesus

In Jesus, God chooses God's own self to be for the sinful human being and the human being to share God's glory.

Karl Barth (1886–1968) diagnoses that kind of Calvinism (Calvinist orthodoxy) in a section of his *Church Dogmatics* that we may schematize by adding another row to our predestination chart.

Author	Identity of the electing God	Identity of the elect	Identity of the nonelect	Nature of election	Nature of nonelection
Wyschogrod	God of Israel; God of Abraham, Isaac, and Jacob; God of the Covenant	The people Israel	Gentiles	Service, witness	Different job, younger brother
Calvin (*sympathetic view*)	God, who is just and merciful to different individuals, plucking some from the burning	At least Calvin's Christians in Geneva	Although we don't know the extent of God's mercy, Calvin acts as if Catholics, non-Christians, and critics of the Trinity like Michael Servetus are damned	Salvation to show God's mercy	Damnation to show God's justice
Calvin (*critical view*) Loosely based on Barth, "The Problem of a Correct Doctrine of the Election of Grace," *Church Dogmatics* §32.	God is a giant sorting mechanism, whose ways are past finding out, like the unknown X in an equation	Although the elect are known to God, they are unknown to us, like another unknown X	The rejected are another unknown X	Mercy without reason is arbitrary (another X)	Damnation without equity is capricious (another X)

Barth diagnoses that version of Calvin as a series of unknowns, an unbroken series of Xs.

The trouble with Calvin's approach, Barth argues, is that Christianity is not in fact a religion in which God is an unknown: Christianity is the religion of God's self-revelation; God is revealed in Jesus. God is not a giant sorting mechanism: God is in Christ. Yes, God is unknown in the sense of being beyond our language and our understanding but not in the sense of vulgar Calvinism. The unknowability of God is no tyranny or caprice; the unknowability of God is grace beyond imagining— that is, that God became human and dwelled among human beings. In a different section, Barth compares the unknowability of God to something very concrete: the virgin birth, in which the Creator impossibly becomes one of us, and God unknows God's distance to come as close to us as our own flesh. It is a miracle, the miracle of Christmas, the miracle of God's self-manifestation as a lover of humankind.[1] Barth tacitly accuses Calvin of becoming briefly, if disastrously, insensible to this center of the Christian faith.

Barth famously writes very, very long. His *Church Dogmatics* takes up thirteen fat volumes. But he sums up his plentiful prose in short, tight, packed, boldface statements called *Leitsätze*, or thesis paragraphs. Typically, everything you need to know is right there in a single paragraph at the beginning, if only you have learned how to unpack it. To understand two hundred pages of the *Church Dogmatics*, we have only to unpack two short paragraphs—seven sentences. Quietly, Barth seems to be trolling Calvin in almost every sentence.

> The doctrine of election is the sum of the Gospel because of all words that can be said or heard it is the best: that God elects the human being; that God is for the human being too the One who loves in freedom. It is grounded in the knowledge of Jesus Christ because He is both the electing God and elected human being in One. It is part of the doctrine of God because originally God's election of the human being is a predestination not merely of the human being but of Godself. Its function is to bear basic testimony to eternal, free and unchanging grace as the beginning of all the ways and works of God. (3, thesis paragraph)[2]

---

1 Karl Barth, "The Miracle of Christmas," in *Church Dogmatics* I/2 (Edinburgh: T&T Clark, 1956), 172–200.

2 The reading for the course was Karl Barth, "The Problem of a Correct Doctrine of the Election of Grace" and "The Election of Jesus Christ," in *Church Dogmatics* II/2 (Edinburgh: T&T Clark, 1957), 3, 94–95, 99–102, 103–6, 115–17, 118, 120–27, 145, 161–65, 166–68, 168–74. Large print only. Only thirty pages; my favorite reading in college. Here, 3. Further references will be by page number in the text. For further reading, see *Church Dogmatics* II/2, 449–506, on Judas.

   For the divine reflexive "Godself," see the chapter on the Trinity. I make God-language nonbinary only for twentieth- and twenty-first-century sources and language for human beings inclusive when the underlying language uses a word for "human being." Barth does not use the divine reflexive; he uses the traditional "Himself," which is gendered masculine but traditionally parsed as inclusive in both the German original and the English translation.

"The doctrine of election is the sum of the Gospel": Barth is trolling Beza's chart, the one titled "the sum of all Christianity." Barth reminds Beza that it's not about "Christianity"; it's about "the Gospel," the Evangelium, as he says in the next clause, the Good News. What about Calvin's doctrine is good news, past the first generation?

Then Barth doubles down: "Because of *all* words that can be said or heard" (he invokes here the context of preaching) "it is the *best*" (my italics). Now, you might argue—on the basis of a sympathetic interpretation of Calvin's audience and context—that Calvin's original doctrine counted as good news to his original, persecuted congregation—but how would you argue that of all the doctrines of Christianity, including the incarnation, the resurrection, and the forgiveness of sins, the doctrine of election is the *best*? Not knowing Barth, you might assume he is some kind of crazed propagandist for Calvinism, taking its worst excesses to even greater extremes. You might ask, "Barth wants to preach what Calvin hid nine hundred pages in and said from time to time should be kept secret?"

That becomes clear in the next, mysterious clauses. These clauses are not mysterious because, like Calvin, they hide something dark and sometimes sinister, the so-called left hand of God.[3] Rather, these clauses are mysterious because *they reveal something that sounds too good to be true.* They are wide open and unquali-fied: "that God elects *the human being*" (my italics). They overcome binaries: "that God is for the human being too the One who loves in freedom."

"That God elects the human being." Note how this differs from Wyschogrod and Calvin. Not, God elects Israel.[4] Not, God elects individual Christians snatched from the fires of sin. Not just some human being(s) but *the* human being, humankind as a whole, as a concrete universal. *Der Mensch*, traditionally translated "man," is German not for the male human (that would be *der Mann*) but for the human being. What does that mean? In spite of its breadth, it means something specific. As we'll see, it means Jesus—and the whole human race "in Him"—as representing the whole.

"That God is for the human being *too* the One who loves in freedom" (my italics). What is the "*too*" doing in that clause? It means that God loves not only within the Trinitarian life, the love of the Father for the Son and so on. It means that God's love extends *also, unnecessarily, gratuitously* to us creatures. It means that love defines God's freedom all the way down. God's freedom is not arbitrary or capri-cious: it is always freedom for love.

I save the Trinity for later. But here is a teaser. It turns out that Barth's previous volume had described God in Godself, God in the Trinity. That section characterized

---

3 For a send-up of church pronouncements against queer people based on biblical language about handedness, see "Dextera Domini: On the Pastoral Care of Left-Handed Persons," Öt Kenyér, November 29, 1995, http://www.otkenyer.hu/halsall/lgbh-dex.txt.

4 God does elect Israel, and Barth devotes over a hundred pages to affirming it. But it's complicated by an unsuccessful attempt also to troll anti-Semitic Nazi rhetoric, which embarrassed him before he died. For a Jewish response, see Michael Wyschogrod, "Why Was and Is the Theology of Karl Barth of Interest to a Jewish Theologian?," in *Abraham's Promise*, ed. Kendall Soulen (Grand Rapids, MI: William B. Eerdmans, 2004), 211–24.

God as "the One who loves in freedom," already in God's own self, apart from creation, apart from us creatures. God in God's own character, in God's own Trinitarian life, already turns toward an Other in love, in that, already in God, God is love: the love of the Father for the Son, the Son for the Father, and the Holy Spirit as the guarantor and witness of their love. God already loves *in God's own self*, and here we learn that God loves humanity too—that God chooses to turn toward the other not only in the life of the Trinity but also outside the Trinity, in the world, in us. This means that God's love for us is not necessary—God has no need of us, God has all love, all riches, all companionship already in Godself—but God's love for us is profoundly *characteristic*; it goes all the way down into God's being. God just is the One who chooses love. The depth of God's being is Trinity, is nonbinary turning toward the Other in love.

"It is grounded in the knowledge of Jesus Christ," not in the knowledge of a logical possibility or an abstract freedom apart from love, and certainly not in the knowledge of a giant mechanical randomness generator or of a plot driven by a mania for drama rather than love.

"Because He is . . . the electing God," not a distant father whom we do not know, whose ways are past finding out. No, Jesus is the electing God. Or, more comprehensively, the Trinity is the electing God, which leaves out neither Jesus nor the Spirit. But Jesus is the person of the Trinity who is principally missing in Calvin's doctrine, because Jesus is also . . .

The "elected human being." Jesus is the God who elects. But in Jesus, God elects *Godself*, elects God's own self to become human, God's own self to suffer and die for us—as we will see in the next paragraph. Just because God chose Godself, the elector is the elected one, and Jesus is therefore fully divine and fully human at once.

To state the obvious, the foregoing paragraphs assume as a premise that Jesus is fully human and fully divine. That has been a central feature of how Christians have attempted to go on talking about Jesus in the ways that the New Testament talks about him, although it took four hundred years for them to work out the rules that would last: talk about Jesus as a human being, *and* talk about Jesus as God. In the next chapter, we will see how Christians can do both. But Barth offers already here an explanation of *why* they talk that way: the full humanity of Jesus was God's decision about God's own life from the beginning. Jesus is (in a book title of Barth's) "the humanity of God."

Now, that may be too abstract for you. For now, just note that Barth has filled in his own answer for two of the boxes in our chart: In the first box, the identity of the electing God is Jesus. And in the second box, the identity of the elect human being is also Jesus. That is what it means when Barth asserts that Jesus Christ "is both the electing God and elected human being in One."

See what Barth did there?

He ends by restating the thesis: "Originally God's election of the human being is a predestination not merely of the human being but of Godself." It's crucial for Barth's argument that God's predestination of the human being is first of all *reflexive*—that is, it is first of all a *self*-determination of *God*; God first of all decides who God wants to be and only secondarily who humans will be; God's self-determination first of all binds God before it frees humans. That self-determination establishes who God is—and therefore it is not inappropriate to use forms of language that call attention by their very oddity to the *reflexive* character of God's self-definition, how strange it is, and how profound. God's self-definition in Jesus is God's going into the far country of the flesh, God's self-orientation toward the other; this is foundational and *sui generis*, one of a kind.[5]

The function of that doctrine—that Jesus is fully human and fully divine—"is to bear basic testimony to eternal, free and unchanging grace [that is, Jesus] as the beginning of all the ways and works of God."

For decades—from the time I was a sophomore in college until I had been teaching for years—I thought "the beginning of all the ways and works of God" was a gorgeous phrase. "Ways and works" goes so well in English because of course their cognates go so well in German: "Anfang aller Wege und Werke Gottes." "Wege und Werke": just as good, maybe better. Such a phrase, I thought, was part of the reason Barth won the Sigmund Freud Prize for the energy and riches of his prose style.

Imagine my surprise when I stated that as fact to a colleague in patristics who returned the stare he reserved for moronic students. "That's Proverbs 8:22," he said witheringly. "Everybody knows that. Athanasius and Arius debated the meaning of that verse." And there too the wordplay is beautiful—because the proverbs are poetry.[6]

Well, that's another way that Barth is trolling Calvin: Calvin has put a giant sorting mechanism at the beginning of all God's ways and works in place of Jesus. Arius too says that the beginning of God's ways and works is something other than Jesus. Athanasius says the beginning of God's ways and works *just is* Jesus. Athanasius won, and as we'll see in the next chapter, Arius became an archheretic.

Barth follows Athanasius to lay great stress on John 1:1–3: "In the beginning was the Word, and the Word was with God, and the Word was God. He was in the beginning with God. All things came into being through him, and without him not one thing came into being." The verses refer to the prehistory of Jesus with the

---

5 Those words, Latin *generis* and English *kind*, are related both to each other and to our word *gender*, so it comes not amiss if the unique act of God in destining Godself toward us should also get a distinct pronoun, the divine reflexive. If God makes Godself human by a woman without a man and thus with no humanly supplied Y chromosome, God is showing Godself to be beyond gender. Precisely at the point at which God makes Godself human, God refuses to be defined by masculinity by setting Joseph and his Y chromosomes aside. While Barth stresses both election and the virgin (or fatherless) birth, combining the two to yield nonbinary language for God is my interpretation of Barth, not Barth himself.

6 Both the Masoretic (Hebrew) text and the Septuagint (Greek) have words for *ways* and *works*. But "Wege und Werke" does not exactly appear in either Luther's or Zwingli's German Bible. The Zwingli Bible, which Barth would have consulted first, has *Walten* and *Werke*, God's "reign" and "works"; the Luther Bible collapses the two into one word, *Wege*. Numerous preachers and theologians, including Schleiermacher, took the best of both to speak of God's *Wege und Werke*.

Father. Arius, Athanasius claims, denies that. By tagging that controversy here, Barth takes the side of Athanasius—and suggests that Calvin belongs on the side of the heretics. On this reading, Calvin (or Beza) wants to substitute something other than Jesus as the beginning of all God's ways and works, erecting in Jesus's place the giant, capricious sorting mechanism as an idol.

Barth does not spell that out, and there are other places where Barth is more charitable. But it is a put-down more masterful for its subtlety. I missed it for twenty years. Whoever puts "God, whose ways are past finding out," at the top of their chart *and Jesus farther down on one of the arms* is siding with an archheretic, denying the prologue to John, and putting an idol ahead of the Word.

Now we skip a hundred pages to the next boldface thesis paragraph, which goes like this, just in case you missed it: "The election of grace is the beginning of all the ways and works of God in Jesus Christ. In Jesus Christ God in God's free grace determines Himself for the sinful human being and the sinful human being for Himself. He therefore takes upon Himself the rejection of the human being with all its consequences, and elects the human being to participation in His own glory" (94, thesis paragraph).

Here we learn that it is the *sinful* human being that God chooses to be for. God chooses to make the *lost* cause of the human being God's own cause. God therefore "takes upon Himself the rejection of the human being." That refers to Jesus taking the rejection, the God-abandonment on himself in his suffering, crucifixion, and death (and, Balthasar will add, also in his descent into hell). With that, Barth specifies who the rejected human being is: Jesus. Right? Died for your sins and so on and so on? Rejected of God. God takes the rejection on *Godself*: God chooses to become the judge judged in our place.

So that fills in the third box for Barth's answer in our election comparison. The identity of the rejected human being is also Jesus. That's right: Jesus is the *elect* human being because he is chosen (he chooses himself / the Father chooses him / the Spirit drives him) to fulfill the self-determination of God to be for the sinful human being, *and* the consequence of that choice is to be the one who suffers and dies—who undergoes rejection, God-abandonment, and damnation—for the sake of sinners.

So if you asked Barth, "What about all those biblical verses about election and rejection that Calvin quotes?" he would say, "Yes, yes, that's all true, *only because it applies to Jesus.*" All that election stuff, it applies to Jesus. And all that rejection stuff, it applies to Jesus too. Jesus is the elected and rejected in one; he is elected for rejection, and because he fulfilled that mission, he sits on the right hand of the Father—that is, he is the rejected One *elected*. That's not just a clever trick, Barth would say, *that's the story*—that's *the Gospel. That's the good news!*

Barth even reclaims Calvin's emphasis on the glory of God. He reclaims differential, binary justice and mercy in order to queer the binary. Jesus takes on "the rejection . . . *with all its consequences*" (my italics)—that's the bad stuff—and "elects the human being to *participation in His own glory*" (my italics)—that's the good stuff. So contrary to vulgar Calvinism, damnation is for God, and glory is for . . . us humans.[7]

Note I keep saying "humans" and not "Christians." That's because that's what Barth says. He does *not* say "Christian" in any of those places. "God elects *the human being*" (my italics). "God determines . . . the sinful human being" not for damnation but for "Himself." God "elects the human being to participation in His own glory." Because it's the *sinful* human God chooses to love.

You may well wonder if this is universalism. Well, it is. It's not frank universalism. It's *creeping* universalism. That's a technical term that means an argument *leads up to* universalism but does not explicitly draw the conclusion for you. Barth wants you to draw that conclusion for yourself.

He wants you to draw it by pointing you to Jesus, so the hundred pages—of which I recommend the shorter, large print sections for beginners—is called "The Election of Jesus Christ." In those pages, Barth takes all the biblical talk about God's choosing and rejecting and applies all of it to Jesus. Talk about God doing the electing is talk about Jesus (not without the Father and the Spirit). Talk about the one elected for God's mission is talk about Jesus. And the talk about anyone rejected to show God's judgment is talk about Jesus. To repeat, you can read Barth as if he had said, "Every verse Calvin quotes is true, only it applies to Jesus." Barth's first strategy is always to point you to Jesus, to bring you to look up to Jesus and not into your navel.

His second strategy is to distract you from yourself. So you turn to the doctrine of election in the *Church Dogmatics* looking for yourself. And what do you read? Well, first, you read a hundred pages about "The Problem of a Correct Doctrine of the Election of Grace." This is about how the "unknowns" in Calvin's "equations" need to be replaced with "Jesus." So you expect that Jesus is done now, and you hope to get to yourself. Then you read "The Election of Jesus Christ." How is that different? Well, that's basically a doctrine of the atonement—or how Jesus saves—folded into the doctrine of election. God elects whom? God elects God in Jesus. God decides *what* for God? God decides that God will take the rejection and give humans the glory—in Jesus. That's the doctrine of atonement. The Scots Confession does the same thing. It too folds the atonement into the doctrine of election:

Election

That same eternal God and Father, who by mere grace chose us in his Son Christ Jesus before the foundation of the world was laid, appointed him to be our head, our brother, our pastor, and the great bishop of our souls. But since the opposition between the justice of God and our sins was such that

---

7 I have presented Barth as opposed to Calvin. That's a shorthand. You can also read Barth as *reforming* Calvin. You can point to a christological version of election in Calvin, in which Christ is "the mirror of election" (*Institutes* 3.xxiv.5). The trouble is, if Calvin had taken his own Christology of election seriously, he would have had to rewrite the opening sections, and he didn't.

no flesh by itself could or might have attained unto God, it behooved the Son of God to descend unto us and take himself a body of our body, flesh of our flesh, and bone of our bone, and so become the perfect Mediator between God and man, giving power to as many as believe in him to be the sons of God; as he himself says, "I ascend to my Father and to your Father, to my God and to your God." By this most holy brotherhood whatever we have lost in Adam is restored to us again. Therefore we are not afraid to call God our Father, not so much because he has created us, which we have in common with the reprobate, as because he has given unto us his only Son to be our brother, and given us grace to acknowledge and embrace him as our only Mediator, as is already said.

Further, it behooved the Messiah and Redeemer to be very God and very man, because he was able to undergo the punishment[8] due for our transgressions and to present himself in the presence of his Father's judgments, as in our stead, to suffer for our transgression and disobedience, and by death to overcome him that was the author of death. But because the only Godhead could not suffer death, and neither could manhood overcome death, he joined both together in one person, that the weakness of one should suffer and be subject to death—which we had deserved—and the infinite and invincible power of the other, that is, of the Godhead, should triumph, and purchase for us life, liberty, and perpetual victory. So we confess, and most undoubtedly believe.[9]

That's the doctrine of election? Really? It's just the atonement. It's *how Jesus saves*. It's not about me at all! So maybe the next section is about me.

Then you get over a hundred pages about the election of the community, which turns out to be "the environment of Jesus Christ" and (very ambiguously!) about Israel and the church—a section that was very influential on a Jewish theologian who once visited Barth (and bested him in an argument) named Michael Wyschogrod.[10] Where am I? you ask, in frustration, after 305 pages?

And then, finally, in relief, you come on "The Election of the Individual." And what do you get there? You get "Jesus Christ, the Promise and its Recipient"! Jesus again!

---

8 For reasons that we'll go into when we get to atonement, *punishment* is a word that some theologians fetishize and others avoid. Barth avoids punishment language. For him, God's self-substitution for the sinful human being applies to the whole life and entire existence of Jesus, his solidarity with us in our sorry state, not a moment of punishment from one member of the Trinity to another. For more, see Bruce L. McCormack, "The Ontological Presuppositions of Barth's Doctrine of the Atonement," in *The Glory of the Atonement: Biblical, Theological & Practical Perspectives*, ed. Charles E. Hill and Frank A. James III (Downers Grove, IL: IVP, 2004), 346–66.

9 *The Book of Confessions* (Louisville, KY: Office of the General Assembly of the Presbyterian Church, 2004), section 3.08, https://tinyurl.com/y3uwrmas.

10 Michael Wyschogrod, "A Jewish Perspective on Karl Barth," in *How Karl Barth Changed My Mind*, ed. Donald K McKim (Grand Rapids, MI: Eerdmans, 1986), 156–61; here, 161.

Then in the next section, you get (finally?) "The Elect and the Rejected." And yes, this section, starting on page 340, is about individuals. But not you. *Biblical* individuals who are always in pairs. This is one of the most impressive parts of Barth. You get elected/rejected individuals yoked together: Cain and Abel, Jacob and Esau, Isaac and Ishmael, Rachel and Leah, Moses and Pharaoh, Saul and David—this is what Barth calls *praedestinatio gemina*, twinned predestination, where the elect and the rejected come in twos, down to the dove sacrificed and the dove set free, the goat sacrificed and the scapegoat driven into the wilderness with the sins on its back. And *both* members of each pair lead up to Jesus: Jesus represents and brings to a head both the series of the elect, as the heir of Isaac and Moses and David, *and* on the cross the rejection suffered by Cain, Esau, Ishmael, Leah, Pharaoh, and Saul. Jesus embodies both series: the series of the elect throughout the whole Bible and, also throughout the whole Bible, the series of the rejected. Jesus is both the elect and the rejected one.

If you don't buy this (and it's a tour de force), there is one final pair from the New Testament. Who is the rejected one, other than Jesus, in the New Testament, the one who deserves damnation in his own right, if anyone does? That would be Judas. And who replaces him among the apostles, if anyone does? Technically that's the unknown Matthias. But effectively it's Paul. So Judas and Paul are Barth's final pair. He argues that Paul, who persecuted Christians before his conversion, and Judas, who repented of his betrayal, are much alike. The Middle Ages developed the strictest test for repentance. They required three things: *contritio cordis*, contrition of the heart; *confessio oris*, confession of the mouth; and *satisfactio operis*, satisfaction in works. Judas had all three: he had regret, he confessed, he gave the money back, he even hanged himself. What further proof could you have of Judas's sincere repentance? Barth concludes,

> The answer can only be as follows. [God] wills that [Judas] too should hear the Gospel, and with it the promise of his election. God wills, then, that the Gospel should be proclaimed to him. God wills that he should appreciate and live by the hope which is given him in the Gospel. God wills that [Judas] should believe, and that as a believer he should become a rejected person elected. The rejected as such has no independent existence in the presence of God. [The rejected one] is not determined by God merely to be rejected. He is determined [that is, God determines him] to hear and say that he is a rejected person elected. This is what the elect of the New Testament are—rejected persons elected in and from their rejection, those in whom Judas lived, but was also slain, as in the case of Paul. They are rejected persons who as such are summoned to faith. They are rejected persons who on the basis of the election of Jesus Christ, and looking to the fact that He delivered Himself up for them, believe in their election. (506; modified for inclusive language)

In other words, Barth ends up preaching election to Judas. Put on your magnifiers and read the whole fifty-page, small-print section. It's worth it.[11]

It's so riveting that in the meanwhile, you have finally forgotten about yourself. At the end of 506 pages of avoiding the election of the present-day individual, Barth has accomplished the impossible: he has distracted you from yourself, immersed you in the strange new world of the Bible, directed you to Jesus, and succeeded in unasking the question, "What about me?"

Barth thinks it's a terrifically bad, sub-Christian question, because it's self-centered and self-absorbed, and it needs to be ruled out of court. For Augustine, the very definition of sin is to be turned in on yourself, *incurvatus in se*, so that you become smaller and smaller like a tightening curve or diminishing circle. But it's like this: if the prosecutor asks the witness, "When did you stop beating your wife?" and the defense attorney yells, "Objection! Objection!" the jury remembers the bad question even more. So Barth has to *distract* his audience with something even more interesting, like a defense attorney who turns cartwheels across the courtroom. Barth's lengthy exposition is a *therapy* against self-absorption; it aims to take you out of yourself and fill your eyes with Someone Else.

According to legend, a radio interviewer once put Barth on the spot in a live broadcast where he couldn't evade for five hundred pages. The host asked Barth point-blank, "Do you teach universal salvation?" And Barth replied equally bluntly. According to legend, he said, "I don't teach universal salvation. But I preach it until the end of the world."[12]

What does that mean? "I don't teach it" means Barth didn't have the data from the New Testament and the tradition to prove that it's true. He's a careful scholar; he knows that the New Testament assumes eternal punishment and puts it onto the lips of Jesus and into parables attributed to him. "I preach it," on the other hand, is an observation about the grammar of correct Christian speech.

Barth's strategy arises from *how Christians talk* about salvation; he makes an observation about the grammar of their speech: that grammar works like conjugating a verb. It works differently for "I," "you," and "he/she/they." In the first person, in the mode of prayer and confession, I know only one person worthy of damnation—myself. So I pray, "O God, have mercy on me, a sinner." In the second person, in the mode of preaching and exhortation, I say (if I am a preacher), "Hear the good news of the Gospel: Jesus Christ died for *you*!" In that second mode, I cannot preach, "Hear the ambiguous news of the sorting machine: Jesus Christ died for the people on the right, but the people on the left are out of luck!" The preaching of Jesus to all marks the second person grammar of sermons and missions. In the third person, I cannot know what God wills to become of each person; about any concrete him/her/them, I cannot speak because I cannot speak for God.

---

11 Barth, *Church Dogmatics* II/2, 449-506.
12 I don't have a source for this story, but this version is similar: Karl Barth, *Barth in Conversation*, vol. 1, 1959–1962, ed. Eberhard Busch (Louisville, KY: Westminster John Knox Press, 2017) 1:129–30.

Knowing what God wills for each person—that the person know their election—Barth regards the nonelect person as simply *not elect yet* or even *not yet aware* of their election. So nonelection (or nonawareness) is not a negative but a not yet, a placeholder for where an elect person might be. In mathematics, a placeholder is not a negative but a zero. That puts us in position to revisit our chart.

Author	Identity of the electing God	Identity of the elect	Identity of the nonelect	Nature of election	Nature of nonelection
Wyschogrod	God of Israel; God of Abraham, Isaac, and Jacob; God of the Covenant	The people Israel	Gentiles	Service, witness	Different job, younger brother
Calvin (*Barth's mathematical view*)	Unknown X	X	Rejected X	Positive number	Negative number
Barth	Jesus	Jesus	Jesus	Suffering servant (Jesus)	Not yet elect; placeholder for election (like zero)

Christians Talk about Incarnation, or God Chooses Humanity

6 Athanasius Talks about a God Who Becomes a Human Being

Christians speak of a God who chooses to become a human being. Biblical narratives require two ways of describing the unitary character of Jesus, human and divine. Doctrine calls the two ways of talking two natures in one person, or two whats in one who.

In many cases, Christian-speak develops in an attempt to *go on talking the way the Bible or the New Testament talks.* There is a character in the New Testament who acts both as a human being and as God. This character bears various names, including "Jesus," "Christ," "Word," and "Son," all for the same character. The question arose very early in Christianity about how to go on talking about this character. To go on talking about him as the New Testament did, the earliest Christians tended to think they had to decide whether to talk about him as a human being or as God. It took them almost four hundred years to figure out how to say both.

You will notice that Athanasius (293–373), like Calvin, Barth, and most of our other interlocutors, is writing in the midst of controversy, because our interlocutory text this time is called *Against the Arians.* That's why I call Christianese a language in which to disagree. In spite of the anti-Semitic way in which Athanasius compares his opponents to "Jews," his is an intra-Christian dispute. Athanasius calls Arians "Jews" in the way that Republicans call Democrats "socialists": not because it's true but as a gratuitous insult. Athanasius does not expect any Jews to be reading it. This is a symptom of the *rabies theologorum,* the rabies of the theologians, by which they foam at the mouth. (By the way, "Arians," named after Athanasius's rival Arius [250/256–336], have nothing to do with German "Aryans.")

The dispute is ugly but instructive. Arius and Athanasius disagree about how to go on talking about Jesus. Arius thinks it's of crucial importance to the worship of the One true God that you draw a line between God and creatures. A creature is any created thing, and for Arius, Jesus has to be on one side of that line or the other. See figure 6.1.

God/world

Figure 6.1. Arius's heretical picture of God and the world classifies Jesus as a supercreature and traps God on one side of the line.

In Arius's view, Jesus can be as powerful as you like, a superman, as long as he is on the world side of the line. Therefore, Jesus is a creature.

Athanasius says, in effect, I agree with you on distinguishing God and creation—but he draws the opposite conclusion. After all, God drew the line. For that very reason, *God can cross that line.* God is not *trapped* beyond creation by God's own line. So I see your line, and I raise it, like figure 6.2.

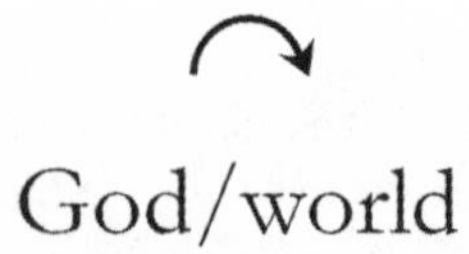

$$\curvearrowright$$

God/world

Figure 6.2. Athanasius's picture of God and the world interprets Jesus as God the Word crossing the line.

Athanasius had found a way to say both. The line is real, and Jesus belongs on both sides of it. Yes, human and divine are not the same, *and* Jesus is not only one or only the other or a third, mixed thing. God does not erase or fuzz the line; God just steps over it. Although it takes several generations for Arians to die out, and Arians exist today without knowing it in every congregation, Arius has been outflanked, and Athanasius wins. To go on talking the way the New Testament talks, you have to let God out of the box. You have to speak of Jesus as human *and* as God.

Because God the Son—or, as Athanasius prefers, God the Word—steps over the line, the line does not run through Jesus or divide him. It's his line; he is not its creature. So the character of Jesus is unitary, not divided.

There are several narrative reasons the character of Jesus has to be unitary. First is the sort of "magic realism" of the text. If you're reading a South American novel in the genre of magic realism, you have to just accept—or suspend disbelief—that someone can pass through a wall or return from the dead, or you need to stop reading the novel because it won't make sense as a novel anymore.

But there is a deeper reason. That reason is that *the story ceases to make sense if part of the plot happens to one character and part of the plot happens to another.* If part of *Romeo and Juliet* happens to Juliet, then Mercutio dies, and Romeo lives to marry somebody else and live happily ever after, you have a completely different story. *Romeo and Juliet* depends on the idea that the one who loves the other dies. Similarly, the New Testament story requires that one who was crucified is raised. If the crucifixion happens to Jesus and resurrection happens only to Lazarus, the Gospel doesn't make sense.

And there is a deeper reason still. The story also ceases to make sense if the human who is crucified is not also *God*, since the crucifixion and resurrection have to be of salvific significance. They have to change human nature from the inside. Even if Lazarus had been crucified before he was raised, that wouldn't change human nature or the relation of the world to God. Only God can *use* the events to change the world. Traditional exegesis sees that in what doubting Thomas exclaims when he puts his finger into the side of Jesus: "My lord and my God" (John 20:28). "My lord," according to Thomas Aquinas (1225–74; not the same Thomas) refers to the human being, his teacher, and is an act of human recognition. "My God," however, refers to the Creator and Redeemer of the world and is an act of faith. What the disciple really understands, according to Aquinas, is that the two are one: his teacher is the Re-Creator of human nature.

The character Jesus seems to act with two sets of capacities. One set identifies him as a human being: he weeps, speaks, eats, dies, and is born. Another set of capacities identifies him as divine: he forgives sins. A voice from heaven identifies him as God's "Son," and the opening of the Gospel of John rewrites Genesis to identify him as God and credit him with creating the world: "In the beginning was the Word, and the Word was with God, and the Word *was* God. . . . All things were made by him; and without him was not any thing made that was made" (John 1:1, 3; my italics). The reason we need to talk about Jesus as human and as God is that the New Testament talks about him as acting in those ways.

Athanasius answers a similar question with a similar answer: "What is the basic meaning and purport of Holy Scripture? It contains, as we have often said, a *double account [Logos] of the Savior.* It says that he has always been God and is the Son, because he is the Logos and radiance and Wisdom of the Father. Furthermore, it says that in the end he became a human being, he took flesh for our sakes from the Virgin Mary, the God-bearer."[1]

The simplest way to say this is that the Christian tradition speaks of Jesus as two *whats* in one *who*. Two *whats*, or two sets of capacities, and one *who*, or one singular, unitary agent. The one character acts, that is, from two categories and requires, therefore, two ways of speaking. The traditional language for the two *whats* in one *who* is two natures (*phuseis*) in one person (*hypostasis*). As a *who*, a person in this sense is just the bearer of a nature, of a set of capacities.

It's simpler first to consider other "natures." Suppose you have this set of capacities: "woofs, wags tail, bears or begets puppies." In that case, you have a canine nature. But in order for that to be more than an abstract possibility, you need an *actual dog*—that is, a *who*, like Rover, Lassie, or Spot. Jesus is *one* bearer of *two* sets of capacities, *but the capacities cannot act on their own.* Only the bearer of the capacities can act. The *idea* of a dog cannot bear puppies; only Lassie can do that. We could imagine the nature or even the DNA of a dodo, but we can't have a walking dodo without a real dodo. That's very important because it blocks a christological mistake. *You are not allowed to say* "~~the human part did this, but the divine part did that~~." In particular, you are not allowed to make these mistakes:

---

1 The reading for the course was Athanasius, *Orations against the Arians*, in *The Christological Controversy*, ed. and trans. Richard A. Norris Jr. (Philadelphia: Fortress Press, 1980), 83–101. Here the reference is to Athanasius III.29, p. 87; my italics. Further references will be by book and section number in the text with page numbers from Norris.

~~The human part suffered, but the divine part was immune.~~
~~The crucifixion only happened to the human nature, and the resurrection~~
~~only happened to God.~~

Those mistakes would mean that a human nature did something, not a human person, or that free-floating divine capacities did something, not the Second Person of the Trinity. Those mistakes would mean that the incarnation was a fake, and God was only pretending to be with humans. Those mistakes would mean that Jesus was not one Person but that there were ~~"two people in there."~~ Rather, as we will see in the next section, it's important to say (with Cyril of Alexandria) that God the Word or God the Son (not God the Source or the Father) took on suffering and underwent death.

But Athanasius makes the point that Jesus is a singular agent in an elegant way. He points to how the healing stories work.

> Thus, when it was necessary to raise up Peter's mother in law, who was suffering from a fever, it was a human act when he extended his hand but a divine act when he caused the disease to cease. Likewise, in the case of "the man blind from birth" [John 9:6] it was human spittle which he spat, but it was a divine act when he opened the man's eyes. . . . And where Lazarus is concerned, he uttered human speech in his capacity as a human being, but it was a divine act when, in his capacity as God, he raised Lazarus from the dead. (III.32, p. 90)

We may sum up the unity of Jesus's person like this: He does *divine things humanly and human things divinely*. Or to expand it a bit, Jesus does divine things *by human means* and human things *with divine result*. The principle has wide application. Jesus does a human thing, he is born, with a divine result: God is with us. He does a human thing, he dies, with a divine result, everlasting life. He does a divine thing, he forgives sins, by human means, speech. He does a divine thing, reform human nature, by human means: he leads a human life.

7 Tanner Refuses to Talk about Human and Divine as Rivals

The two are not rivals, because the Person of the Word is elevating (saving) human nature.

For the first ten years or so that I taught this material, I drew the human and divine natures side by side, as two sets of capacities that switched, in what theologians call "the blessed exchange." (See figure 7.1.)

$$\left\{ \begin{array}{c} \textit{is perfectly righteous} \\ \textit{lives forever} \\ \textit{understands everything} \end{array} \right\} <> \left\{ \begin{array}{c} \textit{bears sin} \\ \textit{undergoes death} \\ \textit{learns over time} \end{array} \right\}$$

Figure 7.1. The blessed exchange usually pictures divine and human natures as two sets of capacities on the same level.

In figure 7.1, a blessed exchange takes place in Jesus, whereby he takes on the human features of bearing sin, death, and learning over time in order to bestow on us the divine features of righteousness, everlasting life, and consummate understanding, or the beatific vision. The two arrows mean exchange: Jesus takes on the bad stuff so that we get the good stuff.

But when I place the two sets side by side, a lot of tension remains. It's not immediately clear why some divine capacities are left out (creating your own worlds from scratch and saving them) and why some human features are mere limitations (like learning over time) while others are just plain bad (like sinning). That's because the side-by-side presentation implies, even if it never says, that the two are *rivals*. But Jesus, in saving human nature, *befriends* human beings, putting them on the same side. Or, as Barth put it, God makes the lost cause of the human being to be God's own cause. So no rivalry.

Kathy Tanner has taught me a better way.[1] (This is not Athanasius anymore.) The two sets belong one on top of the other—*because divinity and humanity do not belong on the same level.* God *made* humanity, so divinity is humanity's *source.* And humanity is no stable category but one meant for *change*—that is, to grow. The destiny of the human nature is *to grow into God,* which we'll see more about in the next section. In short, the divine features belong *above* the human features, as in figure 7.2.

---

1 The reading for the course was Kathryn Tanner, "Who Is Jesus?," in *Jesus, Humanity and the Trinity* (Minneapolis: Fortress Press, 2001), 1–34.

$$\left\{ \begin{array}{l} creates \\ redeems \\ sanctifies \\ elevates \end{array} \right\}$$

$$\downarrow\uparrow$$

$$\left\{ \begin{array}{l} bears\ sin \\ dies \\ learns \end{array} \right\}$$

Figure 7.2. Tanner's revision of the blessed exchange pictures the divine set of capacities creating, redeeming, and elevating human nature from above.

In that case (figure 7.2), the double arrows mean Christ comes down and human beings, by his Spirit, go up. The elevation of human beings by Christ's descent and indwelling of human nature expands human limits and cures human negatives. It also means that divine qualities like creating worlds do not elevate humans out of whole cloth but only grow them into those divine qualities that all Christians associate with life with God in heaven, things like everlasting life, perfect understanding, and stable righteousness. The divine capacities remain God's, but the human capacities are redeemable and expandable. The short version is this: elevation is a better metaphor than exchange. That makes sense because God was always the source-from-above of human life, and life with God was always humanity's destiny.

The priority of God also works better in the incarnation. There are (at least!) two views in the New Testament. In the Gospel of Mark, which (spoiler alert!) has no birth story at all but begins with Jesus's baptism (Mark 1:1-11), it looks as if God uses the baptism to adopt an already existing human being—Jesus—because, perhaps, Jesus is so good or worthy or promising. That's called "adoptionism," an extreme form of "Christology from below." In the Gospel of John, on the other hand—which (spoiler alert!) also has no birth story at all but begins with the preexistence of the Word with the Father before the creation of the world—God the Word comes down to be among us human beings (John 1:1-18). That's called "preexistence Christology" or "Christology from above." All the theologians in this book follow the second option. Among theologians, the strategy of John's Gospel is the overwhelming favorite. The fact that Athanasius refers to Jesus most often as the Logos rather than the Son shows that he is following the Gospel of John.

"Logos" means the Word, Sermon, Account, Story, or Reason of God. It's the same word as appears in the names of disciplines like biology and theology. To the extent that Christianity is the religion of Jesus, it is also a religion of Reason because Jesus is the Reason of God among us.

The priority of the Logos means that the theological mainstream, including Athanasius, Barth, and the others, prefers to think that the bearer of Jesus's capacities is, both logically and before all worlds, the Logos or Word of God and only later comes down to be a human being among us. The Logos first has a divine nature and only in time comes to take on a human nature. (That doesn't answer the question of whether the Logos always already intended to take on a human nature, as Athanasius and Barth think, or decided "later," after humans sinned.) The priority of the Logos means that there was *not* a preexisting human being for the Logos to inhabit, indwell, or possess. It means that the human being Jesus was created when the Logos took on a human nature. The human nature had a bearer, the Logos, so the human being was real. But there wasn't anybody "else" in there, *only the Logos or Word of God*. (This Christology is called "enhypostatic," which means that the human nature of Jesus exists only in the hypostasis, or Person, of the Word, not by itself.) That means that whatever happened to Jesus happened to God, because there wasn't anyone else in there for it to happen to.

Here's another way to see why priority has to go to the divine nature. What if the human being did come first (contrary to theological consensus) and only then took on a divine nature so that the bearer of the divine nature was originally human? Then stories other than those of the canonical New Testament could make sense, like the stories in the *Infancy Gospel of Thomas*,[2] where the kid Jesus, learning to use his divine powers over time, kills and resurrects his playmates for fun and practice. That doesn't sound like the Jesus you've heard of before? That's because, from a theological point of view, the *Infancy Gospel of Thomas* has the incarnation upside down. You can recognize that the *Infancy Gospel of Thomas* is working with a human being using divine powers with caprice, whereas this book has already interpreted Jesus in the orthodox way, so that Jesus is God using human nature to accomplish the elevation of human beings. To repeat, priority of the Logos doesn't mean the human being Jesus is less a human being, because by definition to be a human being is to be a bearer of a human nature, and the Logos *is* a bearer of a human nature once it takes on a human nature to be its very own. What the priority of the Logos does mean is that the *way* in which Jesus is a human being really matters (his *tropos hyparxeos*, or way of existing). According to Christian orthodoxy,[3] he exists as God with us in the flesh, not as a fallible human with superpowers.

---

2 *The Infancy Gospel of Thomas*, in *The Other Gospels: Accounts of Jesus from Outside the New Testament*, ed. and trans. Bart Ehrmann and Zlatko Plese (New York: Oxford University Press, 2013), 3–14.
3 "Christian orthodoxy" is a mental practice of social consensus supported by texts and other authorities and subject to dispute.

Now, God existing in the flesh[4] does lead to all kinds of paradox, which Cyril of Alexandria glories in.[5] I owe to David Yeago my attention to these two: "Impassibly he suffered," and "One of the Trinity has suffered for us in the flesh."[6] "Impassibly" means "without being able to suffer": it is no part of divinity to suffer, but God took on flesh precisely to be *able* to suffer. It's as if Cyril had written, "Bullet-proof vested, he exposed himself"—except that human nature was something that God in Christ took on rather than divine nature something the Logos took off. The paradoxes stress that God's suffering and death in Jesus were voluntary. They mean that there is no one else in Jesus to whom to ascribe his suffering and death but the Person of the Word. In Jesus, for our sake, the Logos of God underwent death. Death was possible for the Logos because the Logos took on a human nature, and there was no independently existing human being to bear it, only the human being who *was* the Logos.

That does not mean, however, that *the Father* suffers and dies. "Was crucified, died, and was buried" means that God underwent death in Jesus but not God the Father. God the Son (or God the Word) underwent death in Jesus. It's somewhat as if I stub my toe. The pain applies to me as a whole, but it's not in my hand; it's in my toe. The death applies to God as a whole, but only *one* of the Trinity has died, not the Father and not the Spirit, only the Word.

The orthodox conclusion that the subject of the suffering is God the Word is called "theopaschism," God-suffering, whereas the idea that the suffering of Jesus also infects the Father is traditionally regarded as the heresy of "patripassianism," Father-suffering. In the twentieth century, it became popular to ascribe a different suffering to the Father, not in the flesh but in sympathy. That way, through solidarity with the Son, the Father and the Spirit are not left out of solidarity with the human being (for example, Jürgen Moltmann). Critics reply that if the whole Trinity suffers and dies, then there is no one left over to save. That's why Cyril's paradox is precise. *One* of the Trinity has died for us. Not the whole thing.

The rule is this: ascribe everything that Jesus undertakes and undergoes to God in the Person of the Logos. This is called "the communication of the attributes." Catholic and Calvinist theologians tend to read this communication only in one direction so that what you say of Jesus applies to God, because God the Logos is the subject of the humanity—Jesus is the humanity of God—while God the Logos (as well as the Father and the Spirit) exists also outside the flesh. But Lutherans deny that

---

4   "God existing in the flesh" means "God the Logos or God the Son existing in Jesus." When I say "God" in this paragraph, I don't mean "God the Father" unless I specify "God the Father." Rather, I mean "God the Logos" (existing in the flesh) or "God the Trinity" (without further specification). The Trinity comes up in chapter 5.

5   The reading for the course was Cyril of Alexandria, 2d Letter to Nestorius, in Christological Controversy, 131–35.

6   Cyril of Alexandria, Ad Reginas De Recta Fide Oratio Altera 163 (Patrologia Graeca 76, 1393B). Yeago's two theses seem to divide a complex remark of Cyril that Rowan Greer translates, "United with a humanity like ours, he suffered human things impassibly in his own flesh" (unpublished). I owe the citation and translation to J. Warren Smith. See also J. Warren Smith, "Suffering Impassibly: Christ's Passion in Cyril of Alexandria's Soteriology," Pro Ecclesia 11 (2002): 463–83.

God the Logos exists outside the flesh after the incarnation and delight in invent-
ing Cyrillian-style paradox at the other extreme as well. In the Lutheran view, it is
necessary to say, "An infant ruled the world from the manger," because there was
no other place for God except the child; God was *restlos eingefleischt*, incarnate
without remainder. Thus for Luther "a human being sits at the right hand of the
Father." Lutherans follow an additional, disputed rule: ascribe everything that the Word
does after the incarnation to the flesh. See if you want to follow the incarnation that
far. Speaking for myself, I love the Lutheran paradoxes, but I wonder if they follow
from the priority of the Logos. The priority of the Logos says that the Logos is the
sole bearer of the human nature, not that the human nature confines the Logos.
The Lutheran theologian Robert Jenson would call my scruples a failure of nerve.[7]

The profound thing about the Cyrillian paradoxes is that they effectively take
up the statement of the Song of Songs 8:6 NKJV—"Love *is as* strong as death"—and pose
it as a question. Is love as strong as death? Because one of the Trinity becomes a human
being and subjects himself to death. Cyril's answer is that love is stronger than death
because love is able to turn even death to its purposes: this is a death that gives life.
(We will return to that question when we get to Balthasar, Trinity, and Communion.)

The trouble with the Cyrillian approach is that you can misread his paradoxes
to imply a competition between the divine and the human. Kathy Tanner, channel-
ing Irenaeus, wields the antidote. God is befriending human nature by healing it
from the inside, by reliving a human life correctly, so that the Creator can repair
it moment by moment, doing it properly. The beauty of her approach is not paradox
but the harmony whereby Creator and creature are always in accord as the life of
Jesus heals humanity in a human way, over time, with a divine result, re-creation.

We can sum up this section in the words of Richard Norris (1930–2005):

> Jesus Christ is "one hypostasis" but "in two natures," that is, he is a single
> reality, the divine Logos, existing as such, and at the same time existing
> as a human being.
>
> This formula, the final product of the christological controversies, is
> essentially a rule of christological language. Its terms are not calculated
> to picture the way in which Jesus is put together. Rather, they are calcu-
> lated to explain how it is proper to speak of him. Orthodoxy consists in the
> acknowledgment that Jesus is one subject, who is properly spoken of both
> as God—the divine Logos—and as a human being. To give an account of
> Jesus, then, one must talk in two ways simultaneously. One must account
> for all that he is and does by reference to the Logos of God, that is, one
> must identify him as God acting in our midst. At the same time, however,
> one must account for him as a human being in the ordinary sense of that

---

7   For more about this controversy, see Robert W. Jenson and Eric Gritsch, *Lutheranism: The Theological Movement and Its Confessional Writings* (Philadelphia: Fortress Press, 1976) 97-101.

term. Both accounts are necessary. One cannot understand Jesus correctly by taking either account independently, even while recognizing that they really are different accounts. There is a sense, therefore, in which it is true that the Council of Chalcedon solves the christological problem by laying out its terms. Its formula dictates not a Christology but formal outlines of an adequate christological language.[8]

---

8   Norris, *Christological Controversy*, 30–31.

Christians Talk about Atonement, or God Chooses the Lost

8 Athanasius Talks about God Becoming Human to Make Humans Divine

If God becomes human, is God subject to death? How can human beings join the Trinitarian feast if death divides it? Christians offer various accounts of why God became a human being. Did God become human to die for sin, or to exemplify love? Did God become human to descend into hell and lead captives to heaven? Athanasius says that God becomes human to make humans divine.

In this, the longest part of the book, we consider six or seven versions of how Jesus saves. Each atonement theory attempts to retell the story of Jesus so as to pick out what is logically important about the stories. The nice thing is that the stories always contain more than the theories. That means that none of the theories is exhaustive; none captures all the important bits. No church has outlawed any of the other theories. Whether you are reading this book just because you want to know how Christians talk about these things or because you adhere to a church that favors one theory, you are always free to take features you like from the others. Because the theories are not really self-contained but commentaries on the stories, it is always appropriate to mix and match. Each theory encapsulates a narrower view of what the problem is with human beings and how the work of Jesus solves it—that is, how Jesus saves. If you feel compelled by a different aspect of the work of Christ, you perceive a different problem, and if you start with a different problem, you get a different solution. In the most famous and popular atonement theory, that of Anselm, the problem to be solved is sin regarded as a debt. But what if the problem is death? Or sin regarded as social? Or suffering? Or what if the problem is a transaction in heaven that fails to deliver love on earth?

• • •

What follows was inspired by reading Athanasius, but I'm not sure that it is Athanasius any longer. I have been changing it over many years until, one semester at a time, the light dawned in students' eyes. What remains is no longer exposition of Athanasius, or even interpretation of Athanasius. It is more of a fantasia upon Athanasius.

If the works of the Logos' Godhead had not been done by means of the body, humanity would not have been divinized. Furthermore, if the properties of the flesh had not been reckoned to the Logos, humanity would not have been completely liberated from them.

> The Logos himself is impassible by nature and . . . he nevertheless has these passions predicated of him in virtue of the flesh which he took on, since they are proper to the flesh and the body itself is proper to the Savior. . . . And human beings, because their own passions have been transferred to the impassible and abolished, are henceforth becoming impassible and free of them to all eternity.

> The flesh [has now] been "logified" by the work of the divine Logos who on our account became flesh.

Those sayings from *Orations against the Arians*[1] (III.33, pp. 91, 93, 92) vary what Athanasius says several times in different ways: God becomes human that humans might become divine. Here, God the Logos became flesh in order for us humans to become like the Logos. Athanasius acknowledges that God uses flesh, takes on flesh, to save us. But the problem with human beings also begins in the flesh. The flesh is the site where the problem arises and the problem is solved.

The difference between God and creatures is that what God has eternally God wants to give to creatures over time. Time is a creaturely capacity to receive gifts. God brings creatures to Godself by *growing them*. God is stable and creatures are to change. God created creatures to grow them toward, even into God. "Flesh" means, among many other things, the capacity to grow, which is also more neutrally a capacity to change. A foreseen but unintended side effect of flesh is that what was meant for growth (change up) could also decay (change down). A good God, foreseeing the unintended effect, would protect against it. That's why God put the human being into the garden of Eden. It was a safe place for vulnerable flesh. In an anachronistic analogy, it was like putting the flesh into a refrigerator to prevent rot.

So flesh was intended for good, to grow, but under conditions current in Late Antiquity, its defects were even more pungent than they are today. The trouble with flesh, under conditions after the fall, was that it would run down and rot. It ran down in two ways: physically and morally. Physically, the rot led to death; morally, the rot led to sin. But the physical rot was even more impressive. People you loved—your mother, your lover—were subject to disease, as in the time of the coronavirus pandemic, and could slowly or suddenly run down, die, and start to rot. You had to get them into the ground as quickly as possible because they were dangerous to others, and they stank. They stank like rotting meat, because that's what they were. The word for this capacity to change, focused on the negative

---

1 See note 1 in chapter 6.

and physical end of it, was *corruptibility*, and that was the problem to be solved in human nature.[2]

Now, God wasn't at fault for that, according to the theory. God had made provision for the marvel to take place, that humans would grow safely from corruptibility to incorruptibility: the provisions were the garden and the Word. The garden, as I said, was like a refrigerator, or like a sufficiently cool environment (not North Carolina or Athanasius's Egypt), where flesh would remain safe from rot. And the Word was the command, "Don't touch that dial!" which would turn up the temperature in the fridge. Well, you know what happened, and Adam and Eve began the process of rot for the whole human race. But God provided for that, too, because the Word was not only the command, "Don't touch that dial!" but also the Person of God who would take on their flesh with the power of life and revivify it from the inside.

The binary contrast between growth and decay shows that Athanasius was no environmentalist, as I have learned from Aminah Al-Attas Bradford. But Athanasius does allow that life comes from the death of Jesus, which uses death despite itself to grow divinity, so perhaps you can find an environmental Athanasius after all.[3] Changing the metaphor again, the incarnation worked like an inoculation, good infection, or fermentation, the leaven in the loaf or the yeast in the wine that outcompetes the bad bacteria to stop and inspirit the otherwise rotting flesh.[4] The solution was to inoculate (to safely reinfect) the flesh with the life of the Word, to logify or divinize it. The solution, in short, was to replace corruptibility with incorruptibility. God became flesh that flesh might become divine.

"Divinize" was biblical (2 Pet 1:4; Ps 82:6), and it never meant that the humans would get to create their own worlds, forgive the sins of others, or intervene in salvation history from heaven. It just meant the same things that all Christians hope for in heaven: righteousness, happiness, and eternal life—with the recognition that those are divine characteristics. Human divinization was a sharing in the divine life that depended on God. In that vein, even a Methodist hymn could pray God to "receive us as gods to a share of thy Throne."[5] Indeed, in that case, love would be stronger than death.

It's important to note that the Word would have divinized the human being even if the flesh had not run down. The incarnation was not the solution to a botched job but intended from the beginning. To see how, you have to observe that usually

---

2 "Decay" is a frequent metaphor for sin in Christian theology. Environmentalists have taught us to think of decay as a natural process, not a sign of evil. But reformulating the language would take us far from the sources. For an attempt to think that through, see Aminah Bradford, "Symbiotic Grace: A Holobiont Theology in the Age of the Microbe" (PhD diss., Duke University, 2020)—or the book that comes out of that.

3 For a recovery of environmentalist elements in Athanasius, see Virginia Burrus, *Ancient Christian Ecopoetics* (Philadelphia: University of Pennsylvania Press, 2019), 45–53. For a modern environmentalist theology in the Athanasian tradition, see Dumitru Staniloae, *Orthodox Dogmatic Theology*, vol. 2, *Creation and Deification* (London: Bloomsbury T&T Clark, 2002).

4 I owe my attention to metaphors of fermentation also to Aminah Bradford.

5 Quoted from Charles Wesley, "Hymn for Christian Friends," in S. T. Kimbrough, *Partakers of the Divine Life* (Eugene, OR: Cascade Books, 2016), 139. I owe the reference to Kendall Soulen.

we think of creation, fall, and redemption as static. But in Athanasius, they are not states. They are vectors. They are movements; they have direction. They're not static; they're dynamic.

Thus creation is not a floor; it is an up escalator. Fallenness is a down escalator. And the incarnation is God the Word supporting and accompanying us upward. The fall does not necessitate a change of direction for God: God was always going to come down to join us. Under conditions of corruption, the incarnation just reaches down to pick us up on a lower floor. In the beginning, heaven was already in view; there was more in store for human beings even than Eden. In the end, heaven was more glorious even than before, because God had saved the human from hell.

Creation is for the movement in figure 8.1, which we may call elevation.

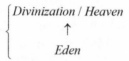

Figure 8.1. Elevation is a movement defined from its upward direction toward life with God.

Fallenness results in the movement in figure 8.2, which is, of course, falling.

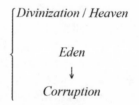

Figure 8.2. The fall is a movement defined from its downward direction away from God.

Redemption is for the movement in figure 8.3, which is "salvation."

Figure 8.3. Salvation is an upward movement distinguished by its origin, the lower position that the human being is saved from.

Elevation is named from its end point, the upward movement. *Falling* is named from its direction, down. *Salvation* is named from its origin, something from which humans need to be saved. Salvation and elevation are named from opposite ends of the one movement in which God accompanies the human being from bottom to top. But salvation and elevation largely coincide. Salvation is just elevation from farther down. It's not a new movement. It's God's persistence in the original plan. Anselm put this very simply in a chapter title of his treatise *Why God Became Human*. He says, "God would complete what he began."[6] God has a sense of dramatic irony, in which God delights to take the worst that human beings have done as the starting point of their elevation.

It is true that the human being ascends the great distance from fall to heaven. But that is not by human power alone. Rather, the ascension of the human being depends on what I call the superball theory of grace, where a superball is one that lands so hard that it bounces back higher than it began. Only because Christ leaps down and pushes off or bounces back from the bottom does the Holy Spirit receive the energy to propel weighty creatures all the way up to heaven. "God becomes human that we might become divine" means God comes down so that we (by the power of the Spirit) might bounce up.

For comparison with other views, we may put Athanasius's theory into a chart.

Author	Problem	Solution	Christ's role	Name	Holiday	How we participate
Athanasius	Corruptibility, especially death	Share the divine nature	Become human to make us divine	Christus Victor	Easter	Join a desert monastery

The last three columns require comment. The name Christus Victor, or "Christ the Victor," became popular only in the twentieth century in a book of that name by Gustaf Aulén. He coined it to contrast with Anselm's, which he called *Christ the Victim* and which comes next. Aulén used it not primarily for Athanasius but for an even earlier theory called the "ransom" theory, which we'll encounter later because Anselm and Abelard make fun of it. (Note how many of these guys start with A: Athanasius, Anselm, Abelard. Remember them by the *second* letter of their names.) In any case, the contrast with Anselm stands: for Athanasius as for his predecessors, Christ was *victorious over death*, and indeed, in early Christian art, Christ looks serene or triumphant even on the cross. Crucifixions depicting Christ as a suffering victim began only much later.

The holiday implied is Easter. Given Athanasius's emphasis on incarnation, you might think Christmas, but evidence for celebration of Christmas at all is thin until the mid-fourth century.

---

6 Anselm of Canterbury, *Why God Became Human*, in *A Scholastic Miscellany: Anselm to Ockham*, ed. and trans. by Eugene R. Fairweather, Library of Christian Classics, vol. 10 (Philadelphia: Westminster Press, 1956), bk. 2, ch. 4.

"How we participate" has two poles. Because God is divinizing human nature as a whole, all humans participate in the grace of Christ. Athanasius thought that people were living longer and wars were ceasing because of the incarnation. (Turned out to be effects of the Roman Empire that disappeared when the barbarians arrived.) But there was a much more intensive way to participate, which Athanasius also listed as a result of the incarnation, a way that modeled the return of the human being to the upward path: asceticism.

In the table above, I have written that the way we participate is to join a desert monastery. That's a bit of a joke. The fairer way to put it is that Athanasius highlights asceticism. *Askesis* in Greek means "discipline" or "training." In Modern Greek, it means "homework." Asceticism is not captured by the notion of "giving things up." Rather, it's the pearl of great price: giving something up that you won't miss because you'd so much rather have the prize. We do this all the time today and for many of the same reasons, if somewhat less effectively. We diet and we go to the gym, all for something we'd much rather have—not just a beautiful body, but one that other people will love. Really, we do it in hopes of love. And dieting and going to the gym are not very effective at procuring love. But ancient asceticism, including the desert monastery, had better prospects. The wager was that life with or apart from others would be training for life with God.

You don't see it in our selection from *Orations against the Arians*, but Athanasius also wrote the first biography of a hermit, the *Life of Anthony*. In Athanasius's time, monasteries were breaking out all over the desert. For him, divinity involved getting free of the passions. So divinization involved abandoning the self-regard of hunger, sexual desire, and (more troublesome than either) anger.[7] To be logified is to subject the flesh to reason. In that way, monks, nuns, and hermits began to display in their bodies the transparency to the divine that also marked the angels. This was no holy anorexia but an availability to others that swept the body up into a great spiritual venture, to retrace the descent of Christ into flesh by rendering flesh ethereal on the way back up. Properly understood, asceticism sweeps the body up into such a glorious venture. I also called it "join a desert monastery" because it's the only bit of Athanasius's theory I'm not attracted to.

---

7 There is good anger, the desire for justice. There is bad anger, the desire to justify yourself. The self-abandonment of the desert is about learning the difference.

9 Anselm Talks about Christ Paying a Debt of Honor

Anselm originates the most popular atonement theory, that Christ pays a debt for our sins. But "debt" doesn't mean money, and you don't accept the payment with your mind. You accept it into your mouth.

Imagine you're riding down the highway. You see a billboard of Jesus with his arms outstretched on a cross. The words on the billboard say what? (Of all the sections in the book, this is the one where you're most likely to guess what's coming.) "He died for our sins." Or, if you wanted another verb, "He died to pay for our sins." This is the most familiar atonement theory in Western Christianity, Protestant and Catholic. Because it's the most popular atonement theory among Catholics, at over a billion, it's also the most popular among Christians, period.

It's the theory that picks out Christ's *death* as the most important moment in the story; death is the moment that makes the theory work. It's the theory in which the human problem is sin. And it's the one that uses payment as a metaphor. See how Anselm's theory already differs from Athanasius's. For Athanasius, death appears in the problem column; for Anselm, it appears in the solution. For Athanasius, both death and sin are only two *results* of the underlying problem, corruptibility, with death arguably the most salient, especially to the nose. For Athanasius, the solution is life—divine life—not death. God in Christ passes through death, of course, but for Athanasius, death is not a means but an irony. And for Athanasius, "payment" or "satisfaction" is not the moving metaphor but divinization, sharing in the death-defying life of God.

In what follows, I want you to make a sharp distinction between what Anselm says and intends, on the one hand, and the ways in which readers have developed and misinterpreted him, on the other. Both the intention and the history of interpretation matter. In the most charitable version, Anselm really does focus on life and gift—and resembles Athanasius—more than it first appears. In the most critical version, interpreters blame Anselm for the faults of his heirs, so that an implication Anselm denies looks to others like cosmic child abuse.

Of all the sections in the book, this section on Anselm is the one where you're most likely to guess what's coming—except for the context in which it comes. The outlines you've learned from highway signs are there, but other features will surprise. Here is the familiar part: "He [Jesus] took on all the debt that sinners ought

Anselm

to pay, and this when he himself owed nothing, so that he could pay the debt for the others who owed it and could not pay."[1]

That is the familiar shape of *Why God Became Human*. The human being owed but could not pay, God had infinite riches but was not human. So the solution was for God to become human. But that's where the familiarity ends.

The Nature of the Debt

First of all, the most obvious word here—the nontheological, everyday word that seems to make it all concrete—does not mean what you think it does. This is not the kind of debt you have in mind.

When Anselm was alive (1033–1109), there were no banks. Banks as we know them began to be established three to four hundred years later. The great Medici Bank was founded in 1397, almost three hundred years after Anselm died; the oldest bank that still exists, the Bank of Siena, was founded in 1472, more than four hundred years after he was born. There are considerably more years between Anselm's birth and formal banks than between the founding of the United States and the present day. So the debt that Anselm talked about was not like a credit card or mortgage that had to be paid off. No doubt our twenty-first-century culture of mortgages and credit cards resonates for us with Anselm's eleventh-century language, but that's accidental. There are payment metaphors in Anselm's atonement theory. Not banking metaphors.

In the Middle Ages, money persisted in the form of coins. But western Europe did not mint gold coins until after Anselm's death, and even then the rich might prefer to store value in a gold object rather than a gold coin. As an ordinary person, your main debt was to your feudal overlord, in a system not far from sharecropping, and you paid those debts—your taxes and your rents—in crops and service. In the markets, too, you might prefer to barter or to pay "in kind," or with goods. Part of the point of a market was to bring all the barterable goods together to facilitate their exchange among people who used little money.[2] Although you will find the verb *pay* in Anselm and in the New Testament, you will not find any words for *money* in Anselm's atonement theory.

If the debt of which Anselm speaks is not a debt in money or for a bank, what other kind of debt can there be? Anselm speaks repeatedly of a debt of *honor*. He says, for example, "sin is to dishonour God" (l.97, 232), and "Whoever sins should give something better to God in return for the honour of which he has deprived him,

---

1 The reading for the course was Anselm of Canterbury, *Meditation on Human Redemption*, in *Prayers and Meditations of Saint Anselm*, ed. and trans. Benedicta Ward (New York: Penguin, 1973), 230–37; here, 233. Further references will be by line and page number in the text. References to other works of Anselm are footnoted separately.

2 For a survey, see Gaspar Feliu, "Money and Currency," in *Money and Coinage in the Middle Ages*, ed. Rory Naismith (Leiden: Brill, 2019), 21–40; also online at https://tinyurl.com/y2qxl68p.

that is more than the supposed good for the sake of which he dishonoured him" (ll.100–102, 232–33).

Sometimes Anselm compares the dishonor to the destruction of a work of art; the work of art is the image that God makes of Godself in creating the human being. In sinning, that is, humans deface the image of God in themselves. To use an anachronistic metaphor, we are like the guy in 1972 who took a sledgehammer to Michelangelo's *Pietà*. But mostly, Anselm uses the metaphor of "satisfaction." This is not the good kind of satisfaction, like the blues song. This is a sinister sort of satisfaction. The two instances of satisfaction are alike, however. Both are interpersonal—they don't involve money or a statue as an intermediary. And both are bodily. I'm not saying Anselm's God wants punishment or revenge. But Anselm's God does seem to want reparation—repair of the human being for the human's own sake—which God takes on Godself in Christ.

Unfortunately, the reflexive aspect is not nearly as clear in Anselm as it is in Barth. Whereas Barth emphasizes that the Father and the Son are both God—so that the Trinity acts on itself and the Judge is judged in our place—Anselm only sometimes speaks of God suffering for us without further specification, and other times he separates God the Father from God the Son so that what the Son undergoes is said to "please" the Father (p. 234, ll. 139, 142, 145).

Now, Anselm is careful to state that Christ "did not submit to violence, but freely embraced it out of goodness, to the honour of God and the benefit of other human beings" (p. 233, ll. 132–34). This formulation is meant to stress voluntariness—but what it takes for granted is that what Christ undergoes in any case is "violence." Again, "What Christ understood would please the Father and benefit humanity, that he did of his own free will. . . . Such honour could not but please the Father, when the Son freely obeyed the Father, when he willed freely to do what he knew would please him" (p. 234, ll. 142–45). Abelard will ask, in the next section, what kind of father this is, who demands such an honor from his son, who could be "pleased" by such a thing.

The Nature of the Necessity

Anselm is also careful to guard against misunderstandings about the necessity involved. Why couldn't God just forgive, without violence? Anselm agrees: God could have done that. But "God was not obliged to save humankind in this way, but human nature needed to make amends to God like this. God had no need to suffer so laboriously, but the human being needed to be reconciled thus. God did not need to humble himself [note reflexive], but the human being needed this, to be raised from the depths of hell . . . so that human nature might be restored to that for which it was made" (p. 232, ll. 80–88).

We have already seen Anselm insist that what Christ did, he did freely, and Anselm is also careful to supplement the metaphor of debt with others. We find metaphors of revivification, liberation, awakening, resurrection, strengthening, elevation, deliverance, inheritance.

The Nature of the Setting

The strangest feature of all, especially to Protestant readers, is the setting. What's going on here? Where are we when we hear this *Meditation on Human Redemption*? "Christian soul, . . . rouse yourself and remember. . . . Consider again the strength of your salvation and *where* it is found. Meditate upon it, delight in the contemplation of it. . . . *Taste* the goodness of your Redeemer. . . . *Chew* the honeycomb of his words, *suck* their flavor which is sweeter than sap, *swallow* their wholesome sweetness. Chew by thinking, suck by understanding, swallow by loving and rejoicing. [He's not finished yet.] Be glad to chew, be thankful to suck, rejoice to swallow" (p. 230, ll. 1–12; my italics).

A few pages later, he's at it again: "*See*, Christian soul, *here* is the strength of your salvation, *here* is the cause of your freedom, *here* is the price of your redemption. . . . Chew this, bite it, suck it, let your heart swallow it, when your mouth receives the body and blood of your Redeemer. Make it in this life your daily bread, your food, your way-bread, for through this *and not otherwise than through this*, will you remain in Christ and Christ in you, and your joy will be full" (pp. 234–35, ll. 163–71; my italics).

So where is he? He's at Communion. You are supposed to both "taste" and "see" the wafer (echoing Ps 34:8: "Taste and see that the Lord is good"). Have you ever sat through a Communion service and thought, *This is taking longer than I expected. When are we going to get lunch? Maybe I should psych myself up into a more spiritual state of mind. Should I try to make myself* feel *something?* Addressing his own soul and his fellow monks, Anselm is clearly trying to elevate his hearers' minds at Communion. Here, in this wafer, in your mouth, is the Christ who died for you. All his lines are biblical tags, down to the honeycomb. I know, however, that some of you have also heard sexual metaphors, metaphors about the exchange of bodily fluids. Could Anselm possibly have meant such things?

Medieval Christian authors wrote commentaries most often of all on the Psalms and next most often on the Song of Solomon or Song of Songs. That's secular erotic love poetry that won its place in the Bible because Jewish readers have always applied it to the love of God for Israel, and Christian readers have always applied it to the love of Christ for the church. The Song of Songs primed a medieval Christian audience of monks both to hear and to write about the love of God in erotic terms. Anselm is a *very* careful writer. He writes some of the most beautiful Latin of the Middle Ages. Anselm is incapable of leaving an implication in a text if he doesn't want it there. If he wanted to avoid something, he would say it another way. The erotic implications may be avoidable, but Anselm chose the double entendre. This very treatise ends with more erotic language that does not have Communion as a cover text:

Draw me to you, Lord, in the fullness of love. I am wholly yours by creation; make me all yours, too, in love. Lord, my heart is before you. I try, but by myself I can do nothing; do what I cannot. Admit me into the inner room of your love. I ask, I seek, I knock. You who made me seek, make me receive; you who gave the seeking, give the finding; you who taught the knocking, open to my knock. . . . By you I have desire; by you let me have fulfillment. Cleave to him, my soul, and never leave off. Good Lord, do not reject me; I faith with hunger for your love; refresh me with it. Let me be filled with your love, rich in your affection, completely held in your care. Take me and possess me wholly, who with the Father and the Holy Spirit are alone blessed to ages of ages. Amen. (p. 237, ll. 254–71)

A student once exclaimed, on hearing me read those passages aloud, "I don't like that nasty man!" Well, there is a perfectly plausible cover story. This is a man, Anselm, delivering an address orally to other men, monks. And yet the trope is that God is male to the soul's female. Anselm, impersonating his soul, is gendered female. The Middle Ages gendered all souls female to God's male. Now, Anselm was a good enough theologian to deny that God belonged in any human category, including the category of male, and yet Anselm would also have told you, after you explained the verb, that God was "gendered" male. So the cover story with complete clarity orients the encounter between God and the soul heterosexual.

On the other hand, to use an anachronistic category, Anselm was almost certainly gay, as we can see from his letters. Unlike Abelard, whom we get to next, there is no scandal whatever attached to Anselm's name. As far as anyone knows, he kept his vows of celibacy completely. And yet medieval writers did not have Victorian standards of prudery to go by. Instead, as I said, Anselm was a careful writer always in complete control of his metaphors and his wording. It is hard to fathom that a gay man speaking to male monks, some of whom we would nowadays also read as gay, would not have noticed that the relationship he described in terms of sucking and swallowing would arouse other images in the minds of at least some of his hearers. And if he wanted to avoid those images, he could have confined himself to the chewing and biting. But the background of the Song of Songs positively encouraged erotic metaphors. In my view, Anselm decided to let the ambiguities stand—because the destiny of desire was to be devoted to God.

Anselm wrote the most important atonement theory ever. In many of the churches that adopt his theory above all others, all you have to do to participate in its effects is to "accept Christ." You do this, more or less, by believing; you do it, that is, with your mind. Anselm is not against faith, of course. He's in favor of it. One of his most important lines—in another treatise—defines theology as "faith seeking understanding." But I defy you to find the word *faith* in this *Meditation*. In Anselm, note well, you do not accept Christ into your mind. *You accept Christ into your mouth.* You do it faithfully, of course. But faith is not the salient element in this *Meditation*. It's precisely fitting, Anselm thinks, to accept Christ *into your mouth* because Christ wrought your redemption *with his body*. Therefore, it is only appropriate to accept his redemption *with your body*. If you refuse your body to Christ, when he has offered his for you, how can your withholding be faithful? Anselm is perfectly literal (and paraphrasing John 6:53) when he writes, "Through this and not otherwise than through this, will you remain in Christ and Christ in you"—through taking the bread, Christ's body, into your mouth. Anselm's context was not our own. Keep those things in mind the next time you're in the vicinity of Communion and the next time you hear about accepting Jesus.

We can put these results into the following table to contrast them with Athanasius.

Author	Problem	Solution	Christ's role	Name	Holiday	How we participate
Athanasius	Corruptibility, especially death	Share the divine nature	Becomes human to make us divine	Christ the Victor	Easter	Practice asceticism
Anselm	Sin as debt	Pay the debt	Pays the debt	Satisfaction	Good Friday	Take Communion

Anselm anticipates and guards against almost every objection you can come up with, especially in the longer version *Why God Became Human*. And yet the critique of Anselm continues to stick to every vulgarization of the theory. Three things seem to be true and yet remain at odds: Anselm anticipates all the objections, the critique never goes away, and the theory remains popular. We'll see more about the critique in the next section, when we come to Abelard.

10 Abelard Talks about Christ Teaching Love by Word and Example

Abelard abhors the idea of the Father sacrificing or punishing his Son. Abelard never uses Anselm's name. Is he criticizing Anselm or helping us to understand him properly?

Abelard (1079–1142) was thirty years old when Anselm died. In his *Commentary on Romans*, he pauses in his exposition of Romans 3:25 and seems to criticize Anselm's theory and propose his own. He develops his critique in a series of rhetorical questions:

> In what way does the apostle [Paul, whom Abelard is interpreting] declare that we are justified or reconciled to God through the death of his Son [Rom 5:10; Abelard is not disputing this, but offers his own interpretation later], when God ought to have been the more angered against the human being, inasmuch as humans acted more criminally by crucifying his Son than they ever did by transgressing his first command in paradise through the tasting of a single apple? For the more human sins were multiplied, the more just it would have been to be angry with them. And if that sin of Adam was so great that it could be expiated only by the death of Christ, what expiation will avail for that act of murder committed against Christ . . . ?[1]

That is the paradox of sacrifice: How does the killing of an innocent victim make *up* for an earlier sin—rather than making it worse? Anselm tried to escape this problem by making the victim's death voluntary. But Abelard only uses Anselm's defense to make his own critique more pointed and precise: "How did the [even voluntary] death of his innocent Son so *please* God the Father that through it he should have been reconciled to us . . . ?" (283; my italics).

That is, a father whom it would please to see his innocent son killed would be a monster. A father who would torture an innocent, much less his innocent son, would be hard to tell from the devil. In fact, Abelard has just said as much about Satan in the previous paragraph, to which we will come later. In short, sacrifice

---

1 The reading for the course was Peter Abelard, *Commentary on Romans*, in *Scholastic Miscellany*, 10:280–84; here, 282. Further references will be by page number in the text.

seems to make things worse rather than better. And how do you tell such a god from the devil?

> In what manner have we been made *more* righteous through the death of the Son of God than we were before, so that we ought to be delivered from punishment? [Should we not deserve more punishment?] And to whom was the *price of blood* paid for our redemption but to him in whose power we were—that is, to God himself, who (as we have said) handed us over to his torturer? For it is not the torturers but the masters of those who are held captive who arrange or receive such ransoms. Again, how did he release these captives for a price if he himself exacted or settled the price for release of the same? (283; my italics)

Now, that seems to tell against both Anselm and an earlier theory, to which we will come, called the ransom theory, because both of them depend on paying a price. But the whole idea of paying a price to God implies that God is both the parent who wants the child back *and the kidnapper who wants the payment*! There's nothing wrong with wanting your child back, but on Abelard's account, *there can be no talk of payment*—because only a kidnapper demands it. Abelard says, "Indeed, how cruel and wicked it seems that anyone should demand the blood of an innocent person as the price for anything, or that it should in any way please him that an innocent man should be slain—still less that God should consider the death of his son so *agreeable* that by it he should be reconciled to the whole world!" (283; my italics).

Anselm would reply that God had no need to do it like that, but we humans needed the dignity of paying the debt ourselves. To be such a victim serves dignity only if the debt is just. So you could argue that the debt is owed neither to God nor to the devil but to justice. But that still involves justice with torture and separates justice from God. Critiques like this keep coming back, especially the more popular Anselm's theory becomes and the further it gets from his nuances.

So what does Abelard propose instead?

> Now it seems to us that we have been justified by the blood of Christ and reconciled to God in this way: through this unique act of grace manifested to us—in that his Son has taken upon himself our nature and *persevered* therein in *teaching us by word and example even unto death*—he has more fully *bound us to himself by love*; with the result that our hearts should be enkindled by such a gift of divine grace, and true charity not now shrink from enduring anything for him.
>
> Yet everyone becomes *more* righteous—by which we mean a greater lover of the Lord—after the Passion of Christ than before. . . . Wherefore, our redemption through Christ's suffering is that deeper affection in us which not only frees us from slavery to sin, but also wins for us the true liberty

of sons of God, so that we do all things out of love rather than fear—love to him who has shown us such grace that no greater can be found, as he himself asserts, saying, "Greater love than this no man hath, that a man lay down his life for his friends [John 15:13]." (283–84; my italics)

This then is Abelard's theory. Christ is a voluntary martyr who gives his life for his friends. There is no talk of payment or requirement but only of gift. That gift then inspires love rather than fear. No particular moment is this gift, but everything that Christ undertakes and undergoes teaches us, by word and example, how to love one another.

We may sum up Abelard's theory and contrast it with the others like this:

Author	Problem	Solution	Christ's role	Name	Holiday	How we participate
Athanasius	Corruptibility, especially death	Share the divine nature	Becomes human to make us divine	Christ the Victor	Easter	Practice asceticism
Anselm	Sin as debt	Pay the debt	Pays the debt	Satisfaction	Good Friday	Take Communion
Abelard	Failure to love	Teach love	Teaches love by word and example in all he says and does	Exemplary or moral theory	No one holiday because it all counts, every day of the calendar	Love your neighbor

The way we participate, you see, is elegantly obvious: love your neighbor. Abelard puts forward a great hope: That, starting from Jesus, love could break out. That it could spread. That it could become contagious, gift from gift. And that humanity—so far from looking vertically to heaven for a cosmic transaction—could actually *change*, in a love made visible from person to person horizontally, on earth as it is in heaven.

On the topic of love made horizontally, however, is an interlude for gossip. We have seen that Anselm was what we would now call a gay man with a reputation for celibacy. Abelard however gained a different reputation—one that may well bear on a theory whose hallmark is love.

Abelard was—and certainly thought himself—the smartest man in Europe. He was teaching at the University of Paris. He had formalized a method with deep roots in theology, which he called *Sic et Non*, or "Yes and No," which required practitioners to hone their skills in debate by learning to argue both sides of a question. Like many of our authors—Calvin and Athanasius among them—he was infected with the *rabies theologorum*, the rabies of the theologians. He enjoyed himself, and he liked to win.

Heloise (?–1164) was the smartest woman in Europe, at least as it appears from her writings. Before she met Abelard, she was already famous for her mastery of Hebrew, Greek, and Latin. The University of Paris, however, admitted no women. But Heloise was also rich. Her uncle met Abelard when he and Heloise moved to Paris in 1115, and he arranged for Abelard to teach her medicine and philosophy, privately. She was probably around twenty. He was thirty-six.

Abelard taught her philosophy by debating, for example, whether love must be free. They began an affair, older teacher and younger student, in her uncle's house, which continued until Heloise became pregnant. Abelard offered to marry her, but he wanted to keep the marriage secret, and when he sent her to a monastery to protect her from gossip, her uncle suspected Abelard of wanting to get rid of her. The uncle sent his henchmen to castrate him. He stashed Heloise and Abelard in separate monasteries.

Heloise—intelligent, practical, and good at administration—eventually found herself the abbess of her monastery. She had not chosen the monastic life, and as she wrote later, she didn't even believe in God. She considered herself a hypocrite. Who could understand and advise her?

Abelard. Years after their separation, Heloise wrote him a letter. If you have ever written a letter to an ex, you know that it's cathartic to write—until you receive a response. Abelard wrote back. Heloise had written that she still loved him. He said he had never loved her. She said she still believed in their philosophy of love. He said she needed to give up on him and love God. She said that was the problem: because of him, she didn't love God—and she was running a monastery. To cut things short, he was a jerk. He was a highly intelligent man and a great writer; surely he must have seen that he was writing himself as a jerk. The only question is, Was he doing it on purpose to take the blame and help her get over something that could never resume?

Heloise comes across as the consistent, reliable, virtuous one; Abelard as the one who talks about love and can't manage it. (The technical term for this is *sloppy agape*.) What does this say about his theory? That Abelard's solution—for love to break out—is hopelessly naive? Or that Abelard works from a realism born of painful experience, so the problem that humans need solving is, like his own, their failure to love?

After an excursus on the use and abuse of Anselm and Abelard from the Reformation to 1830, we turn to Stephen Ray, in whose work we meet not only involuntary martyrdom but a social failure to love that shades into hatred.

11 Excursus

Protestants Talk about Anselm and Abelard to Debate Punishment

The major debates about the atonement among Protestant churches in the twentieth and twenty-first centuries—with interested observers from Catholicism and Orthodoxy—are staged as debates between Anselm and Abelard. I say "staged" because the debates hardly touch Anselm and flatten Abelard.

The debates really concern a distinct atonement theory that I have refrained from teaching for twenty-seven years.[1] It is a descendant of Anselm's. It is one that Anselm distinguishes from his own and twice dismisses in a few words as if beneath consideration.[2] It is called the "penal substitution" theory. It supposes that the problem with human beings is law breaking and that the solution is punishment. Note that Anselm's *Meditation* never uses the word *punishment*, and his longer *Why God Became Human* denies it. The heyday of the penal substitution theory (1500–1830) was one marked by spectacular public punishments like hanging, beheading, crushing, flogging, and the stocks. At the end of this section, I will list several texts that defend penal substitution, but I have chosen none of them as an interlocutor. That's because I think that in every way, penal substitution is inferior to Anselm. If you are attracted to the penal substitution theory, I urge you to consider Anselm instead. Not because you confuse the penal substitution theory with Anselm's, but because you have come to recognize Anselm's as better. The penal substitution theory claims Anselm as a parent by exploiting ambiguities in the concepts of *satisfaction, agency, honor, obedience,* and *flesh*.

Satisfaction. Suppose you're hitting baseballs in the backyard.[3] You've been warned not to do that because the guy next door is a stained glass maker and has replaced all his windows with the most beautiful leaded glass. Sure enough, the ball goes sailing into a window and smashes it to smithereens. This is especially painful to you because you are always doodling in your Elements of Christian Thought class, and when the lecture is really dull, you have lately been dividing your drawings into small, curved cells in just the way that the lead next door divides the glassmaker's window into smaller colored panels. It may even be that

---

1 I surface it here at the urging of Kendall Soulen and Joseph Mangina.
2 Anselm of Canterbury, *Why God Became Human*, bk. 1, near the ends of chs. 13 and 15.
3 I owe the example but not all of its elaboration to Kendall Soulen.

the baseball hit the window because you couldn't take your eyes off it. Now it's ruined, and it's your fault.

What's the best solution?

1. Your parents turn you over to the glassmaker for a thorough whipping. Everybody in the neighborhood can hear it. In this way, justice is restored in the same way as the window broke: by loud noise and public display.
2. Your parents turn you over to the glassmaker, who forgives you without penalty. But you can never look at the windows again without feeling guilty, and you avoid the glassmaker from then on. You no longer carve your drawings into tiny crosshatched cells.
3. Your parents turn you over to the glassmaker, whose kid, secretly or openly in love with you, volunteers to be whipped instead.
4. Your parents turn you over to the glassmaker, who requires that you pay a fine in money.
5. Your parents turn you over to the glassmaker, who requires that you make amends in labor. The labor is to restore the window. You can't do it yourself. But he requires that you do it together. In doing it together, you will become his apprentice. You will become more like him.

Like most multiple-choice lists, this one is clearly set up so that the last choice sounds best. Number one might be penal substitution, so might number three. Anselm, however, is different from both: he is number five, and number one is an option he rejects. As far as I know, nobody is actually in favor of number two, although most insist that God could do that if God so chose. Some readers mistake Anselm for number four, but as we have seen, he never actually mentions money. You can use the story to think through your own variations. But note a common problem with all atonement theories: in trying to identify what's important in the biblical story, they end up first simplifying and then replacing it. In this case, for example, Jesus represents both the glassmaker and the apprentice, God and sinner. And the image that the glass breaker ruins is him or herself, made in the image of God. Careful with the replacements! They are indispensable to thinking the matter through, but all are inadequate, and some of them are bad.

Anselm uses the Latin word *satisfactio* so frequently that it comes to be one of the names of his theory. In Medieval Latin, it means "putting in order," "penance," "indemnification," "wergild," "amends," or "giving reasons." In his *Meditation on Human Redemption*, Anselm shows how Christians at Communion can participate in the reasons for Communion with God that God's Reason, the Logos, presents to restore that Communion on the night on which he was betrayed. In that movement of love, God (the Trinity) satisfies Godself, because in a lovely chapter title from *Why God Became Human* (bk. 2, ch. 4), Anselm writes that "God would complete what God began"—that is, the enjoyment of fellowship—in a great thanksgiving meal with the creature. God satisfies (puts in order) God's plan by engaging the human being in repairing the damage. Indeed, the damage is to God's image, which is not just a window but the human being created "in the image of God." "Satisfaction" in the real Anselm is supposed to mean God's repair of the human being.

The *agency* of the crucifixion Anselm assigns to sinners who do not realize what they are doing. God uses this occasion, but the crucifixion reveals no "congruence or parallel between what God intends to do in the crucifixion and what [sinners] intend to do."[4] "Sinners" includes everybody, not only the authorities of Rome and Jerusalem, but even the disciples who by their betrayal, denial, or falling asleep show that they had no idea what *God* intended to do with their malfeasance.

Honor in Anselm means *not* that the artist is so proud and self-absorbed that they need revenge but that they delight in training up others. God considers not only God's own honor, but God honors God's image, the human being. Perhaps the best modern equivalent of the medieval term is *dignity*: God wants to *dignify* human beings by involving them in God's own work. Mere forgiveness would leave them out of their own salvation. God wants to do humans the honor of involving them in it—not separately, as if they made a lonely "decision for Christ," but in intimate relationship, side by side.

Obedience in this case does not mean that God the Son knuckles under to the authority of God the Father: it means that Christ remains obedient to the *mission* of the whole Trinity to repair the broken image, remains obedient to his own commitment to solidarity with the human being. In this, Christ's obedience is like that of Mahatma Gandhi or Martin Luther King Jr.: an obedience to a *joint cause*, not obedience to an *external authority*.

Flesh in this case is the means of solidarity by which the glassmaker and the glass breaker work side by side. It is only accidentally the means of suffering by which the glassmaker painstakingly undergoes tedium and cutting and burning in the course of remaking the window alongside an incompetent apprentice subject to fits of frustration, jealousy, anger, and adolescent defensiveness.

Note that in several ways the defense of Anselm brings him closer to Abelard. The attempt to repair *the human being*—not the glass but the glass breaker—requires us to draw out the Abelardian theme of teaching by word and example. The suffering of the glassmaker is due not to punishment or fine but to solidarity with the glass breaker. The obedience of Christ in Anselm as in Abelard *perseveres* in his cause to the end: a word that *Why God Became Human* uses as well. Both in Anselm, properly understood, and in Abelard, the death of Christ comes in foreseeable martyrdom, testifying to his love for his people, as in Gandhi and King. In interpreting Anselm in those ways, I am moving him toward Abelard—or pointing out ways that Abelard has learned from and seeks to clarify Anselm. Certainly,

---

4 Kendall Soulen, private correspondence, June 2020.

Abelard has learned the importance of perseverance and voluntary commitment from his predecessor, even if he neglects to acknowledge those debts.

How Penal Descendants of Anselm Go Wrong

But see how easy it is for Anselm's account to go wrong. In classical Latin, the word *satisfactio* can mean all those things—penance, payment, amends, repair, and punishment, including punishment by death. When Julius Caesar in the Gallic Wars "takes satisfaction" on his enemies, that means he kills them. Because that's within the range of the word, *Why God Became Human* makes clear that the killing of Christ is due to humans, not God.[5] Anselm uses payment language (*solvere*, *persolvere*, which means "to pay," "to solve," "to dissolve," even "to let down your hair") in order to avoid the language of punishment. After all, as David Yeago points out, if you pay someone's debts (Anselm elsewhere suggests, the debts of Christ's bride), it's not the same as punishment; on the contrary, you pay them because punishment is what you want for your spouse to avoid.

But the trouble is that the crucifixion doesn't look like a debt payment, it doesn't look like a fine, and—precisely if satisfaction language is in question—the kind of satisfaction it looks like is punishment. That's what the Romans intend by it. But is that what God intends by it? Anselm would say logically exactly what Abelard says more forcefully, that the crucifixion is none of those things: it is a further sin by human beings, and what it brings about is not justice but martyrdom. Christ undergoes it because he is maintaining solidarity with sinful human beings—indeed, with the thief on the cross—in pursuing his mission to the end. Only humans still in thrall to oppression and violence could look at God's attempt to satisfy God's hopes for the human being by maintaining solidarity even unto death—and still see a god constrained by a law of punishment. The notion of a law of punishment implies something higher than God, which Anselm's theory disallows. Putting something in place of Jesus at the top of the flowchart—whether a sorting mechanism or some kind of law—would be Calvin's and Arius's mistake.

For all those reasons, penal substitution seems to think that you can *read off the agency of God* from the agency of sinners: that there is some congruence or parallel between at least what the "left hand" of God intends to do with the crucifixion and what Pilate, the Sanhedrin, Judas, Peter, and the sleepers intend (or by omission fail to intend) to do with it. You might think, to be fair, that what God intends is the restoration of justice, and what sinners intend is injustice. Even so, God ought not to use such creatures unironically as his henchmen; God and sinners ought not to share their wrath. That confusion is what makes it hard to distinguish God from the devil.

---

5 Anselm of Canterbury, *Why God Became Human*, bk. 2, ch. 15.

Under the heading of *honor*, I want you to think of an honor culture prominent in movies and on TV. In those movies and series, people in power demand honor and satisfaction. Need a hint? Although Anselm moved west to France and then England, he was born in Aosta, in what is now Italy. I'm thinking of an organization now associated with Sicily and New York. I'm thinking of the mafia. Mafiosi want satisfaction in the sense of reparation or punishment for injury, offence, or fault. In the movies, they want bodily satisfaction, by kneecapping or death. You can see how Anselm's heirs—advocates and critics alike—might get to that place. But see how warped it sounds if you apply it to someone who meets their death while leading their people to justice: Would anyone ever say that the violent deaths of Gandhi or King were *punishment*? No, they were perseverance in the face of injustice.

Now, Anselm is careful to state that Christ "did not submit to violence, but freely embraced it out of goodness, to the honour of God and the benefit of other human beings" (*Meditation on Human Redemption*, p. 233, ll. 132–34). This formulation is meant to stress voluntariness—but it does seem to take for granted that what Christ undergoes counts as "violence." The real Anselm specifies that violence is what humans do. What God does is persevere: God would complete what God began in creation.

Obedience is similar. Anselm means obedience to the common cause, the cause of the human being, perseverance in solidarity, but common misunderstandings of Anselm sprang up within a generation. Given the universal experience of sinful oppression and violence, it was easy for people to misunderstand obedience not as a commitment to a common cause but as obedience to an external or even oppressive authority.[6] So when Anselm wrote, "What Christ understood would please the Father and benefit humanity, that he did of his own free will. . . . Such honour could not but please the Father, when the Son freely obeyed the Father, when he willed freely to do what he knew would please him" (*Meditation*, p. 234, ll.142–45). Abelard could pounce and ask what kind of father that is, who demands such an honor as death from his son, who could be "pleased" by such a thing. Only a godfather, Abelard implies. That is why feminist (white) and womanist (Black) theologians detest penal substitution and suspect Anselm.

Anselm's advocates tend to take Abelard's critique of obedience as unfair. But what if the authority Christ obeys is his love for the thief? What if we read Abelard as trying to *clarify* Anselm by reducing the penal interpretations to absurdity?

Obedience language in penal substitution theories also implies that God the Father and God the Son are two parties rather than one. The obedience problem goes away when God is obedient to God's own commitment to the thief, to complete what God began, to grow the sinner into fellowship with God. But as soon as you speak of the Son's obedience to the Father, the problem of external authority looms,

---

6 Christian speech has usually insisted on the possibility of a good and loving authority, one that may originate on the outside but moves the heart from the inside. We'll see more about that when we get to freedom.

rather than shared purpose. What in the doctrine of election I called the reflexive aspect is not nearly as clear in Anselm as it is in Barth. Whereas Barth stresses that the Father and the Son are both God, so the Trinity acts on itself, the one whom God predestines is Godself to be for us sinners, and therefore the Judge is judged in our place; Anselm on the other hand only sometimes speaks of God suffering for us without further specification and other times separates God the Father from God the Son, with the result that the phrase "the Godfather" sounds like more than a pun.

Advocates of penal substitution see an advantage in Anselm's over Abelard's theory in that penal substitution is objective, whereas Abelard's theory is subjective. On Abelard's theory, according to this critique, what changes is my attitude: I become grateful and therefore loving. But you might observe that by that standard, penal substitution is doubly subjective. First, it too relies on a change in attitude, this time God's. What matters is not my sin as such but God's anger at my sin, and what changes is God's attitude,[7] from angry to placated. Furthermore, the whole attraction of the penal substitution theory is that it valorizes Christians' feelings of guilt, and it helps those feelings go away by the public spectacle that at least somebody gets the punishment. In penal substitution, "the real work is done as we contemplate the cross, feel awful about ourselves, but at the same time are flooded with gratitude for Christ's suffering for our sake."[8] Without implying that changes of attitude are necessarily bad, I observe that both of these are: ours and God's both sound like a bad family dynamic.

Finally, "flesh." "By His stripes we are healed" (Isa 53:5 NKJV; compare Matt 8:14-17). The original meaning of the suffering servant in Isaiah and Matthew is once again God's dramatic irony: that God takes the worst that creatures can do—kill God—and chooses it as the *occasion* of their repair. Christian theologians who practice the blessed exchange will always love paradox and reversal, and such verses will never lose their power. But they don't have to mean that the flesh is a place of punishment. They can mean that flesh is a place of solidarity.

Windows, like flesh, are vulnerable to breakage. What we want is real repair, real change. You might see a similar irony when Black Lives Matter protestors, marching for justice, are undermined by a few who break windows—even of a few Black-owned businesses. And then what happens is that artists decorate the plywood with powerful antiracist art that not only goes up overnight but changes from day to day and brings visitors daily to contemplate the visions of community, justice, and repair.

For the last fifty years—just as the prevalence of credit card and mortgage debt has grown—Black liberation and feminist theologians have argued that Anselm's theory makes the atonement dangerous for Blacks, women, and all those lacking

---

7 I owe this observation to David Yeago, "The Problem of Atonement," in *Apostolic Faith* (unpublished typescript), 309. That book is far better than this one, if any publisher can pry it out of Yeago's hands.
8 I owe the analysis to Joe Mangina.

in privilege because those benefiting from privilege will cite the example of Jesus to say, "Take up your cross and follow him." Oppressors use the example of Jesus to justify the suffering of those they oppress. Not all suffering is unjustified. But you must learn to ask diagnostic questions when someone tells you to take up your cross and follow Jesus: (1) Who is carrying the hammer and the nails? And (2) Are you willing to climb the cross with me? The contemporary complaints are not new but began to arise with Abelard's *Romans Commentary* at the latest—that is, in the 1130s, within twenty-five years of Anselm's death. They have been with us for nine hundred years.

Why does Anselm's theory bear up and even flourish under such a critique? The reason seems to be the enduring appeal of sacrifice. Sacrifice seems to make a problem go away. It is, in Anselm's case, a transaction in heaven, above our pay grade, that takes human sin seriously and rescues humans with what anthropologists call "costly signaling."

Critics of Abelard, on the other hand, find his theory namby-pamby or warm and fuzzy and complain that Abelard does not talk enough about "blood." The blood of Christ works like a Christian totem, in the technical, Durkheimian sense. Closely allied with the body of Christ is his blood, which the New Testament cites three times as often as his "cross" and five times as often as his "death." The blood from the cross is the blood of Christ, the wine of the Eucharist is the blood of Christ, the means of atonement is the blood of Christ, the unity of the church is the blood of Christ, the kinship of believers is the blood of Christ, the cup of salvation is the blood of Christ, icons ooze the blood of Christ, and the blood of Christ is the blood of God.[9]

But the critique is unfair. Abelard constantly talks about blood. His theory occurs as a *quaestio*, a quest or difficulty, to be addressed when his commentary on Romans reaches verse 3:25: "Christ Jesus, whom God put forward as an expiation by his blood" (282). His treatment begins like this: "A most pressing problem obtrudes itself at this point, as to what that redemption of ours through the death of Christ may be, and in what way the apostle declares that we are justified by his blood" (282). He repeats the question in the passage we quoted before. He speaks of both the "price of blood" and the "blood of an innocent person" (283). And he opens his own theory with this announcement: "Now it seems to us that we have been justified by the blood of Christ and reconciled to God in this way . . ."—that is, through the blood of a voluntary martyr (283).

Abelard does not say how this blood counts as an "expiation," which certainly sounds like sacrificial language. But an explanation is not far to find. God chooses the *occasion* of a voluntary martyr to *count* that death as an expiation. God's "putting forward" is not the deliberate sacrifice of an innocent person, which would

---

9   The last two sentences form a refrain in Eugene F. Rogers Jr., *Blood Theology: Seeing Red in Body- and God-Talk* (Cambridge: Cambridge University Press, 2021).

make God resemble the devil, but the dramatic irony of using the worst that *humans* can do—execute an innocent person by torturous means—as the occasion for their salvation. In this, Abelard and Anselm are alike. It is the irony of "his blood be upon us" turning out to be the blood that saves us. Mixing in a metaphor that Abelard eschews, the Welsh poet David Gwenallt Jones puts it this way: like wolves, we (and not God) lift our snouts and go "howling for the blood that ransomed us."[10]

We may sum this up in the chart:

Author	Problem	Solution	Christ's role	Name	Holiday	How we participate
Athanasius	Corruptibility, especially death	Share the divine nature	Becomes human to make us divine	Christ the Victor	Easter	Join a desert monastery
Anselm	Sin as debt	Pay the debt	Pays the debt	Satisfaction	Good Friday	Take Communion
Abelard	Failure to love	Teach love	Teaches love by word and example in all he says and does	Exemplary or moral theory	No one holiday because it all counts, every day of the calendar	Love your neighbor
John Calvin, Jonathan Edwards	God the Father is angry at sin	Someone takes the punishment to placate the Father	Voluntary victim	Penal substitution	Good Friday (as experienced in individual soul-searching)	Feel guilt and relief

That brings us to another kind of martyrdom, involuntary martyrdom. Stephen Ray revives the ransom theory with several improvements to show the significance and Christlikeness of even an involuntary death.

If you want to read more about penal substitution, here are some decent samples:

- For further reading, see John Calvin, *Institutes*, 2 vols., trans. Ford Lewis Battles (Philadelphia: Westminster, 1960) II.xii.2–3, vol. 1, 465–67.
- For further reading, see Jonathan Edwards, "Concerning the Necessity and Reasonableness of the Christian Doctrine of Satisfaction for Sin," §9, in *Works of Jonathan Edwards*, vol. 2, at https://tinyurl.com/y28j5bha.

---

10   David Gwenallt Jones, "Pechod," in *Twentieth Century Welsh Poems*, ed. Joseph Clancy (Llandyssul, Wales: Gwasg Gomer, 1982), 94.

- For further reading, see Martin Luther, *Lectures on Galatians 1–4, 1535*, vol. 26, *Luther's Works* (Saint Louis: Concordia, 1963), 276–91, which talks about "the Law" as a sinner's perception of God accusing the conscience and administering punishment. Luther treats "the Law" and grace as one piece, one reversal of a comprehensive Athanasian blessed exchange. Although Luther's theory includes wrath and punishment, its emphasis on the blessed exchange brings it closer to Athanasius than Anselm. And although Luther's theory is infected with anti-Semitic tropes and supersessionism, what Luther means by "the Law" is entirely different from what Jews mean by Torah (which is more of a structure that liberates and closer to what Luther means by "command").
- For more about penal substitution, see Stephen Holmes, "Penal Substitution," in the *T&T Clark Companion to Atonement*, ed. Adam J. Johnson (London: Bloomsbury T&T Clark, 2017), 295–314.
- For a defense of Anselm as Athanasian, see D. Bentley Hart, "A Gift Exceeding Every Debt: An Eastern Orthodox Appreciation of Anselm's *Cur Deus Homo*," *Pro Ecclesia* 7 (1998): 333–49.

12 Ray Talks about the Community around a Dead Body

The Spirit, the Giver of Life, gathers a new community (the church) around the martyred body of Jesus. Stephen Ray sees Jesus's Spirit gathering a new community (Black Lives Matter) around the martyred body of Michael Brown Jr. To explain life from the dead, Ray revives the trickster atonement theory of the early church.

Anselm and Abelard have something in common. They both critique a theory—which I have put off presenting, out of historical order, until now—in which God, in Jesus, tricks the devil. There are various versions of the trickster theory, all of which are very short (like a paragraph). In one version, the devil is a bad jailor who keeps a captive (Jesus) he is not entitled to keep, and therefore, as in some contemporary cases about overcrowding or virus transmission in prisons, all the prisoners go free. In another version, which I prefer, death, or the devil, is a great fish—like the one that swallowed Jonah—that gobbles up dead people. Either Jesus is the bait that causes the great fish to vomit up the people he swallowed or the cross is a fishhook that allows God to reel the devilfish in. This is a good story, full of reversal and dramatic irony (a necessary quality in theology), but when parsed into a theory, it brings both Anselm and Abelard to exasperation. Defenders of the story could reply that it's not *meant* to be deductive; it's meant to be narrative. Jesus the Logos is not God's logic but God's story. Specifically, these theories make God's story a trickster story, and tricks necessarily involve catching somebody out in some illogic. The ancient versions are a comedy, and the joke's on the devil.

Here is a far more serious and therefore more successful version of that ancient story set in the present day. This one isn't funny, because the devil's victim is an ordinary person. Still, it too is full of irony, and here too the reversal (this time deadly serious) comes at the expense of the authorities. It is a masterful reworking of an ancient trope.

Stephen Ray makes a pilgrimage to Ferguson, Missouri, where an innocent Black man, Michael Brown Jr., was killed by police and, to add insult, left to lie in the sun for hours while his mother, like Mary at the foot of the cross, stood by (*stabat mater*), unable to cross the police tape.

Using the anthropologist Mary Douglas, Ray argues that "the structures of American public life turn on the idea of Black presence as being defiling" to white eyes.[1] My white Episcopal priest got chased out of a North Carolina parish in the second half of the twentieth century "for baptizing," he says, "a Black baby in a 'white' font." Ray notes how such events illustrate Mary Douglas's sociological definition of *dirt*—that is, "matter out of place." The application, of course, is not that Black people are dirt but that white people can see them as out of place (89).

The problem with human beings that needs to be solved, therefore, is social. The salient example of that problem—in the teens and twenties of the twenty-first century, as in the sixties of the twentieth century and for centuries before—is white racism. A trip to Ferguson brought Michael Brown Jr. to Stephen Ray's mind in a new way. Ray couldn't help himself from thinking about it theologically:

> [A] dimension rarely noticed [in the ancient atonement theories] is that these dark powers of dominion [the power of sin, the bondage to death] are broken because Death simply *could not contain* the power of Life that was manifest in the Incarnation. According to Origen (an African doctor [teacher] of the Early Church), this was a case of the devil overplaying his hand. In Origen's thought, God had baited the Devil with this man who shone forth with the power of Life. Satan knew full well that this was no ordinary flesh bearer . . . but *he thought so little of the flesh that the prince bore* that he saw this as his moment. Thinking he would consume the prince, *made insignificant by the flesh that he bore*, . . . Satan, as he had done with Job, orchestrated things such that Jesus was killed. . . . Satan discovered that not only was the power of Life so great in this One that it broke every bond of Death, *but it also communicated itself to the quick and the dead.* Far from being made weak and insignificant by the particular flesh he bore, Christ was enabled by it to gather a community of witnesses that would herald Life's victory through time and through which this power might be communicated to all. . . .
>
> As with Christ, the flesh of Michael Brown Jr. made him imminently kill-able in the eyes of many and mitigated any claim of empathy on the hearts of too many others. In my own living it was this invitation to violation that was most real to me but, when I experienced the community called into being by the Spirit that was gathered precisely around Mike's Black flesh, our Black flesh, I knew that God had used his death to communicate something to us all. That communication? Simply put, in the unfolding of God's salvific plan for all of creation [in] Black Lives Matter. Michael Brown Jr. is and will be our shining Black Prince for from his death God has brought Life to us all and in his gaze we are enveloped in its power. (91–92; my italics)

---

1 The reading for the course was Stephen G. Ray Jr., "Black Lives Matter as Enfleshed Theology," in *Enfleshing Theology: Embodiment, Discipleship, and Politics in the Work of M. Shawn Copeland*, ed. Robert J. Rivera and Michele Saracino (Minneapolis: Fortress Press, 2018), 83–93, esp. 91–92; here, 89. Further references will be by page number in the text.

In this case, even an involuntary martyrdom gains meaning from the community gathered in its wake. This does not make the police killing an innocent Black man a good thing, but God's dramatic irony brings good out of something that is and remains evil. It is another case in which, as in the case of Jesus, God chooses the *worst* that humans can do, the heart of the fire, as the place to intervene.

In this case, the Black Lives Matter movement works as the church is supposed to, as a community in which love for human flesh and love for one's neighbor breaks out and begins to spread. Racist violence is a bad contagion, but social movements can work like reengineered viruses to increase the goodness in the world and teach human beings how to love. What Origen saw as flesh tricking the devil, Ray sees as flesh tricking the (conscious or unconscious) racist: God endows Black flesh with the power to communicate life to others in Black Lives Matter. That resembles the plot of Good Friday to Pentecost: the Holy Spirit gathers a new community around the body of Jesus.

Author	Problem	Solution	Christ's role	Name	Holiday	How we participate
Athanasius	Corruptibility, especially death	Share the divine nature	Becomes human to make us divine	Christ the Victor	Easter	Practice asceticism
Anselm	Sin as debt	Pay the debt	Pays the debt	Christ the victim	Good Friday	Take Communion
Abelard	Failure to love	Teach love	Teaches love by word and example in all he says and does	Exemplary or moral theory	No one holiday because it all counts, every day of the calendar	Love your neighbor
Stephen Ray after Origen of Alexandria	Social distinctions of flesh such as racism	Imbue the flesh with the power of life to overcome evil	Martyr for the flesh that tricks or reverses the forces of evil	Trickster theory, related to but better than the ransom theory	Pentecost—the day on which the Holy Spirit gathers the church around the flesh of Jesus	Join movements for love and justice. Does the church count?

13 Julian of Norwich Talks about Sin as a Wound

Julian of Norwich proposes a no-blame (if not no-fault) theory of sin and explains it with a vision of a servant in whom Christ and Adam coincide.

Julian of Norwich (1343 to at least 1416) was an English anchorite and mystic. (An anchorite is a religious who has taken a vow to shelter in place for the rest of their life.) I say "shelter in place" because of the coronavirus pandemic occurring while I write this, and Julian lived through the plague, the black death, which ravaged Norwich in waves from 1348 to 1387, killing up to half the population. Not to avoid the plague but to be an anchorite, Julian had herself walled up in a cell, open at the top like a tollbooth, against the wall of St. Julian's Church. (She took her name from the church, not the church from her.) From that anchorage—enlarged now into a side chapel after being bombed in World War II—she gave spiritual advice.

As a girl, she had prayed to come very near death and live, so that she would know what it was like to die and lose her fear. Be careful what you pray for. In 1373, she became so sick—perhaps, although she doesn't mention its symptoms, from the Fourth Pestilence, or wave of the plague, sometimes dated to that year—that a priest administered her the last rites. During that illness, she had a series of visions, which she called in Middle English "showings." She wrote them up twice, first in what we call the "Short Text" and later in the "Long Text." She left out of the Short Text a vision that she couldn't explain in an orthodox way. After many years, an orthodox explanation came to her, which she included in the Long Text. (All quotations come from the Long Text.) That vision with its explanation is known as the "Parable of the Servant." I read it as supporting her theory of sin.

A Different Kind of Honor

Julian also relates sin to honor but not at all in the way that Anselm does. She compares sin not to a debt but to a *wound*.

Julian does not use war metaphors. It's possible she is avoiding war metaphors and wants us to associate the wound with a fall (which the parable of the servant suggests). But I use war and frontier metaphors to contextualize her remark about wounds. When we read Barth before—and when we read him again—we will see that he describes the human being in passing as placed upon a frontier, on the line of battle between good and evil. It's a common trope among theologians. The human being is to acquire the dignity, the honor, even the glory of fighting on the front line with God. God is off the hook for putting the soft, woundable humans in harm's way only (if at all) because God too takes on soft, vulnerable flesh to fight alongside us. But we are subject to wounds and even to death. Because we are frail and finite, we will suffer harm. That harm involves our wills: we sin. But the harm is incomplete. Some goodness remains.

She says, "Our Lord revealed to me that I would sin, by me is understood everyone." But "in every soul which will be saved there is a godly will which never assents to sin and never will."[1] Although she does not mention this explanation, Julian's idea of the godly will accords with other medieval ideas about what distinguishes humans from angels. Angels, being immaterial, assent completely and all at once to either righteousness or sin. In humans, however, the weight of matter lags behind so that when we do good, there is always something leftover to be tempted—and when we sin, there is always something leftover to repent. This inability to commit completely to sin prevents the frictionless chute that condemns the fallen angels. It gives God something to work with in salvaging us.[2] Julian names that grace of incompleteness—the will that God works with—the "godly will." The godly will is that by which "my sin will not impede the operation of [God's] goodness" (ch. 36, 238). The only thing that is complete is the "completeness of his love," the love of the Lord (ch. 37, 241–42).

Julian describes the harm that sin works: "Sin is the sharpest scourge with which any chosen soul can be struck, which scourge belabors man or woman, and breaks a man, and purges him in his own sight so much that at times he thinks himself that he is not fit for anything but as it were to sink into hell, until contrition seizes him by the inspiration of the Holy Spirit and turns bitterness into hope of God's mercy" (ch. 39, 244).

That is, a sin is a war wound in the battle against evil. We have fought against evil and been in part overcome. It is a moral harm, a place where evil has actually struck and diminished human beings in their very substance—made them less good and less human—which is painful in the extreme. Sinners become worse people. Just as wounds in physical wars make us less able soldiers—we can fight less well without an eye or a leg—so too spiritual wounds contract our moral agency. But from this analogy, Julian comes to understand something from her vision that for years had left her shocked:

> And God showed that sin will be no shame, but honour to man, for just as there is indeed a corresponding pain for every sin, just so love gives to the same soul a bliss for every sin. Just as various sins are punished with various pains, the more grievous are the sins, so will they be rewarded with various joys

---

1   The reading for the course was Julian of Norwich, *Showings*, translated into modern English by Edmund Colledge and James Walsh (New York: Paulist Press, 1978), the Long Text, chs. 36–39 and 50–52, or pp. 238–45 and 267–82; here, ch. 37, 241–42. Further references will be by chapter of the Long Text and page numbers from this edition.

2   For more, see Karl Rahner, "The Theological Concept of *Concupiscientia*," in *Theological Investigations*, trans. and with an introduction by Cornelius Ernst (Baltimore: Helicon, 1961), 1:347–82.

in heaven to reward the victories over them, to the degree in which the sin may have been painful and sorrowful to the soul on earth. . . . And this is no shame to [the saints], but everything is turned to honour. (ch. 38, 242–43)

That is, sin is not just a battle wound that harms us. Sin is a *wound of honor*.

I suspect that Julian's interpretation here is influenced by a controversy over the wounds of Christ. The question arose whether the blessed in heaven would be able to recognize Christ by his wounds. The usual answer was yes. More audacious answers asserted that his wounds would continue to bleed. His were not wounds from sins he committed, of course, but wounds from sins that he *bore*. By analogy, the idea arose that the saints, too, would keep the wounds of their martyrdom in heaven, from which, I suppose, Julian transfers the notion that God would see and treat even the wounds of sin as wounds of honor, wounds that God would recognize and even reward for God's soldiers in the war against evil. The wounds of sin would deserve purple hearts. This is another way to get God off the hook for creating a world in which humans are too weak to win against sin.

Consider the alternative. You could say, "But it's better not to sin!" Imagine how that would sound in wartime. John McCain, the American politician and Republican presidential candidate against Obama, was famously a prisoner of war for seven years in Vietnam. He was honored as a war hero—except when he opposed the later Republican presidential candidate Donald Trump. Then Trump struck back, saying he didn't understand why McCain should be treated as such a hero. "He's a war hero because he was captured," Trump said. "I like people who weren't captured."[3]

Julian's God is not like Donald Trump. Julian's God is more like the other Americans whose moral sense urged them to honor, not castigate, John McCain and reward him with (according to Wikipedia) the Silver Star, two Legion of Merit medals, the Distinguished Flying Cross, three Bronze Star medals, two Purple Hearts, two Navy and Marine Corps Commendation medals, and the Prisoner of War medal.[4] Despite their best efforts, sinners have actually been captured by sin. Like those who love soldiers captured in war, "Christ has compassion on us because of sin" (ch. 28, 226). And God rewards them even with "joys" and "bliss." Julian says,

> By contrition we are made clean, by compassion we are made ready, and by true longing for God we are made worthy. . . . For every sinful soul must be healed by these medicines. Though [the sinner] be healed, his wounds are not seen by God as wounds but as honours. And as we are punished here with sorrow and penance, in contrary fashion we shall be rewarded in heaven by the courteous love of our almighty God, who does not wish

---

3 "Trump: 'He's a war hero because he was captured. I like people that weren't captured' (C-SPAN)," YouTube video, July 20, 2015, https://www.youtube.com/watch?v=541Cg2Jnb8s.
4 Wikipedia, s.v. "John McCain," last modified November 17, 2020, 22:30, https://en.wikipedia.org/wiki/John_McCain.

anyone who comes there to lose his labours in any degree. For he regards sin as sorrow and pains for his lovers, to whom for love he assigns no blame.

The reward which we shall receive will not be small, but it will be great, glorious, and honourable. And so all shame will be turned into honour and joy. For our courteous Lord does not want his servants to despair because they fall often and grievously; for our falling does not hinder him in loving us. (ch. 39, 245)

This is almost a "no-fault" theory of sin. It includes a full repentance with contrition, compassion, and longing. But certainly it is a "no blame" theory of sin. Note too that Julian, like Anselm, uses the notion of honor—but not in the same way. For Anselm, sin dishonors God. For Julian, God honors sin's wound.

This is a mystery to Julian herself. Her vision showed her something that she did not understand. Or rather, her vision showed her an absence that she did not understand—an absence of sin. She says,

I did not see sin, for I believe that it has no kind of substance, no share in being, nor can it be recognized except by the pain caused by it. . . . It is true that sin is the cause of all this pain, but all will be well, and every kind of thing will be well.

These words were revealed most tenderly, showing no kind of blame to me or anyone who will be saved. So it would be most unkind of me to blame God or marvel at him on account of my sins, since he does not blame me for sin. And in these words I saw hidden in God an exalted and wonderful mystery, which he will make plain and we shall know in heaven. In this knowledge we shall truly see the cause why he allowed sin to come, and in this sight we shall rejoice forever. (ch. 27, 225–26)

The idea that evil has no existence of its own, whereas pain is real, is a familiar idea in theology, and one to which we will return when we come to the problem of evil. But the idea that sin has no existence of its own, whereas its wound is honorable, is Julian's mystery. That wonderful mystery is the part that Julian suppressed because she couldn't figure out how to explain it. Some twenty years later (ch. 51, 270), Julian's "Parable of the Servant" grounded the no-blame wound theory of sin in a distinctive Christology and theological anthropology.

The Parable of the Servant

The wonderful mystery is a kind of double vision that superimposes the descent of Christ onto the fall of Adam. They are both downward movements, but God sees Christ's compassion rather than our sin. I don't think this means that the fall of Adam and the advent of Christ are the same thing. Nor does it mean that sin causes salvation. Rather, I think this is another case of happy irony. God takes the occasion of the worst that human beings can do, sin, and graciously makes it the occasion of the great thing that God always intended, to befriend us. The friendship of God on the occasion of sin takes the form of compassion for our injury. Julian saw it like this:

> Good Lord, I see in you that you are very truth, and I know truly that we sin grievously all day and are very blameworthy; and I can neither reject my knowledge of this truth, nor see [in my vision] that any kind of blame is shown to us. How can this be? For I know by the ordinary teaching of Holy Church and by my own feeling that the blame of our sins continually hangs upon us, from the first man until the time that we come up into heaven. This, then was my astonishment, that I saw our Lord God showing no more blame to us than if we were as pure and as holy as the angels are in heaven. . . .
>
> Ah, Lord Jesus, king of bliss, how shall I be comforted, who will tell me and teach me what I need to know, if I cannot at this time see it in you?
>
> And then our courteous Lord answered very mysteriously by revealing a wonderful example of a lord who has a servant. The vision was shown doubly. . . . He sends him to a certain place to do his will. Not only does the servant go, but he dashes off and runs at great speed, loving to do his lord's will. And soon he falls into a dell and is greatly injured; and then he groans and moans and tosses about and writhes, but he cannot rise or help himself in any way. And of all this the greatest hurt which I saw him in was lack of consolation, for he could not turn his face to look on his loving lord, who was very close to him, in whom is all consolation; but like a man who was for the time extremely feeble and foolish [that is, stunned], he paid heed to his feelings and his continuing distress, in which he suffered seven great pains. . . .
>
> I was amazed that this servant could so meekly suffer all this woe; and I looked carefully to know if I could detect any fault in him, or if the lord would impute to him any kind of blame; and truly none was seen, for the only cause of his falling was his good will and his great desire. And in spirit he was as prompt and as good as he was when he stood before his lord, ready to do his will. . . .
>
> Then this courteous lord said this: See my beloved servant, what harm and injuries he has had and accepted in my service for my love, yes, and for his good will. Is it not reasonable that I should reward him for his fight and his fear, his hurt and his injuries and all his woe? And furthermore, is it not proper for me to give him a gift, better for him and more honourable than his own health could have been? Otherwise, it seems to me that I should be ungracious. (ch. 51, 268–69)

Julian was confused about whether the servant was Adam or Christ. As in the christological controversies, when it took the church a long time to see that the answer to whether Christ himself was human or divine had to be both, so it was a long time for Julian to see that the servant had to be both Christ and Adam. The idea is not original with her but occurred also to the apostle Paul: "Adam . . . was a type of the one who was to come. . . . Therefore, as one trespass led to condemnation for all, so one act of righteousness leads to justification and life for all" (Rom 5:14, 18 ESV; modified).

For Julian, the insight came in a second version of the vision, when she saw that the servant in the dirt was digging. Julian says, "There was a treasure in the earth which the lord loved. . . . And then I understood that [the servant] was to do the greatest labour and the hardest work there is. He was to be a gardener, digging and ditching and sweating and turning the soil over and over" (ch. 51, 273). A gardener! Where in the Bible is a gardener? Many places. But most importantly, at the beginning, in Eden, and at the end, in Gethsemane. At the beginning, Adam gardens in Eden, and at the end, Mary Magdalene mistakes Christ for the gardener in Gethsemane.

Indeed, Christ buried is a treasure in the earth; perhaps even Adam digging is searching for him. Julian does not spell that out, but Sergei Bulgakov says something similar, that the command to Adam—"In the sweat of thy face shalt thou eat bread" (Gen 3:19 KJV)—is the command that saves, because the wheat that he grows becomes the bread of Communion.[5] In any case, what Julian concludes is this:

> In the servant is comprehended the second person of the Trinity, and in the servant is comprehended Adam, that is to say all humanity. . . . When Adam fell, God's Son fell [that is, descended]; because of the true union which was made in heaven, God's Son could not be separated from Adam, for by Adam I understand all humankind. Adam fell from life to death, into the valley of this wretched world, and after that into hell. God's Son fell with Adam, into the valley of the womb of the maiden who was the fairest daughter of Adam, and that was to excuse Adam from blame in heaven and on earth; and powerfully he brought him out of hell. For in all this our good Lord showed his own Son and Adam as only one man. . . .
>
> . . . Therefore our Father . . . does not wish to assign more blame to us than to his own beloved Son Jesus Christ. (ch. 51, 274–75; modified)

We may comprehend all this in the following table:

---

5 Sergei Bulgakov, *Philosophy of Economy: The World as Household*, trans. Catherine Evtuhov (New Haven: Yale University Press, 2000), 75-104. For a summary, see Eugene F. Rogers, Jr., *After the Spirit* (Grand Rapids, MI: Eerdmans, 2005), 40-44.

Author	Problem	Solution	Christ's role	Name	Holiday	How we participate
Athanasius	Corruptibility, especially death	Share the divine nature	Becomes human to make us divine	Christ the Victor	Easter	Practice asceticism
Anselm	Sin as debt	Pay the debt	Pays the debt	Christ the victim	Good Friday	Take Communion
Abelard	Failure to love	Teach love	Teaches love by word and example in all he says and does	Exemplary or moral theory	No one holiday because it all counts, every day of the calendar	Love your neighbor
Stephen Ray after Origen of Alexandria	Social distinctions of flesh such as racism	Imbue the flesh with the power of life to overcome evil	Martyr for the flesh that tricks or reverses the forces of evil	Trickster theory, related to but better than the ransom theory	Pentecost—the day on which the Holy Spirit gathers the church around the flesh of Jesus	Join movements for love and justice. Does the church count?
Julian of Norwich	Injury and pain of sin	See sin as wound of honor	Accompanies Adam on his fall	Wound or servant theory of sin	Annunciation or Christmas—the day on which Christ descends to earth	Practice compassion—forgive others as you would be forgiven

Our last figure, Hans von Balthasar, only ever read Julian's Short Text—so he missed the Parable of the Servant—but he also sees the solution to sin in Christ's descent, this time all the way down into hell.

14 Balthasar Talks about Christ Emptying Hell

> Barth implied an empty hell because of God's choice of Godself to bear the sin of the human being; Balthasar hoped for an empty hell because of Christ's descent to the dead.

"The mysteries of March are mysteries of descent. In March the Son of God descended into the Virgin's womb, into human life; and in March, too, he descended into human death, into the womb of Hell."[1] Those words of John Saward describe the atonement theory of Swiss Catholic theologian Hans Urs von Balthasar (1905–88). Uniquely in this section, our interlocutor is a secondary rather than a primary source—that is, a book *about* the theologian rather than *by* him. That's because Balthasar's theory is so outlandish and wonderful that he was too cautious to spell it out all in one place. Instead, he dribbled it out slowly over forty years or more among thousands of pages. Even in *Mysterium Paschale*, where everybody thinks the theory is all in one place, it's clearer in the introduction (which is by somebody else) than it is in the book. But Saward has collected into two chapters hundreds of cites and quotes from over fifty sources by Balthasar and his greatest influence, the mystic Adrienne von Speyr (1902–67). Balthasar's work is brilliant and original but sprawling, and it sometimes reads like a first draft. Saward's work about Balthasar, however, is elegant, economical, even poetic.

For Balthasar, the work of Christ reveals that the human problem is suffering. It is the *solidarity* of Christ with human suffering that reveals and solves the problem of suffering. The solidarity and the suffering appear most clearly in the descent of Christ into hell.

As a feature of Christian speech, the descent into hell is attested most clearly by what Christians say or refrain from saying in church and by what icons, if any, they hang there. Traditional versions of the Apostles' Creed read "He was crucified, died, and was buried. He descended into hell. On the third day he rose again from the dead. He ascended into heaven...." When I was growing up, "He descended into hell" appeared in square brackets, after which an asterisk led to a footnote saying, "Some

---

1 The reading for the course was John Saward, "The Incarnation, the Descent into Hell and the Resurrection," in *The Mysteries of March* (Washington, DC: Catholic University of America Press, 1990), 105–43; here, 105. Further references by page number in the text. For further reading, see Hans Urs von Balthasar, *Mysterium Paschale*, with an introduction by Aidan Nichols (Edinburgh: T&T Clarke, 1990; Grand Rapids, MI: William B. Eerdmans, 1993); Hans Urs von Balthasar, *Dare We Hope "That All Men Be Saved," with a Short Discourse on Hell* (San Francisco: Ignatius, 1988); Hans Urs von Balthasar, *First Glance at Adrienne von Speyr* (San Francisco: Ignatius, 1981); and, if you can get hold of it, Adrienne von Speyr, *Kreuz und Hölle*, vols. 3–4, *Nachlasswerke* (Einsiedeln, Switzerland: Johannes Verlag, 1966).

churches omit this." Mine did. Presumably from fear of saying the word *hell* in church. Ephesians 4:9 correctly represents the Greek in saying that Christ "descended into the lower parts of the earth." Late twentieth-century translations of the Apostles' Creed read "He descended to the dead," which is more in accord with 1 Peter 4:6. The traditional Eastern Orthodox icon of the resurrection, or anastasis, shows Christ pushing off from the bottom of the pool, as it were, his feet upon the broken doors of hell.

So what are the "mysteries of March" that provide the title for Saward's account of Balthasar? In short, Holy Saturday and Lady Day: two days of the Christian calendar unfamiliar to most English-speaking Christians—but easy to figure out.

Lady Day is more commonly known in some English-speaking countries as Annunciation. As you might guess from Saward's remark, that's the day on which the Son of God descended into Mary's womb—that is, the day on which the angel announced him to Mary (hence Annunciation) and on which Mary conceived. Given that Jesus is born on Christmas, which is December 25, you could count backward nine months to arrive at a conventional date for his conception. That would be March 25. And in fact, that's the day on which the church celebrates the beginning of Christ's incarnation. It is a mystery of descent, the day on which, according to churchly celebrations, Christ first descended to earth.

Holy Saturday, as you might also guess, is the otherwise unnamed Saturday between Good Friday and Easter, celebrated prominently in Eastern Orthodoxy. It is the day that Christ, having died on Friday and before rising on Sunday, lies among the dead—or in more colorful language, descends into hell. Like the Easter that it precedes, Holy Saturday is a movable holy day, and it most often falls in April, but about a quarter of the time it falls in March.

Because Holy Saturday is movable, and Annunciation is fixed, it can even happen that Annunciation and Holy Saturday fall on the same day. It happened, for example, a spate of times in 1967, 1978, and 1989, and another triplet occurs in 2062, 2073, and 2084. If something happens on the same day of the month during a lifetime, it's a coincidence. But if something happens on the same day of the month on a church calendar, it's a paradox. How do you observe the conception of Jesus, which is a celebration, at the very same time as you are observing the hell of Jesus, which is a solemnity? The liturgy makes an event present: on Easter, Christians sing, "Jesus Christ is risen today." How can Jesus come both to earth and to hell "today"? That's more than a coincidence: that's a collision of opposites and emotions. If you like weird, it's wonderful.

It's common for atonement theories to center on the death of Jesus, on Good Friday, and for them to speak of his suffering and death. But why stop there? Depending on how you understand Holy Saturday, there is more suffering to come—and certainly more death. Furthermore, Holy Saturday is arguably the most salvific day as well. For Holy Saturday is the day on which Christ preaches to the dead (1 Pet 4:6) and empties out Sheol. For Balthasar, Holy Saturday is the very deepest part of the Christian paradox. To stop at Good Friday looks like a failure of nerve. And Balthasar likes it because it presents a whole series of paradoxes.

How can Christ liturgically become alive and lie dead? In Western churches (Protestant and Catholic), Annunciation moves to another day. Eastern churches have special combined liturgies if Annunciation falls on a day of Holy Week. John Donne wrote a poem about the coinciding of Annunciation and Good Friday in 1608:

> This doubtful day
> Of feast or fast, Christ came and went away.
> . . .
> This Church, by letting these days join, hath shown
> Death and conception in mankind is one:
> Or 'twas in Him the same humility
> That He would be a man and leave to be:
> Or as creation He had made, as God,
> With the last judgment but one period,
> His imitating Spouse [the church] would join in one
> Manhood's extremes: He shall come, He is gone.[2]

The poet makes clear that to remove the feast from the fast is to lose an opportunity. It is the opportunity to experience the coincidence of opposites, which also happens spatially: tradition also appoints the spot on which Christ died—Golgotha, as covered by the Church of the Holy Sepulchre in Jerusalem—as the spot where God created Adam. Such paradoxes are not to be avoided but prove productive in many religions.

How can Christ lie dead and yet preach? Balthasar's problem is that he wants to respect both the full humanity of Jesus and the biblical witness. If Jesus is fully human, then dead means dead. But 1 Peter 4:6 says that the Gospel "was proclaimed" to the dead, in the passive voice (εὐηγγελίσθη); the passive is a clue to Balthasar, a clue that deepens rather than dispenses with the mystery: it opens the possibility of passive preaching. What if Jesus does a human thing—lie dead—with divine result, that the dead receive the Word? Jesus, even as a dead human being, is the dead humanity *of the Word*. Remember, there is nobody else in there to assume a human nature but the Person of the Word. So the Word can be even more *with* the dead, in *solidarity* with the dead, if he is dead. In that way, they can receive the Good News unspoken: that God is with even the dead. The paradox of the Life being dead becomes the paradox of the Word keeping silent—but still, somehow, able to "move" the dead. This does not diminish but deepens the paradox: it is still a paradox that the dead could be moved; it is just as much a paradox that the dead could "hear," receive, or be moved as that the dead Jesus could preach, come, or act.

And yet my own experience at a funeral suggests that Balthasar has recast the paradox in a productive way. My mother died suddenly of a cerebral hemorrhage.

---

2 John Donne, "The Annunciation and Passion," in *The Poems of John Donne*, ed. Edward Kerchever Chambers (London: Lawrence and Bullen, 1896), https://www.bartleby.com/357/109.html.

And the only thing that helped was the Balthasarian idea that God (God the Son) had died, too, not in the sense that God was gone but in the sense that wherever my mother was—*still dead*, not in some life that I could not, in new grief, imagine—God was too. She died in October, and when Easter came, six months later, it was still too soon. Resurrection was offensive that year. I didn't want to hear about renewal of life when I was still getting used to dead. So it mattered that Balthasar had a way of keeping God by keeping God dead, that Jesus could show solidarity by staying dead, could accompany by keeping still, could speak by keeping silent.

If Jesus empties out hell while he is dead, you might ask, why does he threaten with hell when he is alive? Balthasar, like Barth, is a creeping universalist. That means, in both cases, that neither theologian claims to know what God is going to do. They don't claim to have the scriptural authority to say that God saves all, and they don't claim to have a special revelation (like a biblical prophet) that tells them so. But the phrase also means, in both cases, that Barth and Balthasar present a logic that *leads right up* to the conclusion that God saves all. It's a piece of inference, not a piece of information. They would probably both admit to having drawn an inference, even as both would insist that they do not possess the information. And each of them would like *readers to draw the same inference for themselves.*

In Balthasar's case, the inference is clearest in a little book called *Dare We Hope "That All Men Be Saved," with a Short Discourse on Hell.* Balthasar does not claim to know what God will do, but he does claim to know what God wants: "that all men be saved" (see 1 Tim 2:4; compare the much-ignored John 3:17). Given that universal salvation is what God wants, it would be a *sin not to hope* that God will get what God desires, the salvation of all. Hope is one of the great theological virtues—faith, hope, and charity. Not to hope that would be the sin of despair. In that case, the one deserving of hell would be the one refusing to hope.

But the inference is most profound, in Balthasar as in Barth, where the theologian does the Christology. In Barth's case, as we saw, the deepest form of Balthasar's question "Dare we hope?" was this: if anybody deserves damnation, it would be Judas, but Judas is hard to distinguish from other apostles like Peter and Paul, and in any case, Judas completed the strictest standards for repentance. In Balthasar, the deepest form of the question takes place not on the cross of Jesus or in the heart of Judas: it takes place in hell. Jesus descends to the dead to take them by the hand and join them to the resurrection. Balthasar has in mind the great Greek Orthodox icon of the anastasis, or resurrection, but by convention this icon depicts Jesus not rising from the earth or even the tomb but pushing off from the deepest place—hell—with the devil and the doors of hell under his feet, completing resurrection and ascension in one great upward sweep, and bringing Adam and Eve, by the hand, up with him into heaven. In Balthasar's picture, Jesus has emptied out hell. It is not a doctrine of no hell. It is a doctrine of an empty hell. There is such a thing as hell. But we are required to hope that it's empty. (See figure 14.1.)

Figure 14.1. The fresco anastasis from the Chora Monastery (now Kariye Camii) in Istanbul shows Christ pushing off with his feet on the broken doors of hell to bring Adam and Eve by the hand up with him into heaven.[3]

Now, Balthasar is a decent biblical scholar, for a theologian. He knows, for example, that purgatory is not biblically attested. And more to the point, he knows that Sheol, the place of the dead in the Hebrew Bible, *does not function the same way* as hades, or Gehenna, in the New Testament. Sheol is a holding pen for the dead, good and bad alike. Hades, or Gehenna, is worse. It is a place of punishment. Many Christians fail to recognize that "the God of the New Testament" is actually meaner than "the God of the Old Testament." In the "Old Testament," God prevents Abraham's sacrifice of his son; in the New Testament, God goes through with the sacrifice and kills his own. In Wyschogrod, as we have seen, the opposite of election is a different job; in Calvin, the opposite of election is rejection. Balthasar does not deny that the New Testament—even Christ's activity of emptying out Sheol—makes things worse for anyone whom Christ consigns to Gehenna. The New Testament hell, like the New Testament heaven, is a new reality created by Christ. But there is tremendous ground for hope in the way the story goes. Can Christians really believe that God, having cleared out Sheol, returns to populate hades? Are Christians not

---

3 Gryffindor, *Anastasis Fresco*, 1310–20, painting, Kariye Camii, Istanbul, Wikimedia Commons.

required at least to *hope* that God will see God's will done, and Gehenna will prove an empty possibility? Given that human freedom is finite and God's freedom is infinite, can God's will really be thwarted? Dare we not hope that all will be saved? What would it mean, Balthasar would like to know, if you wanted or needed some to be damned so that you could be saved? Paul asks the question another way: Are *you* willing to be damned for *others* to be saved (Rom 9:3)?

That possibility is the premise of a Presbyterian joke. The search committee of a church is interviewing a candidate for minister. They ask him (it would have been a "him" when the joke was current) if he is willing to be damned for the glory of God. He answers that he is willing for the *committee* to be damned for the glory of God. It is not recorded whether he got the job.

How can a dead man raise the dead? This consequence of Balthasar's theory resembles Origen's and Stephen Ray's. The Word, who was life itself, could voluntarily undergo death but not stay dead. Or, if that sounds like special pleading, credit the resurrection to the Spirit, the Giver of Life. Death separates the Son from the Father: the Holy Spirit reunites them. That solution has the advantage of following Romans 8:11, which identifies all three Persons of the Trinity by their role in the resurrection of Jesus—a verse to which we will recur when we come to the Trinity.

How can Christ be God and suffer God-abandonment? How can the Trinity survive when one of its members is dead? How can the Trinity maintain Communion when the Father and the Son are infinitely separated? Here again the declaration of the Song of Songs—that love is as strong as death—reappears as a question: God has become a human being; God has undergone death; *is* love as strong as death? After the crucifixion? After the descent into hell? Really?

It is a common criticism of Balthasar that he separates the members of the Trinity so far from one another that he treats them as three gods, and the Trinity comes apart. I don't see that at all. Because the whole point of the Trinity, when Christ descends to the dead, is to allow the *Holy Spirit* to stretch, infinitely, beyond whatever created distance lies between the Father and hell and hold both the Father and the Son in one embrace. Whatever the human being can do or suffer, God is more encompassing: more encompassing than death, separation, and God-abandonment. It is part of the proper office of the Spirit to be the bond of love between the Father and the Son, even in the face of death, and even in the face of abandonment. Mystics from Teresa of Ávila and John of the Cross to Adrienne von Speyr and Mother Teresa experience God-abandonment, and they know, too, that God comes back. Balthasar proposes that the Spirit, whose name is Love, is God's way of return.

How can a theologian proceed when he[4] has received much of his information from the visions of a mystic? And not a mystic who has acquired the respectability

---

4 I use the masculine pronoun deliberately. Is he, Balthasar, bad for women theologians because he appropriates the insights of a woman? Or is he good for women theologians because he—even

of five hundred years, like Julian, but a contemporary unknown except to him? The footnote to some novel claim surely cannot read like this: "A mystic told me." And yet Adrienne von Speyr is the source for some of the most interesting aspects of the theory.

Adrienne von Speyr was born a Protestant. She experienced visions from a young age. She found that Protestant ministers don't deal well with visions. Nowadays we would send people with visions to a psychiatrist for drugs. But Catholic priests are taught that, at least in theory, *some* people might (rarely) receive visions from God. It's not impossible. Eventually, von Speyr[5] got a medical degree—no small feat for a woman in mid-twentieth-century Switzerland, where women got the right to vote only in 1974! She converted to Catholicism. Balthasar became her spiritual director. A spiritual director is like a psychotherapist, except that instead of meeting once every week or two, you typically meet once a month or less, and instead of being asked to talk about your mother, you might be asked to read the angry psalms.

Well, Balthasar got an earful. The "normal" pattern for many Christian mystics in the West (yes, mystics have patterns) is to experience the sufferings of Christ on the cross from noon on Good Friday until three o'clock, when Christ liturgically dies (according to each mystic's own time zone, because the pattern is a liturgical one). But von Speyr was different. She not only suffered with Christ on the cross: she accompanied him on his descent into hell. She went to hell with Jesus, and she *could say what it was like.*

For example, she saw effigies being burned up. What are these effigies? As on Guy Fawkes Day, effigies are usually papier-mâché models of people, models that are easy to burn. In the hell of the damned (not Sheol), according to von Speyr's visions, the effigies are made up of the moral substance that people have lost by sinning. So it is the person-shaped tissue of sins that they have sloughed off that burns up.

She observed that Jesus had to go down into hell (Sheol) in order to get back to the Father, a normal trope of journeys into hell but not one that Christians expect to hear, and odd, too, because the Father isn't there.

Now, that puts Balthasar in an interesting position. Von Speyr's visions have lots of fresh theological content that seems to go Barth one better. It appeals to Balthasar that the problem with human beings is suffering. In the twentieth century, we learned a lot about suffering. There were trenches and mustard gas and the first aerial bombings from World War I. There were the gas chambers and atom

---

more than Barth, who has another story—fosters and celebrates a unique theological partnership with a woman?

5   Both Hans Urs von Balthasar and Adrienne von Speyr have the nobiliary particle *von*, pronounced "fon," in their names. English sources vary freely in their use or neglect of the von. My sense is that in face-to-face interactions, you would refer to someone present using their von as you would use their title (Dr., Prof., etc.). But the more they become public property, the less their titles survive. So Beethoven, Goethe, and Schiller have all lost their "van" or "von." But our interlocutor, Saward, refers to von Speyr only by her *first* name, which I find unconscionable. In compensation, I insist on the particle for von Speyr but (inconsistently!) not for Balthasar.

bombs of World War II. There was new interest in psychological suffering from Freud and Jung. Adrienne von Speyr suffered both from ailments causing physical pain and from visions causing psychic pain. One of my former students who was bipolar found von Speyr's visions both triggering and inspiring—inspiring because von Speyr had found something constructive to do with her pain.

But how was Balthasar going to write up all this? He couldn't just say a mystic told him. Balthasar was alone among our modern theologians in lacking a university post. He was a maverick. He left the Jesuits to found his own order, the Johannesgemeinschaft, the Community of John, and he started his own publishing house, Johannes Verlag, the St. John Press. He had little institutional capital. He had no university, no established religious order, no distinguished publisher behind him. To raise the ante, he wanted to write the kind of theology Barth wrote, the kind that might last five hundred years. The last thing he could do is quote an unvetted, contemporary mystic.

So he allowed von Speyr to give him ideas, and then he read the whole Bible, the whole history of exegesis, the whole theological tradition, and a whole cloud of older mystics to find other time-tested sources for her ideas. If he could quote the Bible, its ancient interpreters, mystics from centuries past, or famous theologians—standard sources, even if some of them are obscure—then no one could fault him. That is why his material on the descent into hell is so scattered and so rich.

Balthasar both promoted and protected von Speyr. He wrote a whole book about her titled *First Glance at Adrienne von Speyr*. It is clearly a brief for sainthood. Its refrain is that von Speyr never desired to teach anything at odds with the magisterium of the Catholic Church. Mystics and institutions are often at odds; the ones who seek influence within the church often balance their innovations with protests of not wanting to innovate. Also in Julian of Norwich we see constant obeisance to Holy Mother Church. Balthasar took the very long view: How would he protect von Speyr's reputation so that her ideas live on to influence the church of the future?

Some of the most interesting quotations in *The Mysteries of March* come from a book that is a mystery all its own. Footnotes abbreviate it *KuH*. I looked up the abbreviation in a list at the back to see that *KuH* stands for a book of von Speyr's called *Kreuz und Hölle*, which sounds like the name of a horror movie: *Cross and Hell*. So immediately I went to the university library catalog and looked it up. Nothing. I got onto WorldCat, which includes all libraries in English-speaking universities and many in other European countries. At that time, in the early 1990s, I found two copies in university libraries in the English-speaking world. Of those, neither circulated. That is, I would have to get on a plane, go to Widener Library at Harvard in person, pass through security, present my credentials, wait for a librarian to retrieve the book, and read it in the building. That was weird. Now I wanted it more.

At a conference, I ran into a Balthasar biographer, and I asked him,

"Do you know this book by Adrienne von Speyr, *Kreuz und Hölle*?"

"Yes, what about it?"

"What's the deal? I can only find it in two libraries in North America, and they don't circulate."

"It's privately published."

"Wait, 'published' means it's available. 'Private' means it's not. Which is it?"

"'Published' means Balthasar ran the presses. 'Privately' means it's not for sale."

"Why would you print it and not make it available to sell?"

"Balthasar decided the church wasn't ready for it yet." (At this point, both Balthasar and von Speyr were dead.)

"Do *you* have a copy?"

"Yes."

"How did you get it?"

"The printed copies are stacked up in an apartment in Basel. You write to the literary executor, Cordelia something. You say you're a scholar and you're not intending to write anything bad about Balthasar or Speyr, and maybe she'll send you a copy. I can get you her address."

Then, cravenly, I gave up. But I told the story every year. And years later, a graduate student came up to me with a sly smile on her face.

"Guess what I found?"

"I don't know, what?"

"*Kreuz und Hölle.*"

"Really? How? It doesn't circulate."

"Things have changed. I got one from St. John's Seminary Library. You want a copy?"

Those are some of the reasons a theologian might love Balthasar's theory: not because the answers are so good but because the questions are. Mysteries about the Trinity, mysteries about hell, mysteries about church politics, mysteries about how to get hold of the damn book. In theology, it is usually better to be adequate than to be consistent.

This then is what the final version of our atonement chart looks like:

Author	Problem	Solution	Christ's role	Name	Holiday	How we participate
Athanasius	Corruptibility, especially death	Share the divine nature	Becomes human to make us divine	Christ the Victor	Easter	Practice asceticism
Anselm	Sin as debt	Pay the debt	Pays the debt	Christ the victim	Good Friday	Take Communion

Author	Problem	Solution	Christ's role	Name	Holiday	How we participate
Abelard	Failure to love	Teach love	Teaches love by word and example in all he says and does	Exemplary or moral theory	No one holiday because it all counts, every day of the calendar	Love your neighbor
Stephen Ray after Origen of Alexandria	Social distinctions of flesh such as racism	Imbue the flesh with the power of life to overcome evil	Martyr for the flesh that tricks or reverses the forces of evil	Trickster theory, related to but better than the ransom theory	Pentecost—the day on which the Holy Spirit gathers the church around the flesh of Jesus	Join movements for love and justice. Does the church count?
Julian of Norwich	Injury and pain of sin	See sin as wound of honor	Accompanies Adam on his fall	Wound or servant theory of sin	Annunciation or Christmas—the day on which Christ descends to earth	Practice compassion—forgive others as you would be forgiven
Hans Urs von Balthasar, Adrienne von Speyr (as described by John Saward)	Suffering	Solidarity in suffering	Descends to the dead	Descent into hell theory	Holy Saturday	Offer up your suffering for others

The last cell of the chart requires some explanation. What does it mean that we participate in this atonement of Balthasar's by "offering up suffering"? The phrase requires some familiarity with 1950s Catholic popular piety. (This is my explanation of Balthasar's move, not his. He doesn't refer to popular piety.) Think back if you know an older Catholic, probably a grandmother or great aunt, who may once have tired of hearing you complain about a broken leg or a long quarantine. The suffering is real, but she's tired of hearing about it. She says, "Offer it up for the souls in purgatory." Now, Balthasar is skeptical about purgatory, and he doesn't quote your grandmother, but he shares the sentiment. The person who uses that construction of Christian speech assumes that you can devote or dedicate your suffering to a useful purpose, to benefiting others. "Offering it up for the souls in purgatory" even assumes that *your* suffering can lessen *others'* suffering. Here's how that works.

When Christ suffered, he lessened or ended the suffering of others by suffering in their place. He can do that because he is also God, and God can remit punishment for or purification from sin. Apart from empathy and solidarity, other humans can do no such thing. But there is a work-around. God already plans to reduce the suffering required to purify others. God can graciously decide to take my suffering as the occasion of reducing the suffering of others, so that I get to participate in both purification and mercy. Once Christ has established a "treasury of merit," God can graciously allow others to make deposits. The grace of depositing your suffering in the treasury of merit is that the suffering is no longer in vain. This idea is a marvel of popular religious thought, and the marvelous thing about it is that it gives ordinary people something *constructive* to do with their pain.

This idea does not mean that anyone should increase or seek pain in order to help others. Don't try that at home. Rather, the saying assumes that there is enough suffering to go around, and the problem is what to do about it—or with it. This aspect of Catholic Christian grammar creates a constructive outlet for the unavoidable suffering: devote it to others.

That completes our survey of atonement theories. We have seen that they vary widely on the human problem that the work of Christ solves: the devil, death, debt, society, injury, suffering. To see the variety, try reading down each column rather than across. The way you participate might be to join a desert monastery, to take Communion, to love your neighbor, to join a movement, to dedicate your suffering. Despite the critiques that several authors raise against their predecessors, no church has officially declared that their adherents may use only one theory. You are always allowed to mix and match. All theories pare down the myriad of possibilities raised by the stories of Jesus, and adequacy always requires switching back and forth among the theories to recover the riches of the narratives. The theories raise several questions, questions like these:

1. One of the Trinity suffers, dies, and undergoes separation from the Father: Does the Trinity break, or does the Spirit stretch? How does the Trinity work, anyway?
2. Does solidarity in suffering solve the human problem, or does it consign humans and God to all sink together in the same boat? What does the resurrection have to add to Good Friday and Holy Saturday, other than a happy ending?
3. Several atonement theories raise the question of how, apart from their careful texts, they actually get used. How does Christianity guard against the misuse of commands like "Take up your cross and follow Jesus" or "Offer up your suffering for the souls in purgatory"?

Those and other questions will accompany us through the next sections of the book.

Christians Talk about the Trinity, or Love Stronger Than Death

15 Christians Ought to Talk about the Trinity Joining Them to Itself

The doctrine of the Trinity is a set of rules to enable Christians to go on talking the way the New Testament talks about the Three who are God. Jesus's relations with those he calls "Father" and "Spirit" presuppose that God is a community interacting among themselves and sharing one activity beyond themselves or towards creatures. The Three seek always and in everything to join us to their fellowship; the New Testament makes analogies to prayer and feasting.

How to Go on Talking the Way the New Testament Talks

The doctrine of the Trinity is an attempt to *go on talking about the Three in the way the New Testament talks.*

In the New Testament, there are three characters running around who are God: Jesus, the one Jesus calls "Father," and the one he calls the Spirit. Christians call all three "God": God the Father, God the Son/Word (= Jesus = Christ), and God the Holy Spirit.

At the same time, Christians claim not to have changed the Jewish commitment to worship only one God. They base that claim on the further claim that the Three have only one activity in the world. Unlike three humans, the three members of the Trinity only ever work together in the world. We can distinguish their activity only among themselves, or on the inside, as if they were a single human agent or psyche that has one activity but can distinguish on the inside among memory, reason, and will.

The New Testament talks as if the One God is also three. *They are three* whos *in one* what. The word for the "what," as in we don't know what it is, is *God*. The word for the three "whos" is "persons," "members," "hypostases," or just the Three.

Do not refer to the three as "parts." There are only two approved nouns for the three: persons or members (or the Greek word *hypostases*). That's not because those words are so good. It's because all the other words are worse. It's not because we know what we're talking about. It's because we know that we *don't* know what we are talking about, because we don't know *what* God is. (For more about language for God, including gendered language, God's pronouns, and "Father"/"Son" language, see the end of the chapter).

What are the pattern and the rules that allow Christians to go on talking that way?

The Pattern of How the New Testament Talks

The *pattern* is not the same as the *rules*. The pattern is a way of talking, like a pattern in language. Consider the ridiculous pattern for the verb *to be*. It goes like this: "I am," "you are," "he/she/it is." "Am," "is," and "are" seem to have nothing in common and even less in common with "be," "was," and "were." Nevertheless, we get used to the pattern, and after a while we never make mistakes with it.

The so-called Athanasian Creed supplies the *pattern* of the New Testament's talk about God.[1] The basic pattern is this: the Father is God, the Son is God, the Holy Spirit is God, but there are not three gods, only one God. Read it rhythmically, out loud. Not because you believe it or are reciting it in church. Read it out loud because you are practicing the way the language goes. It's like a verb pattern in Christianese.

What the Athanasian Creed is not: it's not by Athanasius, and it's also not by somebody named Mr. Vult. The phrase *Quicunque Vult* is simply Latin for the first line ("Whoever wants"). You know how some people call the Lord's Prayer by the first words, the Our Father? You may have also heard them call it the Pater Noster, which is "Our Father" in Latin. It sounds a little bit like Spanish, in which you call it the Padre Nuestro. When students referred to Mr. Vult as the author of the Athanasian Creed, I wanted to go back on Facebook. Finally, the Athanasian Creed is *not* only Catholic just because it refers to the "catholic" faith with a small c. The word *catholic* with a small c means "universal." Someone with "catholic tastes in music" likes all kinds of music. In the Athanasian Creed, it means that all Christians talk about the Trinity in this way. It's true; they do. Here's your proof: this creed about how to adhere to the "Catholic faith" appears in the *Lutheran Book of Worship*. As you remember, Lutherans were the first to rebel against the Catholic Church (capital Cs).

To sum up: stop and read the Athanasian Creed out loud to get the pattern. You can find it on the internet. You will find yourself getting bored. That's good. That means you're getting the pattern. Keep reading so you won't forget it.

---

1 "The Athanasian Creed," in the *Lutheran Book of Worship* (Minneapolis: Augsburg, 1978), 54.

The Rules of How the New Testament Talks

Now you've got the pattern. But it's not actually as bad as "I am," "you are," "she is" "to be." There are also rules. The pattern is more important than the rules. But three simple generalizations hold for New Testament talk about God.

1. *Opera trinitatis ad extra indivisa sunt:* "The works of the Trinity toward the outside are indivisible" (Augustine). "Toward the outside" means "toward us," "toward the world," "toward creation." If God (the Trinity) saves you, Father, Son, and Spirit are all involved. If God (the Trinity) creates the world, Father, Son, and Spirit are all involved. And so on.

2. Another way of saying the same thing. *The Three are distinguished only among themselves.* In iconic New Testament scenes, like the baptism of Jesus, the Three are interacting among themselves, and if onlookers or readers can see the Three separately, that's because those onlookers or readers are getting a *glimpse into the Trinitarian life, into the interior of God.* At the baptism of Jesus, we see Jesus in the river, see the Spirit hovering over his head, and hear the voice of the Father saying, "This is my Son, my Beloved, with whom I am well pleased." In (Eastern Orthodox Christian paintings on wood with lots of gold, the source of computer icons), the voice of the Father can't be painted and is represented by a small hand or blue field at the top. (See figure 15.1.)

3. "Appropriations." In natural language, some things are idiomatic—that is, usually said that way, even apart from rules. So it's polite to put myself second, "she and I," not "I and she." Or we say, "That's me," whereas in German, you say, "Das bin ich," or "That am I," which sounds totally weird in English, even though it's not wrong. There are ways of talking idiomatically about the Trinity, too, called "appropriations" because they are appropriate. Here are the three most common examples:

   Christians say, for example, "I believe in God the Father Almighty, maker of heaven and earth." That's idiomatic. But it does *not* mean that the Son and Spirit are left out of creation. That would violate rule A. Indeed, John 1:3 insists that "all things were made by him [Jesus]; and without him was not any thing made that was made." Similarly, in traditional Christian exegesis, Genesis 1:2—"the Spirit of God was hovering over the face of the waters"—is taken to mean the Holy Spirit. (Obviously, Jewish readers see poetic variation between "God" and "Spirit of God.") Finally, it's idiomatic to say "Jesus saves," but again that never means that the Father and the Spirit are left out.

   The pattern of "appropriations" even affects the word *God* itself. Technically speaking, the word *God* is not a name; it's a *description of the Three.* Other gods are named Jupiter, Zeus, Wotan, and so on. So "God" is not a name. But the word *God* is most often appropriated to the Father. Nevertheless, when theologians say "God," they almost never mean "only the Father." They almost always mean "the Trinity without further differentiation." They almost always mean all of the Three: Father, Son, *and* Holy Spirit. Therefore, from now on, *if you mean the Father, say the Father.* If you want to avoid masculine language for God, see the end of the chapter.

Figure 15.1. In this mosaic from Hosios Loukas (St. Luke Church) near Distomo in Boeotia, Greece, the members of the Trinity (represented by the hand of the Father, the body of the Son, and the dove of the Holy Spirit) catch humanity up into the Trinitarian life.[2]

2 *Baptism of Christ*, 1050, mosaic, Hosios Loukas, Greece, Wikimedia Commons.

To sum up: The Three are one because they always work together on the outside. If they are working separately, you are getting a glimpse into their interior. And if it's usual to give one of the Three credit for something that happens in the world, that doesn't mean the other two are left out.

Three Analogies about How This Works

The Analogy from Psychology

From the One God to the Three Persons. In this model, due to Augustine, God as a whole is like a human person. I, as a human being, have unified action toward the outside. Only within myself can I distinguish three, as if my memory, reason, and will were three persons all by themselves. This model emphasizes the oneness of God. It's called the psychological model.

The trouble with this model is that I distinguish my memory, reason, and will only when something goes wrong, and presumably things don't "go wrong" with God. Suppose I am supposed to call you, and I don't. Then I can blame my memory ("I forgot"), or my reason ("It didn't seem necessary anymore"), or my will ("I'm sorry, I just didn't want to!"). But supposedly, God's not like that, so the analogy breaks down.

A greater disadvantage of this model is that it seems to have little or nothing to do with salvation, so it's hard to see why the Trinity might matter.

The other model starts from the Three and goes to their unity. On the second model, the Trinity is a community to join. I have divided the second model into two. One is an analogy from Jesus's parable of the wedding feast. The other (the third overall) is an interpretation of Romans 8:11.

The Analogy of the Wedding Feast

God is love in the Trinity.[3] There is one to love, one to receive love, and one to witness, celebrate, and guarantee love. Even in human relationships, the love of two is insufficient; the love of two exceeds itself in hospitality to others, including children, and even early couples crave to proclaim their love to witnesses: that's why they spray paint their names on highway bridges, "John loves Mary" or "David loves Stephen." Christian Trinity-talk has deliberately avoided the imagery of a ménage à trois, of parent-parent-child, or parent-child-grandchild: both Augustine of Hippo and Richard of St. Victor warned against the procreationism of the pagan gods and the dangers of a fertility cult. Yet they held fast to the idea that the Three of the Trinity represent the love of two and their bond. The promise and problem of

---

3 For more about the analogy of the wedding feast, see Deirdre Good, Willis Jenkins, Cynthia Kittredge, and Eugene F. Rogers Jr., "A Theology of Marriage Including Same-Sex Couples," *Anglican Theological Review* 93 (2011): 51–87; and Deirdre Good et al., "Liberal Response," *Anglican Theological Review* 93 (2011): 101–10.

traditional Trinity talk (at least in the West) is to speak of the Spirit as the "bond" or "chain" of love, the *vinculum caritatis*, uniting the Father and the Son. The problem with the chain of love is twofold: chains sound unfree, and chains are not persons.

I have proposed that we upgrade the role of the Spirit to that of a witness. A witness is a person, and the New Testament frequently associates the Spirit with bearing witness (John 15:26, Acts 15:8, Rom 8:16, 9:1, Heb 2:4, 10:15, 1 John 5:7). Because love is incomplete à deux, it is the office of the Holy Spirit to witness, glorify, rejoice in, celebrate, multiply, and bless the union between the Father and the Son. Where does a witness have duties to celebrate and uphold love?

Jesus said, "The kingdom of heaven may be compared to a king who gave a wedding feast" (Matt 22:2 ESV). Christians believe that heaven will be like a great feast—"Thou preparest a table before me . . . ; my cup runneth over" (Ps 23:5 KJV)—with the members of the Trinity, like the hospitality of Abraham with the three visitors under the oaks of Mamre (Gen 18). This is not the wedding alone but the celebration, the feasting. As Augustine and Richard of St. Victor warned, we want to do this without reducing it to sex (even though all forms of love arise kaleidoscopically from the love that is God): but a wedding is about covenant. In a wedding, there are *three* who make vows, not only two, because the congregation promises also. The minister or priest not only requires vows from the couple but asks the people, "Will you uphold this couple in their marriage?" And the people answer, "We will!" That is the office of the Holy Spirit. This model fits in well with ecclesiology, or how Christians talk about the church, because it is the office of the Spirit here below to call forth more witnesses, witnesses to love. And if you have been reading Balthasar, it also fits in well with the role of the Holy Spirit in reuniting the Father and the Son after the death of the Son. For the role of the witnesses who promise to uphold a couple at their wedding is to help them over times of difficulty, when the one flesh seems to die. The couple, with their witnesses, becomes a school for virtue, making each other better; practicing faith, hope, and charity toward their nearest neighbor; and bearing, according to the Greek tradition, the crowns of marriage, which are crowns of martyrdom. Thus weddings are parables of the Trinitarian life, exchanges of gift and gratitude guaranteed by a third, the Holy Spirit, multiplying a host of witnesses. Weddings—like prayer, resurrection, Bible reading, good deeds, and everything the Trinity inspires in the world—catch humans up into a parable of the Trinitarian life, into a life of grace, gratitude, and guarantee that generates a community gathered by the Spirit and a likeness of God's Child.

The Analogy from Prayer

In the third model, we also start from the Three and work to the One.[4] The advantage of this model is that it has everything to do with salvation. *The Trinity is a community to join. Or better, it is a community that joins human beings to itself.* Call it the communitarian model.

This model arises from Paul's descriptions of prayer in Romans 8:11–29 and Galatians 4:6. The *Spirit* prays in us and for us, even when we don't know how to pray (Rom 8:26). The Spirit teaches us to call God "*Father*" (Rom 8:15; Gal 4:6). What happens is that the person in whom the Spirit prays is conformed to Christ (Gal 4:7; Rom 8:23). That means, the person who prays is caught up in the Trinitarian life, where the Spirit prays to the Father and what happens is becoming a child of God. Prayer is a means by which the Spirit puts humans in Son position—that is, in the Spirit, mortals address their prayers to "Our Father, who art in heaven." They acknowledge their (adopted) Son position by concluding their prayers "in Jesus's name." This is not a human achievement. This is what happens when the Spirit catches humans up into the very life of God in the Trinity, when the Spirit sweeps them into the prayer by which the Spirit approaches the Father, and what happens is Jesus.

This is salvation. Life in heaven is life in fellowship with the Trinity—that is, when other human beings are brought by the Spirit into being children of the Father and siblings to the Son. Salvation is nothing else but the Spirit's bringing human beings to share the Trinitarian life of God. This is why the Trinity matters: the Spirit brings humans to the Father, and what happens is Christ-likeness, becoming a child ("son"[5]) of God.

The Trinity, the Resurrection, and Salvation

The most important verse in the New Testament about the Trinity is Romans 8:11. It defines all three Persons of the Trinity in terms of the resurrection of Jesus. It goes, "If the *Spirit* of the *One Who* raised *Jesus* dwells in your mortal bodies, you too will be raised from the dead" (my translation, influenced by Robert Jenson). Let's take the sentence backward, from the end to the beginning.

"You too will be raised from the dead" clearly implicates salvation. That happens if the *Spirit* dwells in your bodies. Like prayer, resurrection also begins with the Spirit.

---

4 For more about the analogy from prayer, see Sarah Coakley, "Living into the Mystery of the Holy Trinity," in *The Holy Spirit: Classic and Contemporary Readings*, ed. Eugene F. Rogers Jr. (Oxford: Blackwell, 2009), 44–52; and Robert W. Jenson, *The Triune Identity* (Philadelphia: Fortress Press, 1982), 50–52.

5 "Sonship" language prevails in Paul because in Greco-Roman society, sons were heirs who could inherit. Christian women were also placed into the son-position to the Father, since they would also inherit eternal life. Therefore, Paul genders both women and men as inheritors or "sons."

In resurrection as in prayer, the Spirit connects humans to "the One Who raised Jesus," here, the Father. (You can also refer to the Spirit as one who raised Jesus because the Spirit is—obviously!—not left out of the resurrection, but here the phrase clearly means the Father.)

In resurrection as in prayer, what happens is Christ-likeness. Just as the Spirit flowed through Christ at *his* resurrection, so too—as a gift to the Son—the Spirit flows through Christians at *their resurrection*.

This shows that *salvation itself* has a Trinitarian shape. *For all things related to salvation, the Spirit moves the human toward the Father, and what happens is Christ-likeness.*

For a surprising example, take sexuality and marriage. Their point is to bring humans into a relationship in which the fruits of the Spirit can appear: faith, hope, and charity. Marriage is a school for virtue. The other person is both an occasion of joy and hard to live with over time, so the Spirit brings the partners to turn joy into faith, hope, and charity, the fruits of the Spirit. What begins in eros, ends in agape. God binds two for life with each other, to prepare them for life with God. This makes them Christlike. Here too the pattern is *through the Spirit, to the Father, on the pattern of Jesus*. Unless of course it makes them worse, in which case, according to parts of the Eastern tradition, the "one flesh" (the marriage) "dies," and they can get divorced, since remarriage is always allowed after death.

The Trinity and Gendered Language

The Bible uses gendered language to talk about God: gendered relationships like "Father" and "Son" and gendered pronouns, almost always "he," but in rare cases, "she" (keep reading).

An important theological principle governs *all* language about God: because God transcends the world and created the world out of nothing, God is not in any human or created category. To say, *God is not in a category*, is to make a rule: *don't put God in a box*. To say, *God is not in a category* in the traditional way is to say it in Latin: *Deus non est in genere*. The word *genere* is a form of the word *genus*, which means "category." It is the origin also of our word *genre*. But it is almost as if the Latin says, *God is not in a gender*, and "gender," of course, also descends from the Latin words *genus, genere*. (The native word for this in English is also related: kind. God is not in a kind.) But to say, *God is not in a gender*, is to make the most salient contemporary application of the ancient principle.

God is not in a gender for an important substantive reason: God is the *source* of gender, all of it. Therefore, God is not *under* the category of gender; God is *beyond* gender as the source of it all. Furthermore, if God is not in a category, God is not binary.

In the year 693, the sixteenth Synod of Toledo (a meeting of bishops) emphasized the divinity of the Son by saying that he emerged *ex utero patris*, "from *the womb of* the *Father*." In case you're not paying attention, fathers don't usually have wombs, unless of course they are transmen. The bishops meeting in Toledo helped themselves to the principle that if God is beyond gender, then they have the freedom to refer to God's uterus, even, to make the paradox more pointed, the uterus of the "*Father*." So yes, "Father" is masculine language, but it does not prevent God the Father from having female characteristics, like a womb.

The language of God's womb is no aberration of crazy bishops but derives from Psalm 110:3, which the Latin Bible translated as "out of my womb before the morning star I bore you."[6] Even earlier than the sixteenth Synod of Toledo, around the year 420, Augustine had commented on that Psalm. He asked this rhetorical question: "If God hath a Son, hath He also a womb? Like fleshly bodies, He hath not; for He hath not a bosom either; yet it is said, 'He who is in the bosom of the Father hath declared Him'" (John 3:18).[7]

Similarly, in Cistercian monasteries and elsewhere in the Middle Ages, monks were directed to crawl up into the wound in Jesus's side to be born again there: the wound was also a womb. In Latin, too, the words for "wound" and "womb" sound alike, *vulnus* and *vulva* (which means "womb" in Latin). In the Middle Ages, both the Father and the Son had wombs.

So the Father and the Son are figures with male-gendered names but other female-gendered characteristics.

Meanwhile, Christians spoke of the Holy Spirit in different languages with words of different genders. In German and Old English, *Geist* (Holy Ghost) was masculine. In the Latin of the Vulgate, *spiritus* was masculine as well. But in the Greek of the New Testament, *pneuma* is neuter—and in the Semitic languages, including Hebrew, Syriac, and Aramaic, the words for "Spirit" (*ruach* in Hebrew and *rucha* in Aramaic) were feminine. Jesus would have spoken of the Spirit in Aramaic with feminine words and referred to Her as She. Many Middle Eastern Christians worship in Syriac, a language very close to Aramaic, and although they now refer to the Holy Spirit as He, they referred to Her as She for hundreds of years. We see some remnant of this usage in Paul, who refers to the Spirit as groaning in travail—that is, like a woman in labor—to bear believers and even the new creation (Rom 8:22–27).[8]

So all three Persons of the Trinity have female characteristics, and one gets female pronouns in other languages.

---

6   This is the way Augustine understood the Old Latin translation of the Psalms (the Vetus Latina.) The English comes from Augustine, *Homily on Psalm 110*, in *Nicene and Post-Nicene Fathers*, ed. Philip Schaff, first series, vol. 8 (Buffalo: Christian Literature, 1888), ch. 10. The translation is a mess, but it was very influential. The Vulgate (the Latin translation made by Jerome) numbers the Psalms differently, where this verse appears as 109:3. Bibles in the English tradition translate the Hebrew differently from the Vetus Latina, which depends on the Septuagint (that is, it went from Hebrew to Greek to Latin).

7   Augustine, *Homily on Psalm 110*, ch. 10.

8   The word often translated "sighs" in verse 26 is related to the word translated "groan in travail" in verse 23. To translate them differently is a bit of a cover-up.

If you want to avoid masculine language for the Persons of the Trinity, there are some work-arounds. You can call the Father and the Son the First Person and the Second Person of the Trinity. You can call the First Person the Source or the Origin. You can follow the Gospel of John and call the Second Person the Word. Those words are all traditional and unobjectionable.

Speaking for myself, I think paradox is better. Even Pope John Paul I said in a public audience (or speech) that God "was like a father but even more like a mother."[9] There is no problem with "mother" as a metaphor for the Trinity as a whole, even among people who want to keep "Father" as the name of the First Person. People are especially conservative about the words of baptism, which have never been in dispute among Catholics, Protestants, and Orthodox: "I baptize you in the name of the Father, and of the Son, and of the Holy Spirit" (Matt 28:19). But there is nothing wrong with adding, as happens at the famous Riverside Church in New York, "I baptize you in the name of the Father, and of the Son, and of the Holy Spirit—Mother of us all." In that way, feminine language is used for the Trinity as a whole but not for the Trinitarian Persons. (The word *Trinity* is itself also feminine in Latin, German, and other gendered languages.)

In some churches and divinity schools, people try to avoid gendered language for God at all. That means they avoid pronouns. Or it's as if God's pronouns are God, God's, Godself. You've seen me do that sometimes. At Yale, we thought that if you slipped up and called God "He," then lightning would strike. It would be blasphemous to limit God in that way. (But God was merciful and lightning never struck.) That was in the late 1980s, long before trans and gender nonbinary people were teaching us to name our pronouns. If you want to try out this way of speaking about God, note that "Godself" is just the reflexive. The direct object is still "God." It works like this: God created the world. I believe in God. God revealed Godself in Jesus.

It's awkward repeating the word *God* all the time, and *Godself* is a mouthful. So the objection is obvious that this way of talking is uncomfortable and maybe even distant rather than intimate. But here's the interesting thing. Because God transcends language and the world, talk about and to God has always been awkward. Here is a parallel example from Judaism.

In the practice of avoiding pronouns, some Christians are substituting the word *God* over and over. Jews have had a similar practice of avoidance: they avoid saying God's proper name. In the Hebrew Bible, God has a proper name. Have you ever noticed that in most Bibles, God is sometimes referred to as "the Lord" in small caps? That's a substitution for God's name based on ancient Jewish practice.

Hebrew was originally and is still mostly written without vowels. If you already know the words, it's clear enough: f y lrdy knw th wrds t's clr ngh.

---

9 Because the first John Paul was pope for only thirty-three days, this quote is hard to document although it is well known. See Carol Glatz, "Pope Approves Foundation Promoting Example, Works of Pope John Paul I," Catholic News Service, April 28, 2020, https://tinyurl.com/y5lbq6gj.

There is an A and two semivowels, Y and W, which give you some hints, but half the vowels are still missing. Originally, the Hebrew Bible consisted of all consonants. Later, "vowel points" were added above and below the consonants, as if we wrote English like this: ᶦf yᵒᵘ ᵃlrᵉₐdy knᵒw thᵉ wᵒrds ᶦt's clᵉₐr ᵉnᵒᵤgh.

What stands in the Hebrew, where English Bibles have "the LORD," is four consonants: YHWH, without vowels. Although various reconstructions exist, there is no unanimity on what the vowels might be. English reconstructions include "Yahweh" and "Jehovah." Observant Jews not only don't spell out those names; they even leave out the vowel in *God*, spelling it "G-d." By long Jewish practice, you *avoid* saying the name, and you say the Hebrew word for "the Lord" *instead*. That is, you say, "Adonai," which, to repeat, is not God's proper name but simply means "Lord." To remind yourself to say, "Adonai," instead of pronouncing YHWH, you add to YHWH the vowels *for an entirely different word*, Adonai. If you put the consonants from one word with the vowels for another, it would be nonsense, like pig latin. But that's not what you do. You see the consonants, and you make a substitution. You say, "Adonai." Or, like Wyschogrod did, you say, "Hashem," which is one remove further: it means, "the Name." This is why praying something in "the Name of Jesus" is powerful.

All this means that awkwardness in speaking about God is normal and pious and has an ancient history.

Christians Talk about God Enabling Difference in Creation and Freedom

16 Barth Talks about the Trinity Enabling Creation

Because God loves others already in the life of the Trinity, God can love others also outside the Trinity, in the world.

In Christian-speak, the primary case of otherness, or of difference that enables relationship, is the Trinity. God is love, and God has otherness already in God's own life, so love of another makes sense even in God. In the Trinity, there is already one to love, one to receive love, and one to witness and celebrate love. The famous sermon that begins with God saying, "I'm lonely! I'll make me a world," is wrong.[1] God is not lonely; God has perfect love and companionship already in God's own, triune life.

The second case of otherness is unnecessary, gratuitous, extra. It is extra in the Latin sense of "exit" or "outside": it is outside the Trinity. It is creation.[2] "Creation is the temporal analogue, taking place outside God, of that event in God Godself in which God is the Father of the Son. The world is not God's Son, it is not 'begotten' of God; but it is *created*. But what God does as the Creator can in the Christian sense only be seen and understood as a reflection, as a shadowing forth of the inner divine relationship between God the Father and the Son."[3]

Thus creation is pure grace, strictly unnecessary, entirely gratis. But it is *possible*, in Christian-speak, because Trinitarian relationships precede it.

> The mystery of creation on the Christian interpretation is not primarily—as the fools think in their heart—the problem whether there is a God as the originator of the world. . . . [But] whether it can really be the case that God wishes to be not only for Godself, . . . that *we* exist alongside and outside God. . . . We must be astonished at the fact that there are ourselves and the world alongside and outside God. God has no need of us. God has no need of heaven and earth at all. God is rich in Godself, God has fullness of life; all glory, all beauty, all goodness and holiness reside in God. God is sufficient unto Godself. God is God, blessed in Godself. To what end, then, the world? Here in fact there is *everything*, here in the living God. How can there be something alongside God, of which God has no need?

---

1 James Weldon Johnson, "The Creation," in *God's Trombones* (New York: Penguin, 1955), 17–20; here, 17.
2 I believe I have learned this not only from Barth but also from listening to David Yeago. But if he disagrees, then I am mistaken!
3 The course reading was Karl Barth, "God the Creator," in *Dogmatics in Outline*, trans. G. T. Thompson (London: SCM Press, 1949), 50–58; here, 52; modified. Further references by page number in the text.

This is the riddle of creation. (*Dogmatics in Outline*, 53–54; modified for ungendered God-language)

Therefore, creation is neither *necessary* for God nor *arbitrary* for God: it is however *characteristic* of God. God loves in the Trinity: therefore, God can *also* love the world. Pavel Florensky (1882–1937), speaking of God as "the Subject of the Truth," goes a step further. God loves in the Trinity: therefore, God can *also* initiate unnecessary, gratuitous others into participation in the Trinitarian life. Florensky says, "But more than three? Yes, there can be more than three—through the acceptance of new hypostases into the interior of the life of the Three. But these new hypostases are not members which support the Subject of the Truth, and therefore they are not inwardly necessary. . . . They are conditional hypostases, which can be but do not have to be in the Subject of the Truth. Therefore they cannot be called hypostases in the strict sense, and it is better to call them deified persons. . . ."[4]

Where Barth says the Trinity makes creation possible, Florensky goes one better and says the Trinity makes salvation possible—that is, it makes possible the participation of created persons in the Trinitarian life. I think Barth would agree, since (as we saw in election) the purpose of creation is to "elect the human being to participation in God's own glory."[5]

Note that here too Barth is trying to unask a question. In his doctrine of election, we saw that Barth was trying to unask the question, "But what about me?" and point to Jesus. Here Barth is trying to unask the question, "Is there a God?" and point to Jesus. In the first line of his thesis paragraph, Barth writes, "In that God became human, it has also become manifest and worthy of belief that God does not wish to exist for Godself only and therefore to be alone" (50). "In that God became human": there's a lot packed in there.

For Barth, God did not create human beings without choosing them to be God's own; for Barth, God always already willed to have fellowship with human beings by becoming one of them in Jesus. So the creation of human beings belongs to God's decision to become incarnate as a human being.

And the destiny of human beings to be with God in Jesus also gives point to their ability to change and grow: God will draw them to Godself. This God-given possibility to be God-moved is human freedom. It's not a possibility that humans have alone, of themselves: it's the possibility to be attracted, which exists only in relationship. More about that in the next section.

Why would it *not* be manifest or worthy of belief that there is a God? Because unaccountably (but of course), there's evil in the world. Barth says,

---

4 Pavel Florensky, *The Pillar and Ground of the Truth*, trans. Boris Jakim (Princeton, NJ: Princeton University Press, 1997), 38.
5 Barth, *Church Dogmatics* II/2, 94, end of the *Leitsatz*, translation modified for inclusiveness and to fit the sentence in which I have placed it. For more, see chapter 2.

I am speaking here now . . . to make clear that this whole realm that we term evil—death, sin, the Devil and hell—is *not* God's creation, but rather what was excluded by God's creation, that to which God has said "No." And if there is a reality of evil, it can only be the reality of this excluded and repudiated thing, the reality behind God's back, which God passed over, when God made the world and made it good. "And God saw everything that God had made, and behold it was very good." What is not good God did not make; it has no creaturely existence. But if being is to be ascribed to it at all, and we would rather not say that it is non-existent, then it is only the power of the being which arises out of the weight of the divine "No."

That's not entirely a satisfying answer. Unsatisfactory explanations of evil are another reason Barth begins his account of creation with "In that God became human, it has also become manifest and worthy of belief" that God created the world. Because it is finally Jesus, and not a suspicious piece of metaphysics in which evil arises out of the weight of the Divine No, that makes the Christian response to the question of evil. (As we'll see two sections from now.) God has placed human beings in a position of great vulnerability on the front lines of the struggle that finite creatures experience to do good with God. The only thing that gets God off the hook for creating such fallible creatures is that God does not leave them alone on the front lines but joins them there *in their own condition, as one of them* in Jesus. That is why Barth says creation first becomes manifest and worthy of belief "in him."

Because creation is what God makes out of nothing, the creature has no self-standing being of its own but only leaning being, being that leans upon God. God will slowly grow the creature into uprightness—always in relationship with God—over time. If the creature ceases to lean, it falls back into the nothingness from which it came.

I said, carefully, "the struggle that finite creatures experience to do good with God." I was avoiding the word *evil*. Perhaps the hint of evil is already hidden in the word *struggle*. In any case, Barth, like the authors in the section after the next, denies that evil has any existence of its own and insists that freedom is only the power to do good. Freedom is the power to grow into uprightness in relationship with God.

This section has raised two questions that it can't answer: freedom and evil. The next three sections turn to those. The way that Christians speak about Jesus as the answer to the question of evil comes to a head in the fourth section, on Communion with him. In Communion, Christians do more than speak about Jesus; they expect him to join them again.

17 Augustine Talks about God's Freedom Empowering Human Freedom

After God becomes human, does God leave other human beings to their own devices, or do they participate in the humanity of God? In other words, are God's freedom and human freedom in competition?

How to Read Augustine's *On Grace and Free Will*

Augustine (354–430) began his career with a treatise on free will. In the middle of his career, he got into a dispute with Pelagius (354–418), who would become known as the greatest heretic after Arius. Arius had denied the divinity of Christ; Pelagius seemed to deny the grace of God. Pelagius seemed to say that after baptism, you saved yourself.[1]

In the fourth century, many Christians believed that baptism washed away only *prior* sins. They didn't believe in infant baptism or even adult baptism. They believed in *deathbed* baptism. You wanted to wait as late as possible—until the point of death—to be baptized. Augustine writes in his *Confessions* (book 4) about a friend who held this view.

Augustine and Pelagius agreed that was a crazy idea, at odds with the practice of Jesus and destructive to the Christian life. The point was baptism as the *beginning*, not the end or even the absence of a Christian life. But they disagreed on how to *understand* the Christian life.

Pelagius saw the Christian life as a kind of heroic striving. Baptism cured you from previous sin. After baptism, for Pelagius, you strove to be perfect. If you were not strong enough, you could pray for help. At least in the view of Pelagius's critics, such as Augustine, that was all. Either you did it yourself or you asked for help. I think that many Christians today share Pelagius's view.

Later theologians saw at least three problems with that.

---

1 This section explains Augustine by adopting his view of Pelagius, which is probably unfair to Pelagius. In Pelagius's defense, see Gisbert Greshake, *Gnade als konkrete Freiheit: Eine Untersuchung zur Gnadenlehre des Pelagius* (Munich: Matthias-Grünewald, 1972).

Augustine's View

Pelagius's view implied that you were cured. Augustine knew that you sinned after baptism and *would still need forgiveness*. He thought of the Christian life as one *not of cure but of convalescence*. You might be getting better, but you were still injured, still damaged by sin; you still needed God's continual care. The lungs are still healing after the virus is gone.

Luther's Development of Augustine

Luther sees in Pelagius's view a *choice of damnations*. Either fall into the sin of *pride* and think you can achieve salvation all by yourself, or you realize you can't and fall into the sin of *despair* (in which you don't believe God can save you). Just because what *God* does is reliable, you realize that all the weak links in the chain are due to you, and you fall into despair. You have to ask God for help at so many points that the whole chain is weak, and you and God are never really in it together.

My View, Influenced by Tanner and Compatible with Augustine

This is my interpretation, influenced by Kathy Tanner, whose views I think Augustine implies. Pelagius's view is of a really bad relationship. God and the human being are not really friends, not really in the project of salvation together. Rather, in Pelagius's model, human beings are on their own unless they ask for help. What if you were about to marry someone and you learned that your betrothed's model of marriage was "You go ahead and do it all yourself, and if you need help, call me." Is that a good marriage? Is that intimacy? *Augustine wants to promote real intimacy between God and the human being*. Grace is a form of intimacy.

At this point, Augustine wrote several treatises against Pelagius and in favor of grace. Augustine's friends were confused. They said, "Thirty to forty years ago, you wrote in favor of free will; now you're writing in favor of grace! Which is it?"

Augustine set out to explain *how you could have both: grace and free will*. That treatise, *On Grace and Free Will* (ca. 426), is this section's interlocutor.[2]

---

2 The reading for the course was Augustine, *On Grace and Free Will*, in *Anti-Pelagian Writings*, trans. Peter Holmes and Robert Ernest Wallis, Nicene and Post-Nicene Fathers (Grand Rapids, MI: William B. Eerdmans, 1971), 5:436–65. For further reading, see Kathryn Tanner, *God and Creation: Tyranny or Empowerment?* (Minneapolis: Fortress Press, 2004), 46–48. The Council of Orange (529) shows where later bishops drew the heresy line between double and single predestination. See "The Council of Orange," sourcebooks.fordham.edu, March 15, 1994, https://sourcebooks.fordham.edu/basis/orange.txt.

Aquinas, *Summa Theologiae*, I.105.4, I.22.4, I.23.6, puts the matter very simply. Grace is eminently resistible, but God's will is nevertheless infallible. God wills what will happen *with its mode* so that what God wills to happen necessarily happens with necessity, what God wills to happen contingently happens contingently, and what God wills to happen freely happens freely. Unlike Calvin, this does not mean that God "controls" the free actor in such a way as to bind their freedom. Rather, God *inspires* the free actor to act most freely.

Augustine Attempts to Go on Talking about Grace and Free Will the Way the Bible Does

Augustine's strategy is to read the whole Bible from cover to cover looking for passages about grace and free will.

He discovers that the word *grace* appears frequently in the New Testament, particularly in the letters of Paul. Furthermore, he discovers synonyms for *grace* frequently in the Hebrew Bible, primarily the Hebrew word *hesed*, חֶסֶד, which is traditionally translated into English as "lovingkindness" and sometimes "mercy." Grace and *hesed* appear 261 times in Hebrew or Greek in the Bible.

Augustine discovers that the words *freedom* or *free will hardly appear* except for the technical and unrelated phrase "free will offering." Words like *free will* appear only nineteen times. The crude quantitative analysis is that words for *grace* appear almost fourteen times as often as words for *freedom*. *Freedom* and especially *free will* are *philosophical* vocabulary, not biblical vocabulary.

But Augustine was smarter than to count as I just did. He concluded that the *idea* of free will was implied *every time God made a command*. Where God commanded, God expected humans to respond, and *that* counted as freedom, whether the word appeared or not.

So both: freedom responds to God's command, *and* everywhere God shows mercy, or grace. God's mercy is the crown to God's gift of freedom.

The Christian life, therefore, is to live not by one's own strength (against Pelagius) but by God's mercy: *but part of God's mercy is that God engages or empowers human freedom so that humans are not "left out" of their own salvation but led to participate in it. This participation in one's own salvation is God's gift of freedom. But this is nothing independent of God: this is the gift of participation in God's own project.*

But What Is Freedom?

Imagine a child's intonation when asking the meaning of a new word: "Mommy, what's *freedom*?" Augustine had actually defined this word in his original treatise on freedom. Freedom is *the ability to seek the good for yourself by reason.*

Notice how vast the difference is between Augustine and contemporary views of freedom. Consider some: Freedom is having more choices. Freedom is the choice of good or evil. Freedom is doing what you want, where "what you want" is entirely open. Freedom is doing something on your own. *Augustine, and every single interlocutor in this book, is against all those views.* None of the authors in this book holds a modern view of freedom.

That's because the modern view of freedom is bivalent or multivalent. It doesn't *head* anywhere. It's arbitrary. It's in a vacuum. It's value-neutral.

All the Christian views of freedom in this book give freedom a direction, a heading, a vector. *Freedom is the power to do the good for yourself.* It's not value-neutral.

It's value-oriented all the way down. It's a way to the good. See, this is fundamentally different.

I would like you to practice, between now and the end of the book, the strange, unfamiliar Christian version of "freedom." You're practicing it like a foreign word. It's *not the same* as political freedom. It's a way of pursuing the good.

You may object that this is circular. The end of freedom is built into Augustine's definition. The defenders of the traditional definition of freedom might well agree that it's circular. They would just deny that there's anything wrong with their circle. It's not a *vicious* circle, they might say: it's a *virtuous* circle. Freedom is the way of the Lord, which is good to walk in.

How God Moves Creatures

You should be experiencing a lot of cognitive resistance now. This is not a version of freedom that you've heard of before, even if you went to Sunday school. Let me put this notion of freedom into the context of the whole creation.

God moves creatures, and creatures move themselves. God is an "unmoved mover," and every created thing is a "moved mover." God creates all things to move toward their own good. That means God gives every thing a movement native to it, which moves that thing toward its good. Animals seek their good by instinct, which is the movement proper to them; they smell and move toward food. Down the chain, plants seek their good by growing; they move toward light and water; their proper movement is called "growth." Rocks seek their good by gravity. The deepest desire of a rock is to reach the center of the earth. See how the rock yearns! (push something off the table). Human beings are also subject to instinct like animals, to growth like plants, even and perhaps most obviously to gravity like rocks. But humans move toward their good by something distinctive. They move toward their good by reason. That means they can deliberate about the means to reach their good. God gives them a share not only, like all things, in God's movement but also, distinctively, in God's reason—or in Greek, *Logos*, the Person of God who became incarnate in Jesus. The distinctive movement of human beings, which distinguishes them from plants and other animals, by which they seek their good by reason is called "freedom."[3]

On that picture, "freedom" only makes sense if it's reason directed toward the good of the human being. If it's not reason and if it's not directed toward the good, it's not freedom; it's something else. It's captivated or enslaved. Augustine elsewhere

---

3 This is, I suppose, a version of a medieval idea—"the great chain of being"—that has recently received a lot of critique. It's hierarchical, it's human-centered, and it's bad for the environment. I feel sheepish confessing I like it. But I don't think of it as elevating the human. (Although it does. I see that it does. I accept the critique.) I think of it as elevating the dumb rocks. They too get a share in agency. Falling is their freedom; parabolas are their playfulness. The great chain of being is about how everything is *related*. The teaching question is how to *modify* the great chain of being so that we start there and then make the relation a habitat instead of a hierarchy.

expresses that as a paradox and speaks of "free will held captive" versus "free will liberated" (*liberum arbitrium* <u>*captivatum*</u> versus *liberum arbitrium* <u>*liberatum*</u>).

Human Freedom Participates in God's

So human freedom is meant to be a share in God's movement and even in God's Reason, which became incarnate in Jesus. Human freedom is meant to look like the life of Jesus. That means that human freedom is not meant to be in competition with God's freedom. This is Kathy Tanner's great insight: human freedom and God's freedom are *not in competition*. Rather, God means humans to act in an *ever more intimate relationship with God*. That doesn't happen by competition: that happens by closeness. Therefore, *it is not the case* that the more God does, the less I do, or the more I do, the less God does. Human and divine freedom are related not inversely but directly. Kathy Tanner and Augustine of Hippo are *against* the slogan that "I must decrease, thou must increase." Rather, God *empowers* human freedom, and the more Christians want to do, the more they must tap into God's infinite supply.

How to Talk This Way: Some Linguistic Exercises

You may not buy this theory. You don't have to buy this theory. *I just want you to* practice *it until the end of the book.* It's like learning a language. You don't have to like Spanish; you don't have to become a Spanish citizen; you just have to *practice* speaking Spanish until the end of the semester. You can go back to being Pelagian heretics or righteous atheists as soon as you finish the book. But for now, we are going to do some linguistic exercises.

1. If we were in class together, I would say, until the end of the semester, especially in posts and tests, *do not use these verbs:*
    God ~~makes~~ or ~~forces~~ the human being.
    God ~~compels~~ the human being.
    God ~~pushes~~ the human being.
2. Use these verbs instead:
    God <u>*empowers*</u> the human being.
    God <u>*engages*</u> the human being.
    God <u>*involves*</u> the human being.
    God <u>*activates*</u> the human being.
    God <u>*motivates*</u> the human being.
    God <u>*inspires*</u> the human being.
    God <u>*attracts*</u> the human being.
    God <u>*pulls*</u> the human being.
3. Notice that several (if not all) of those verbs—*activates, motivates, inspires*—follow the pattern that God *works so that we work.* This pattern occurs because God

works within us so that *we want the right things—we want what's good for us.* Among human beings, we can only work on one another from the outside, except, perhaps, in the case of love, which is a participation in the work of the Spirit. *But God can work from the inside, in the heart. And if we are doing what we want and what we want is good for us, then we are free. If we are doing what our heart desires, then we are free.* In that case—*in the case of love*—God and the human being are working together.

Whenever you are reading or thinking about "grace and free will," and you get confused, *try these substitutions.*

For *grace*, substitute	For a verb, try	For *free will*, substitute
infinite freedom	*empowers*	*finite freedom*
the Holy Spirit	*inspires*	*the human spirit*
love	*moves*	*the heart*

Probably the last substitution is the best, right? *Love moves the heart.* Because *love* and *heart* are the *real* biblical words for *grace* and *free will*—and because when you "move someone's heart," you're not "pushing" them. You are engaging their center so that they can move themselves.

The insight that *grace works like love* yields two analogies and two parables.

The Analogy of Gravity

Grace and free will work like the sun and the planets. The sun does not push the planets. It only attracts the planets. So the sun attracts, and each planet has its own motion. Does the planet move on its own? Of course! Does the sun move the planet? Of course! You have to say both. The sun, like God, is an unmoved mover. The planet, like the creature, is a moved mover. The movement that comes from the sun/God (attraction) and the movement of the planet/creature (orbiting) are not in competition but in harmony.

The disadvantage of this analogy is that the sun and the planets are physical objects, not persons. It's a stretch to call the motion of a planet "freedom." That leads us to the next analogy.

The Analogy of Romantic Love

Suppose you're a college student and your roommate is acting very moony. You observe that they are smiling too much, and the smile is unusually broad and goofy. They tend to throw themselves on the bed and . . . contemplate . . . a certain someone . . . for long periods. They develop a habit of hanging out in places where they might meet the someone "accidentally." They identify the someone's dorm room from the outside and constantly check to see whether the light is on. They develop an interest in activities that are strange for them, like opera or baseball, an interest that seems to arise because of the someone.

Eventually, you confront them with the evidence. What's going on with so-and-so, you ask?

Your roommate might have one of two answers (or if they're reading this book with you, even both). The answers may seem incompatible, but they are two sides of a coin.

Your roommate may say, "I don't know what's going on with me. I feel moved by an external force. There's all this energy coming from [person's name]. I'm liking all kinds of new things because they do. It has everything to do with [so-and-so]. I feel desire because of the other person. They're pulling it out of me. [Person's name] has moved my heart." That explanation is like grace. Your roommate describes receiving something from the outside.

Or your roommate may say, "I've never felt more alive! I've never had so much energy! My whole self is expanding. I have so many new interests. This is what I've always wanted. My heart is so full." This explanation is like free will. I am activated, motivated to be more myself by something on the inside.

The two explanations are compatible. The whole point of love is that what's *outside* of me changes me *from the inside.*

The disadvantage of this analogy is that we all know of romantic loves that turn out badly. How do we know which love is really good for us (in this life)? That brings us to a parable of altruistic (rather than romantic) love.

The Parable of the Railroad Tracks

In the twenty-first century, students get readings on internet platforms. But students used to get their readings in a "course packet" of bound xeroxes. It's as if you printed out all your readings at the beginning of the semester and had them spiral bound (such as I bring to class from time to time). You had to buy them at the beginning of the semester from a copy shop.

Now, the copyright law says that everyone can make a single copy from a book for their own use. But a copy shop seemed to be making hundreds of copies from a book for their own profit. So nationwide copy chains like Kinko's were always in danger of getting sued by publishers and asked to pay royalties for making copies. Which caused the copies to cost vastly more.

So faculty and students both preferred to use local copy shops, like King Copy on the other side of Gate City Boulevard (which in those days was called Lee Street). Imagine you were a first-year student. You had to go off campus, cross Gate City in mid-August in the blazing heat, and wait in line, out the door, as the asphalt of the parking lot melted under your feet. The line was slow because dozens or hundreds of students were waiting to buy course packets. The course packets had been xeroxed all summer and were piled to the ceiling. They were hard to find and dangerous to extract from the tottering stacks.

Finally, you get to the counter. You ask for Elements of Christian Thought. They tell you it costs eighty dollars. For a pile of bound xeroxes. You don't have that much money; there is forty dollars in your checking account. It's not even a hardback book. They tell you the cost is high because they're paying royalties to every publisher. And you don't believe that.

And then they tell you that they just sold the last one. They won't have more until next week. You have to come back, wait in line, and listen to the outrageous pricing all over again.

You are not feeling any love. Romantic or otherwise. On the contrary, you're mad as hell. You feel the opposite of love. You're ready to kill somebody.

So you trudge back across Gate City, and you're coming up on the railroad tracks. Two noises pierce through your homicidal mood.

First, you hear a baby crying. At least that's what it sounds like. It's odd. You don't hear a baby often enough on campus.

Then you hear the "woo-woo!" of a train in the distance. A childhood cartoon presents an unlikely image. Surely there's no baby on the tracks.

The baby cries again, and now that you're listening, you can echolocate it. It is on the tracks. Maybe you're in a *Dudley Do-Right* cartoon, but you can't worry about that now. You're running for the baby. You're running as fast as you can—even faster.

When you come to, you're on the campus side of the tracks with a baby in your arms, the smell of brakes behind you, and a microphone in your face.

"How did you come to save the baby?" the reporter asks.

You've got two answers.

1. "I don't know. I was in a terrible mood. I was ready to kill someone, but the baby cried, and it moved my heart. It's like the baby drew me, moved me, pulled me faster than I could have gone myself. It was outside of me. It was like an intervention." (That's the grace narrative.)

Completely compatible with that is this:

2. "I don't know. I was in a terrible mood, but the baby cried, and it moved my heart. My adrenaline surged, and my legs pumped. I've never run so fast. I didn't know I could. I did it, I guess, but I was so involved; I was using every-thing I had. I didn't even have anything leftover to be aware of what I was doing until I saw you standing here and you started asking questions. Now that you mention it, my legs are quivering." (That's the free will answer.)

The cry of the baby draws the rescuer, and the rescuer acts, and nothing the rescuer does takes away from the baby's pull, and nothing the baby does takes away from the rescuer's full activation. Grace and free will are supposed to work the same way.

Examples like that are supposed to show that grace and free will work together *for good*. But this is the next problem: *What about evil?*

That's our topic for the next section. But here I will only say this: deciding for good and deciding for evil *are not symmetrical*. Because free will is the power of doing the *good* for yourself by reason, theologians like Augustine usually think that doing evil *does not count* as a use of *freedom*. It counts as evidence of bondage. The next parable previews that move.

The Parable of the Key

Imagine a happier spring semester in which graduation happens in the normal way. Everybody is healthy; the weather is beautiful. And some relative that nobody ever actually met had died of COVID-19 the previous year, and your parents received a windfall. You understand that it's a little ghoulish, but you didn't know the guy, and you're hoping his money will provide a previously unexpected graduation present.

In fact, you're so hopeful that you've searched your parents' hotel room for a computer box or something. But you haven't found anything. Apparently, all you're going to get for graduation is a free lunch.

Bars and restaurants are back in business, and after the ceremony, you take your parents to Café Europa on Davie Street, near the public library downtown, behind the small park on Elm. You take them there because it's run by this really smart former religious studies major named Jakub, and also because it has tables outside in the sunlight around a fountain. You choose a table along the perimeter.

When it's time to pay, your mother hauls up her pocketbook, sets it on the table, and starts to rummage around. She pulls out not her wallet but a small, flat, rectangular box. She pushes it over to you. You hadn't thought to search your mother's pocketbook. That would be a bit invasive even for you. It's the sanctum sanctorum. But you can think of something great that would fit in a small flat rectangular box. It could be . . .

"Look behind you," she says. Through profusely blooming Knock Out roses climbing a wrought iron fence, you see a red convertible drive up with a big silver bow on the hood.

Taking the key firmly between your thumb and forefinger, you run to the car, kneel down in one fluid motion, and plunge the point of the key into each of the tires in turn until the car is resting on its axles!

• • •

A key, you see, is the *power of driving a car*. Similarly, free will is the *power of doing good for yourself by reason*. To puncture the tires is something you *can* do with a key, but it's no part of "the power of driving the car." Similarly, you *can* use free will to do evil, but it's no part of "doing good for yourself by reason." Rather, it's an unintended by-product or side effect. It's so crazy that it's not even a design flaw. Even now that some cars have electronic keys, it's not because people have been puncturing their tires with the pointy ones. It's so crazy that your parents have had to sell the car to pay for your therapy sessions.

I've adapted this story from the medieval version, in which an old man uses a cane (*baculum*) to trip himself up with. The point of the story is not only that using freedom to enslave yourself is absurd. Rather, if the story has any power, it comes from its *refusal* to account for evil in terms of gift and freedom. But that's the topic for the next section. For now, *do not attempt to account for evil. If you do, you will almost certainly fall into a trap.*

Problems with This Approach

I am in favor of the approach I've outlined so far. But there are problems with it. Here are several.

Freedom in the Time of Earthquake

My version of the "freedom" of physical objects, or the movement by which they seek their good, has strange consequences for rogue asteroids and tectonic plates. John McPhee describes tectonic plates like this:

> The Pacific Plate, sliding, weighs three hundred and forty-five quadrillion tons. Like a city planner, the plate motions have created Los Angeles. The plate motions have shaped its setting and its setting's exceptional beauty, raising its intimate mountains ten thousand feet. The mountains are such a phalanx that air flowing in from the west cannot get over them, and a result is the inversion layer that concentrates smog. Plate motions in Los Angeles folded the anticlines that trapped the oil that rained gold and silver into the streets. Plate motions have formed a basin so dry that water must be carried to it five hundred miles. Plate motions have built the topography that has induced the weather that has brought the fire that has prepared the topography for city-wrecking flows of rock debris. Plate motions are benign, fatal, ruinous, continual, and inevitable. . . . Plate motions are earthquakes.[4]

---

4 John McPhee, *The Patch* (New York: Farrar, Straus and Giroux, 2018), 105, paragraph boundary elided.

Freedom in the Time of Virus

According to the idea that all creatures seek their good by their proper movement, viruses too must seek their proper good. It certainly looks as if the proper good of a COVID-19 virus is to infect a person, and the side effect is illness and even death. Now, it's not clear how much the death of the host really helps the virus, since billions of viruses then die too. The trade-off for the virus is whether it gets to infect more people in the process of driving some percentage of them to death. Whatever the answer from the virus's point of view, from our point of view, a pandemic and an earthquake both raise the question, Who's in charge of *coordinating* the proper movements of creatures so that the whole creation tends toward its good, which is God? The standard Christian answer is that God is in charge of this. Which is not very satisfying. Why doesn't God do better?

In this case—the case of viruses that kill us—I think Christianity could learn something from Judaism. For Judaism, as for Christianity, it matters that some creatures have more intelligence than others. For Judaism as for Christianity, it matters that the creation accounts in Genesis give stewardship over the earth to the human being (Gen 1:26–28). But Judaism develops these ideas in a distinctive phrase, *tikkun olam*. (The accent falls on the second syllable of each word.) *Tikkun olam* means "to repair the earth," or in the motto of the journal *Tikkun*, "to mend, repair, and transform the world." The human being has a responsibility of *repair*. That means that not God alone but the human being too is in charge of ameliorating the bad effects of earthquakes and viruses. Humans receive the dignity of a share in the protection of their brothers; God involves them in the care of their neighbors. In these cases, humans learn to redirect viruses (to attack cancer, for example), to predict earthquakes, to flex buildings, to cure diseases. In this they come to participate in the caring and healing of God.

Freedom and Oppressive Authority

The version of freedom I've presented aligns grace and freedom very closely. Grace liberates us. But the relation of *grace* and freedom is not far from the relation of *authority* or *power* and freedom. Grace is not far from the will of God. What happens when *people* with authority or power invoke the will of God? They can tell you that social structures (class differences, slavery, apartheid, gender roles, property rules) are willed by God and that therefore "true" freedom consists of living in accord with those structures. They can co-opt talk of freedom by misidentifying the good. And because freedom and the good align so closely in the theory, it can be hard to find elbow room to say, "No, this is oppression!" That was a big fight among Calvinist churches in South Africa, for example, where some churches claimed that "true" freedom was acting in accord with racial apartheid. How do you get out of that bind?

The only safe rule is the Golden Rule (Lev 19:18; Matt 7:12; Luke 6:31), traditionally stated as, do unto others as you would have them do unto you. The Golden Rule will expose that the people in power are misidentifying the good. It will expose that they're not seeking for themselves the good that they (mis)identify for you. Watch out for this when there are clear social differences between the people with authority who are telling you what freedom is: when men tell women that freedom is housework, when straight people tell queer people that freedom is conventionality, when rich people tell poor people that "work makes you free" (the slogan the Nazis painted on the gates of Auschwitz).

Augustine Misreads the Story of Pharaoh

You may have noticed that I wrote, "Theologians like Augustine *usually* think that doing evil does not count as a use of freedom." One of the things that makes Augustine so interesting, so long lasting, and so easy for different theologians to use is that he is productively inconsistent. It's not so much that his arguments don't work—usually they do—it's that he can see both sides of things and has often argued on both sides. Augustine's main argument leads to the conclusion that choosing evil is nugatory, in vain, absurd, and doesn't make sense. His logic leads to the conclusion that freedom is only for good. And this is the mainstream of the Christian tradition and one of Augustine's greatest contributions. But . . .

Remember I told you at the beginning that Augustine was trying to go on talking about grace and free will the way the Bible talks? He thinks he's found a passage where the Bible ascribes evil choices to a human being—and even to God. He's found a passage that makes him sound like Calvin.

Calvin tends to act as if good and evil are of equal weight. In predestinarian passages, he can seem to have forgotten that "all things work together for *good*" (Rom 8:28; my italics). Calvin departs from Augustine's main line, where good and evil are *not* symmetrical, *not* on the same seesaw, *not* evenly balanced—and Augustine departs from his own logic, too, in a place where he thinks the Bible is against him.

It can be a good quality (it depends!) to change your tune when you think the Bible is against you, but this time, according to me, Augustine has made a mistake. He has misread the passage. He has misread it because he doesn't know Hebrew. There are even letters between Augustine, who did not know either Hebrew or Greek, and Jerome, who made the longest-lasting translation from those languages into Latin, where Augustine partly envies and partly trolls Jerome for learning Hebrew.

Augustine is reading the whole Bible, looking for evidence. Therefore, when he comes to the phrase "Pharaoh hardened his heart" (Exod 8:32), he thinks that's a statement about free will. But the *story* is not about free will. The story is about a shocking military victory by a band of formerly enslaved people against the greatest power on earth. They are telling the story, standing safely on the far side of the Red Sea, and they're trying to figure out how it happened. They're singing and dancing, and Miriam is shaking her tambourine, and in the oldest musical refrain recorded in the Bible, they sing that "the horse and his rider hath he thrown into the sea" (Exod 15:21 KJV). That is, the only explanation for the little people's success is that God has given them the victory. In this context, they credit God with everything, and they *ring the changes* on God's action in every possible way. ("Ring the changes" means they vary the language like a musical prelude in a very elaborate way.) The changes that work poetically are variations on Hebrew verbs, which can do a lot more things than English verbs do. Hebrew has verb forms with as much variety as "I close the door," "The door closes," "The door is closed by me," "I close the door over and over," "The door closes itself," "I cause the door to be closed," "The door closes intensively" (it slams). Hebrew uses these possibilities for poetic variation.

So the victory celebration on the far side of the Red Sea (in Sinai) affects how the people tell Pharaoh's story. They are not actually concerned with the state of Pharaoh's heart any more than Americans at war concerned themselves with the heart of Adolf Hitler or Saddam Hussein. They just want to give God the glory for the victory. So they tell the story; they don't write philosophy. They say, "Pharaoh hardened his heart," "God hardened Pharaoh's heart," "Pharaoh's heart was hardened," "Pharaoh's heart hardened by itself," "Pharaoh hardened his heart repeatedly," "Pharaoh hardened his heart intensively": all just varying the language. The point of the language is not to distinguish grace and free will. The point of the language is to tell a story in which Moses kept negotiating, Pharaoh kept agreeing, Pharaoh kept reneging, and the Israelites won anyway. Augustine misread the story so that God causes evil. The real point of the story is that God liberated the Israelites. Then they didn't care about Pharaoh anymore.

What's the point of Pharaoh's resistance? It's not part of God's plan, it's nugatory, it's in vain, it can't thwart God: but God can use it. Pharaoh's resistance is not part of God's plan, but God can use it to increase the glory of the victory. It's dramatic irony. Resistance, evil, is not part of the grace and free will story. It's something that doesn't make sense, a place where reason breaks down. Part of the badness of evil is that it doesn't make sense; if evil did make sense, there would be something good about it (the fact that it made sense). But that's our topic for the next section.

Christians Talk about
God's Body Absorbing Evil

18 Chesterton Talks about God Drinking a Cup of Suffering

> If God is good and all-powerful, why is there evil? Theologians answer that evil has no reality of its own, but suffering is real. G. K. Chesterton suggests that in Christ, God drinks the cup of suffering with us.

Except for the section on Pharaoh, where Augustine goes off the rails of his own theory, his treatise *On Grace and Free Will* implies an approach to evil (which is not a theory to rationalize evil). *On Grace and Free Will* defines freedom *in terms of the good* that is sought. *It does not define evil.* We are left to infer that evil is a *lack* of something—a lack of goodness—*rather than a thing in itself.*

Remember the theory of heat? Heat is the movement of particles. The faster they move, the hotter the temperature. Cold, in that system, is not a thing in itself. Cold is "just" the absence of heat. Evil is like that. It is the absence of good.

Other analogies follow that pattern: Evil is like a shadow cast by the good. Evil is like a vacuum—an absence that seems to gain a power of its own—the power of absence.

These analogies allow us to say both that *evil is not a thing in itself* and that *evil gains the power of absence*, like cold, like a vacuum. Cold is the absence that seems to suck heat away from a warmer body; vacuum is the absence that seems to suck air (or other matter) from a place where it's present.

The idea that, analogically speaking, *evil sucks* is parallel to the better formed theological proposition that good is self-spreading. Just as heat and air spread out to fill the space available, rather than cold or vacuums spreading, so even the power of evil is illusory.

Or not so illusory. Evil is not a thing in itself, *but suffering is real.* Just as humans are vulnerable to cold and vacuum, both of which can kill us, so too humans are vulnerable to the absence of goodness—to the absence of love. A person can *suffer* evil (the absence of good) much as they can *feel* cold (the absence of heat). I repeat: suffering, like cold, is palpable, even though evil, like cold, has no existence of its own. The early Christian document called the *Epistle of Barnabas* describes the human being as "earth that suffers."[1] It was such earth that the name Adam recalls and that Christ became.

---

1   John Behr, "From Adam to Christ," in *Orthodox Tradition and Human Sexuality*, ed. Thomas Arentzen, Ashley Purpura, and Aristotle Papanikolaou (New York: Fordham University Press, forthcoming), citing *Letter of Barnabas* 6:9, ed. and trans. Kirsopp Lake, Loeb Classical Library Apostolic Fathers (Cambridge, MA: Harvard University Press, 1985), 1:360.

The name for this theory of evil is "privative," which means to *take something away*. Evil is not *something*; it's *subtractive*. It's *parasitic*, parasitic on good.

In several ways, then, evil "itself" is like zero. It is a powerful nothing, a powerful nonthing, a noncritter—that is, an uncreature, "something" that God did not create.

Evil is so absurd that it's undefined, like division by zero. (For another example of the absurdity of evil, recall the parable of the key in the previous chapter.) Remember division by zero? Suppose we ask, "What's $1 \div 0$?" If we say, "1," then we get $1 \times 1 = 0$, which is absurd. If we say, "0," then we get $0 \times 0 = 1$, which is also absurd. Worse, by that logic, $2 \div 0$ also equals 0. Then $1 \div 0 = 0$, *and* $2 \div 0 = 0$, so $1 = 2$. Something is very wrong. The consequences of division by zero are bad: multiplication stops working. Faced with losing multiplication and division altogether—since if you allow division by zero, $1 = 2$—mathematicians decided to outlaw division by zero. Division by zero is undefined. Similarly, in theology, evil is undefined. The consequences of defining it are worse than outlawing it. "Evil is undefined" means we can't understand or explain it—and if we do explain it, then goodness itself is lessened.

That's OK conceptually because not making sense is part of the badness of evil. If evil did make sense, it would be less bad. This is not an explanation for evil. This is a refusal to explain evil. The mainstream of the Christian tradition has decided that it's better *not* to explain evil, to *refuse* to explain it. Because the "explanation" would treat evil as a thing rather than an absence, and treating evil as a real thing would lead to a dualistic view of the world, with *two* principles rather than one, with a God and a rival to God. Just as in mathematics, if you allowed division by zero, you would have one series of equations in which multiplication and division worked and another set that unraveled the whole system.

For the most part, Christian theology supports monistic (one-agent) theories of goodness rather than dualistic (competitive) theories of good *and* evil. In fact, it's hard to find genuine examples of dualism, with two real opposing principles. The usual suspects for dualism are Gnosticism and Zoroastrianism. But it's not hard to get both Gnosticism and Zoroastrianism off the hook. Perhaps Manichaeism, a semi-Christian philosophy that initially attracted Augustine, is a real dualism: for Manichaeism, the created world was a bad thing, and in some versions of Gnosticism, the "God" who created the world was bad, represented by the serpent, and opposed to the "real" God, the Father of Jesus Christ, who saved the world from him. As you see, that's not the Christian story. Fully dualist systems are either heresies or not Christian at all.

On the other hand, it's also not the case that Christianity has no dualist elements, no traces of a struggle between good and evil. In Genesis, the idea that the Creator had to overcome chaos is a dualist idea, and in the Gospel of John, the theme of light and darkness is very strong, not to mention the book of Revelation. However, those dualist elements have rarely interested systematic theologians. Their very love of system has led them to privative theories of evil.

You may find the privative "explanation" deeply unsatisfying. You may suspect that it begs the question. After all, it's not really an explanation. But "begging the question" means that you claim to give an answer that is no answer. In this case, the privative "answer" or response does not even claim to explain. The privative approach does not cover up that evil makes no sense, nor does it merely "admit" that evil makes no sense; rather, it *insists* that evil makes no sense. This "explanation" insists that it's no explanation at all. It denies that satisfaction on the grounds that the satisfaction would be worse. The satisfaction would deny the part of the badness of evil where evil *doesn't make sense*. It would assign sense where there is no sense.

The privative theory of evil is not meant to be an explanation. It is meant to be a somewhat violent therapy against the question. It is the violence of the blocking maneuver that may be the problem here. Sometimes the blocking maneuver is gentle: it's like division by zero, and it doesn't make sense. But sometimes the blocking maneuver is violent: stop thinking about this. The sometime violence of the blocking maneuver is not necessarily a sign that the theory is wrong but a sign that theory is an inadequate genre. When we have been talking about "evil" in the abstract, we seem to have been treating it as a thing, a definite thing, with no good at all, like absolute zero, the complete absence of heat. Just as you cannot cool anything to absolute zero, so there is no absolute evil, no utter absence of good. The privative theory of evil also implies that *there is always some good*.

This is easier to see in persons. Augustine's theory about evil in persons is that evil is the opposite of being turned outward in love: evil in persons is being turned inward on oneself. Imagine gazing into your navel until you are curled into a ball; the curl gets tighter and tighter, and the ball shrinks smaller and smaller until finally you get so small that you go *pop!* out of existence. This is Augustine's picture of persons turned in on themselves, each one *incurvatus in se ipsum*.

It is also easier to see this in stories than in theories. So in this section, we switch horses. There is only a little theory of evil (here, in these pages). The stories, however, are longer. There are two. One, *The Man Who Was Thursday*, is a novel about evil in general, set as a mystery in which police are looking for terrorists and (spoiler alert) never find them (or perhaps once). The other, "The Unnamed Woman: The Extravagance of Violence," is about personal evil—rape, murder, and dismemberment.

The Man Who Was Thursday is a novel by G. K. Chesterton.[2] It's an allegory. That means that all the characters represent ideas, and it's chock-full of puckish symbolism, symbolism so thick that it makes fun of itself. It's playful and silly even as it's profound. More or less, any symbolism you can see or find is really there.

---

2   G. K. Chesterton, *The Man Who Was Thursday* (London: Penguin, 1986). Multiple versions also exist online. Further references will be by page number in the text. You need to read at least chapters 1–5 and the last chapter. You will not get the point without the final chapter.

The setup is that a "policeman" is trying to infiltrate a cell of "anarchists." *These words had a different valence in 1901 for Chesterton than they do in 2020 for us.* For him, the police are the good guys, and the anarchists are the bad guys. In the time of #BlackLivesMatter, those words have different connotations: we are suspicious of the police, and after Charlottesville, antifa anarchists have a good reputation. Remember that the policemen (they are all men) here are *British* police who *carry no guns.* Think of the "anarchists" here as people who want to overthrow government, not counterprotesters against fascists, and have the cultural valence in Chesterton's novel that the word "terrorist" has for us. Notice, too, that Chesterton gives good lines and good speeches to anarchists and policemen alike.

Some hints on symbolism: *Lucian* sounds like what other biblical character? His red hair symbolizes what? Can you think of any biblical character whose name sounds like Gabriel *Syme*? Where in the Bible are there days of the week? (Think of one place in the Hebrew Bible and another place in the New Testament.) The character Sunday: What does it mean that he is unimaginably big? That he inspires "fear"? That you see his back? (Check out Exod 33:20–23.) What is "the cup that I drink of"?

In Chesterton's *The Man Who Was Thursday*,[3] human beings participate in the battle between being and nothingness, fragile on the frontier, and receive—as also in Julian of Norwich—honor for their wounds. Sunday, the God figure, says to the disciple figures, "You were always heroes—epic on epic, iliad on iliad, and you always brothers in arms. Whether it was but recently (for time is nothing), or at the beginning of the world, I sent you out to war. . . . You did not forget your secret honour, though the whole cosmos turned an engine of torture to tear it out of you."

Syme, the Peter figure, one-ups Sunday to apply the heroism to not just humans but the whole created world.

> Why does each thing on the earth war against each other thing? Why does each small thing in the world have to fight against the world itself? Why does a fly . . . [or] a dandelion have to fight the whole universe? For the same reason that I had to be alone in the Council of the Days. So that each thing that obeys law may have the glory and the isolation of the anarchist. So that each man fighting for order may be as brave and good a man as the dynamiter. So that . . . by tears and torture we may earn the right to say to this [accuser], "We also have suffered."
>
> He turned his eyes so as to see suddenly the great face of Sunday, which wore a strange smile.
>
> "Have you," he cried in a dreadful voice, "have you ever suffered?"
>
> As he gazed, the great face grew to an awful size, grew larger than the colossal mask of Memnon, which had made him scream as a child. It grew

---

3 The end of this section follows the quotations and discussion in Rogers, *Blood Theology*, 157-8.

larger and larger, filling the whole sky; then everything went black. Only, in the blackness, before it entirely destroyed his brain, he seemed to hear a distant voice saying a commonplace text that he had heard somewhere, "Can ye drink of the cup that I drink of?"

What is the cup? A lot of things.

> Thou preparest a table before me in the presence of mine enemies: thou anointest my head with oil; my cup runneth over. (Ps 23:5 KJV)

> James and John, the sons of Zebedee, came forward to him and said to him, . . . "Grant us to sit, one at your right hand and one at your left, in your glory." But Jesus said to them, "You do not know what you are asking. Are you able to drink the cup that I drink? . . . For the Son of Man came . . . to give his life a ransom for many." (Mark 10:35, 37–38, 45)

> Then he [Jesus] took a cup, and after giving thanks he gave it to them, saying, "Drink from it, all of you; for this is my blood of the covenant, which is poured out for many for the forgiveness of sins. I tell you, I will never again drink of this fruit of the vine until that day when I drink it new with you in my Father's kingdom." (Matt 26:27–29)

> And going a little farther, he threw himself on the ground and prayed, "My Father, if it is possible, let this cup pass from me; yet not what I want but what you want." (Matt 26:39)

> Again he went away for the second time and prayed, "My Father, if this [cup] cannot pass unless I drink it, your will be done." (Matt 26:42)

> Jesus said to Peter, "Put your sword back into its sheath.[4] Am I not to drink the cup that the Father has given me?" (John 18:11)

> The cup of blessing that we bless, is it not a sharing in the blood of Christ? (1 Cor 10:16)

When Syme asks, "Have you . . . have you ever suffered?" this God figure allows every creature to say yes, because this is the God who can answer with another question, "Can ye drink of the cup that I drink of?"[5]

---

4   In the Vulgate, the Latin reads, "Mitte gladium tuum in vaginam."
5   G. K. Chesterton, "The Accuser," in *Man Who Was Thursday*, 179–83, quoting the KJV.

In Chesterton, evil may be an illusion, but suffering is real: a wound to be honored and a solidarity to be shared. I don't want to give the whole point away. But notice that there is something to suggest that God, in Jesus, *absorbs evil with his body* and that *Christians remember this in his cup, in Communion.* This is *not an explanation for evil.* This is a story about how God has been together with human beings in *suffering evil.*

19 Trible Almost Talks about God in the Victim of Sin

Human sin renews the question of where God is in the presence of evil. Phyllis Trible parallels the story of the concubine in Judges 19 to the story of Jesus to suggest that God is in the victim.

In Phyllis Trible's account of Judges 19,[1] we meet personal evil. Not evil in general or in nature, like a tsunami or a virus, but personal evil, evil perpetrated by a person. This is a biblical story that is not in children's Bibles, a story you have never heard a sermon about. What is it even doing in the Bible? Furthermore, the biblical narrative is completely straightforward. There is no editorializing, not even any condemnation, and the plainness of the style only heightens the air of menace. In Judges 19, a woman is delivered up, raped, killed or left to die, and eventually divided into twelve pieces.

At the end of her interpretation, Trible lists five or six responses to evil. The article hints at another response, which Trible does not list. She doesn't list it because she doesn't want to prettify the story. She doesn't mind if you think of it; she tries to jog your memory, but she's not interested in pushing it. She's a biblical scholar, not a theologian, and the response she hints at does not belong to the story itself. It's only a faint echo in another place, in the New Testament. But I want to draw it out for you because it chimes with what Chesterton is saying.

Notice two places where Trible cites or echoes the New Testament. In the first instance, she gives you references: "Truly the hour is at hand," Trible writes, "and the woman is betrayed into the hands of sinners (cf. Mark 14:41). . . . No one within comes to her aid. They have all fallen away in the darkness of night (cf. Mark 14:26–42)" (76). As you know, "cf." abbreviates *confer*, which is Latin for "compare." It indicates that you're *not* quoting something, but you're pointing to or even changing something that the reader is supposed to notice.

The second time, Trible omits even a "compare" reference. Like Chesterton, she leaves you to hear the echo on your own. Let the one with ears to hear, hear. She writes, "Her body has been broken and given to many. Lesser power has no woman than this, that her life is laid down by a man" (81). The wording echoes John 15:13—the same verse that was central to Abelard. But the echo is not direct; it is distorted or reversed:

---

1 The reading for the course was Phyllis Trible, "An Unnamed Woman: The Extravagance of Violence," in *Texts of Terror* (Philadelphia: Fortress Press, 1984), 65–92. Further references will be by page number in the text.

> *Greater love* hath no *man* than this, that a *man* lay down his life for his *friends.* (John 15:13 KJV; my italics)

> *Lesser power* has no *woman* than this, that *her* life *is laid down* by a *man.* (81)

Trible is treading a careful line here. She is making the woman a Jesus figure but not directly. She will not make the story all pretty. She laces the comparison with irony, even with sarcasm. The woman is a *reverse* image of Jesus. Do you remember photographs made from film? Before you develop the film, it contains a reverse image, called a "negative." That doesn't mean there's anything wrong with the photograph or the film. It's not "negative" in the sense of anything bad. The woman is innocent. She is a victim; Trible is upholding her memory, not blaming her. Jesus too is innocent. He is a victim; Trible is upholding him, and no one would blame him. But Trible has a second truth to remember and uphold. The woman is not a willing victim. She is not an agent. She does not go to her death with knowledge and freedom. She is a Jesus figure in reverse in the sense that the violence and injustice she suffers are the very things Jesus dies to redeem.

That is, Jesus reverses the valence, or the charge, of what she suffers. He retells her story with a different ending; what for her is purely negative becomes for him a negative made positive. It does not make her story a good one. But her story causes Trible to read his story differently. Trible hints that Jesus suffers with and for the woman. He does not devalue her suffering, but he upholds it; he shares it. Can we say that he makes good on it? Because he upholds and shares it, he makes it less in vain but part of a larger story in which not she but a fellow sufferer overcomes and triumphs. It is as if this soldier or victim fell or still falls to the enemy, but someone else is winning the victory in her name, or at least on her pattern.

"On her pattern" because her name is what we do not have. Note how carefully Trible *does not cite* John explicitly—she omits the reference—because she doesn't want to hit the reader over the head with something she wants to keep subtle. It's a matter of tone. Note that Chesterton, too, refuses to belabor his Christ symbolism. For Trible, this is the case also because, while she writes for a Christian audience, she wants to respect what is first of all a Jewish text. So she invokes Christ *without mentioning his name*, which never appears in the article. That's not disrespectful. Rather, it makes a further comparison to the woman of Judges 19, whose name also never appears in Judges. Her pattern, however, is legible. Trible wants Christians to *remember her* whenever they remember *him*. When he "took the cup" and said, "Do this to remember me," Trible wants us to remember her cup, too, the cup of suffering that the concubine took, so that when Christians take Communion to remember him, they also take Communion to remember her—other victims and sufferers whose stories Jesus took up and retold.

In the end, Chesterton and Trible make almost the same move. He invokes Jesus's cup of suffering to become the cup of Communion when he quotes, "Can ye drink of the cup that I drink of?" The seven, and the woman, *have* drunk of it. Trible and Chesterton both want Christians to remember all who have suffered when they remember him, when they take Communion—because he is in communion with them, the sufferers.

If you have asked yourself, "Where is God in this story?"—the story of the woman raped, killed, and dismembered—the answer is *God is in the woman.* The Gospels put on the lips of Jesus the saying that "as you did it to one of the least of these my brethren, you did it to me" (Matt 25:40 RSV). Usually, that verse is cited to encourage people to do good for their neighbors. Trible extends it to a sister. But it also applies when people do bad, or when neighbors have suffered. The power of the story, and the power of Communion, is to take up and retell stories of suffering so that Christians see God in her as they see God in Christ.

Christians Talk about God's Body in Resurrection and Eucharist

20 Williams Talks about Your Victim as Your Hope

Those responses to evil suggest that God shares suffering. But how does God overcome it? Rowan Williams's account of the resurrection suggests how reconciliation could break out among sinful people with the principle "In your victim lies your hope."

The upshot of the last two sections is this: the Christian tradition insists that no satisfactory account can rationalize evil—because evil is not rational. In that way, evil has no reality of its own but feeds on good. And yet, even if evil is not real, suffering still matters. Part of the distinctively Christian response to evil is therefore not to explain it but to point to the life of Jesus. In what he accomplished, in healing and forgiving, Jesus repaired evil; in what he underwent, Jesus shared suffering. In that way, *Jesus absorbed evil with his body*. Don't try that at home. People will try to persuade you to "follow Jesus" by absorbing evil in which they are complicit or even active. Check to see if they are holding the hammer and the nails. Don't consider "taking up your cross" to "follow Jesus" unless the person advising you to do so is willing to take up their cross along with you. If they are unwilling to accompany you as Jesus accompanied the thief, your suffering is more likely to resemble the thief's than the Lord's—because the body of Jesus was also the body of God. In the event, God took on a body to repair our suffering and to accompany us in it. We, however, were given bodies, in the first place, for joy.

That, by the way, is a reason to suppose that God would have been incarnate if evil had not come. That is, God would have taken a body to usher the human being into joy and to share joy with us. Under conditions of sin, however, God's friendship with us also means suffering with us.

The emphasis of the last two sections has, however, not been on joy and repair. The emphasis has fallen rather on Jesus's absorbing evil in his body by suffering with us—on his solidarity with us. Solidarity goes a long way. But solidarity all by itself is not enough. If Jesus is in the lifeboat with us, that's nice, but if we all sink together, what good is it in the end?

The last two sections, in short, have been "theology of the cross." But after the cross comes the resurrection. Does the resurrection make it all better?

In this section, we have two more-positive readings about the body. Both are by Rowan Williams. At the time of writing, he's still alive. Unlike most of our interlocutors, he has an email address. Williams was Archbishop of Canterbury for ten years. That means he was leader of the third-largest group of Christians in the world: after Catholics (a billion) and Eastern Orthodox Christians (260 million). Williams was leading Anglican, that is, descendants in many countries of the Church of England (eighty-five million, including two million Episcopalians in the United States and twenty million in the Church of Nigeria). He held professorships at both Oxford and Cambridge, and he speaks or uses enough languages to make other theologians jealous: English, French, Spanish, German, Latin, Greek, Syriac, Hebrew, and then two that are less common, Russian and Welsh. Many of us theologians find this unfair. Our first interlocutory text is his chapter "The Judgement of Judgement: Easter in Jerusalem" from his book *Resurrection*.[1] That's about what happens when Jesus comes back in his body.

So does the resurrection of Jesus make it all better? *Resurrection* says, not so fast. Williams is worried that Christians will use Easter as a get out of jail free card, a device that once again attempts to leap right over suffering into bourgeois complacency. Williams would like to see a real change *in the world*, a transformation. He would like to see evil being overcome because *reconciliation is breaking out*. What would it mean for reconciliation to break out, to spread, to spread contagiously, and to change the world?

I read the chapter *as if* it were responding to two Jewish critiques of Christianity. Williams himself never mentions either of the critiques. The conversation is all in my head. This section is therefore not an exposition of Williams. It's an attempt to understand him by putting him into a different context.

One Jewish critique of Christianity is that the resurrection makes light of death and suffering. In this critique, the resurrection is an attempt to evade the human responsibility to work repair in the world that we have. The greatest glory to God, in this view, is to participate with God to mend, repair, and reconcile the world, not to rely on God as a deus ex machina (a machine that comes down from the sky without cause and ruins the plot). On this critique, the resurrection is a fairy tale, not because God couldn't do it, but because it makes a mockery of human responsibility and robs the plot of meaning. Williams himself does not say that the resurrection is a fairy tale. Rather, he tries to make the resurrection teach human responsibility for reconciliation person to person on the ground.

A second Jewish critique is related. In the second critique, the Christian idea that you can apply to God for forgiveness for what you have done to *other people* is offensive. If I murder your sister, what does it matter to you if my father forgives me? Christian atonement seems to bypass victims. It seems to escape vertically, to God, rather than to spread horizontally, among people. The Jewish Day of Atonement, Yom Kippur, works differently. In Judaism, the gates of repentance open on Rosh Hashanah, the Jewish New Year (which happens in September or October). You have ten days, until Yom Kippur, to go to your brother, sister, victim, or friend;

---

1 The reading for the course was Rowan Williams, "The Judgement of Judgement: Easter in Jerusalem," in *Resurrection: Interpreting the Easter Gospel* (Harrisburg, PA: Morehouse, 1994), 7–28. For further reading, see Hans Frei, *The Identity of Jesus Christ* (Philadelphia: Fortress Press, 1975).

make amends; and be reconciled, preferably in person. If you don't try to make amends now—horizontally, among people—you have no right to ask forgiveness on the Day of Atonement from God.

Jesus had that idea in mind when he said, "So when you are offering your gift at the altar, if you remember that your brother or sister has something against you, leave your gift there before the altar and go; first be reconciled to your brother or sister, and then come and offer your gift" (Matt 5:23–24). I once saw Jesus's provision enforced before Communion, and I have never forgotten it. I was in grad school in a religious studies department. But my university also had a divinity school, and every Friday, the Div School had a short, half-hour service with excellent music and Communion, and often faculty preached. "Communion" was the kind where you go forward to the altar or the table to receive rather than receiving in the pews. On this Friday, the preacher was the New Testament professor, who was known to teach, in his New Testament Ethics course, a collection of views that crossed the lines between culture wars liberals and conservatives. Notably, he was a pacifist who was also against same-sex relationships. Same-sex relationships then as now were a very hot topic in the Div School, and the gay-straight alliance, or whatever it was called then, was very active, and in the previous week, conservative div students had struck back. The chapel of the Div School—where we were gathered for Communion—had a very large, gilt-edge Bible on the lectern. Conservative students had taken a yellow highlighter to it to "illuminate" the antigay passages from Leviticus. The New Testament professor had the righteous indignation of a prophet. Although he agreed with the conservative views, he deplored the conservative tactics. That was no way to read a Bible (a topic we finally reach in three sections), and that was no way to treat your fellow students in what was supposed to be a model Christian community. Christians were supposed to listen to one another, learn from one another, even love one another. He preached on "leave your gift there before the altar and go; first be reconciled to your brother or sister, and then come and offer your gift" (Matt 5:24). He said, "I'm serious. This is not a theoretical exercise. Get up. Go. Go now. Mill around. Your brother or sister is here, in this congregation, in this room. You know who you are, and you know who is on the other side. That person is your neighbor with whom you must be reconciled. Go now and be reconciled. Take as long as you need. Don't come to the altar for Communion until you have reconciled with your neighbor."

There was a lot of milling and hugging and crying. When I tell this story in person, I can't keep myself from tearing up, even thirty years later. And then when we came to Communion, it was different. It was not vertical forgiveness from God. It was horizontal reconciliation broken out among people. You could hope that it would spread. It's what Abelard wanted from atonement. It's what the ten days between Rosh Hashanah and Yom Kippur are for. And it's what Rowan Williams wants from the resurrection of Jesus.

How would you have to interpret the resurrection of Jesus so that it's an event from which reconciliation breaks out and spreads, a good contagion? Again, it helps to look at an idea on which Judaism does better than Christianity. What is the unforgiveable sin? In some versions of Christianity, I'm ashamed to say—and I apologize in advance if this is painful to hear—suicide is the unforgivable sin, on the grounds that after you're dead, you can't ask forgiveness from God. To be clear, I think this is theologically stupid and pastorally heartless, but you see how the (rigid) logic works. In Judaism, on the other hand, the unforgiveable sin is *murder*, on the grounds that after *your victim* is dead, you can't ask forgiveness from them. See how that makes more sense? Again, Williams doesn't mention this. But it has direct relevance to Jesus. If Jesus *stays dead*, there is no hope for reconciliation *with the perpetrators*.

First, imagine how fearful it must be if you are a perpetrator—yes, I'm putting you in the position not of the victim but of the perpetrator because the point is that we are all guilty, not that we are all victims—how fearful it must be if you are a perpetrator. Suppose you had gotten caught up in the Pinochet regime in Chile, which disappeared its critics by pushing them out of planes over the Pacific where the bodies would never be found—where they would disappear. You did it. The door of the plane was open. The infinite water was down there. You put your hands on the chest of a tied-up human being. You felt his heart beating. And you pushed him backward into the blue. You'll never forget his face.

In the instant, you're ashamed, but you feel powerful. You're alive; you're invincible. Your sense of yourself is that you feel big. Later, you feel guilt, but you have an identity. You've thought about it so much that, although you don't tell anybody, it's part of who you are. You know what you're capable of. It tells you something about yourself. You can identify with the spies and assassins in novels who kill and live. You're ashamed of it, but it's a special club. It makes you distinctive, even if you can't tell your children.

You keep imagining you see your victim behind the door at night, around the corner of the stairs, in a crowd. One bright, sunny day you're walking down the street, not thinking of his face, when all of a sudden, you see it for real. That's really him. The face isn't fuzzy or ghostly this time. You see details you had long forgotten. You feel your own heart beating. How did he survive? How is he *back*? At least he won't recognize you.

He makes eye contact. He stares. You stare. He slows. You slow. He stops. You stop. He says, "Is it you?"

Then he says something far more shocking. He says, "I forgive you."

A declaration of forgiveness actually takes something away from you, maybe a lot. You're not sure you want to give it up. You're out of the club. Forgiveness seems to diminish your identity; your power seems to seep away. You're no longer quite so special. You lose your distinctiveness. You don't feel so big. You start to feel small. It's unfamiliar. You try to hold on to your identity.

You say, half belligerent, half awestruck, "How can you forgive me?"

He says, "I lost everything. I died—I did die—I already died. I had nothing left to protect. I have nothing left to protect. I'm not back to protect anything. I'm back to offer reconciliation."

It takes away your identity, your sense of yourself, your former life; you've lost that life; that's the punishment. It liberates you; that's the redemption. Now *your* life has been taken away—your bad life—and now *you* have nothing to protect, nothing to hide. You become free to accept reconciliation. You can live differently. That kind of thing could spread.

That's why the most important thesis of Williams's essay is "In your victim lies your hope."[2] In *your* victim. In the one you have harmed. In the one to whom you could make amends. But it starts with the one who has no victims. That's why it starts with Jesus, who comes back to offer the judgment, the judgment of—forgiveness.

Williams wants to keep this horizontal. He wants it *not* to be all about Jesus, if Jesus-talk elides and evades the concrete victims that I have harmed in my own life. Therefore, Williams wants to be very careful about Acts 4:12: "There is salvation in no one else, for there is no other name under heaven given among mortals by which we must be saved." Out of context, the verse sounds like a blanket statement. But in context, it's very concrete. The martyr Stephen is talking to the Sanhedrin. Like a good preacher, Stephen is using "we" pronouns. But the victim he's talking about is Jesus, who is, concretely, their victim (and the victim also of Romans). This is not about picking out Jews. Williams is careful to say that everybody in Jerusalem is guilty—Romans like Pilate, disciples like Peter. Rather, Stephen is telling perpetrators that in their victim lies their hope. The general principle is not Jesus. The general principle is Jesus is in your victim—*your* victim, the one you have harmed. The one you have harmed is your Jesus, and *their* name is the one in which reconciliation lies for you.

This is a dangerous teaching. Let me try to qualify it.

This does not mean you should approach everyone you have harmed. Even AA, which makes a formal practice of going to make amends to all whom you have harmed, includes the proviso "except when to do so would injure them or others" (step nine)—as when you demand forgiveness to silence your victim.[3]

Williams's instruction is not to victims. It's to perpetrators. As a victim, you don't have to entertain the attentions of a perpetrator. Jesus has already died and been resurrected—presumably that's not your situation. Once, I was staying with an Episcopal priest and invited her to dinner on Saturday night. She said she couldn't go because she was writing the next day's sermon. It was about "the lion shall lie down with the lamb."[4] I was being persecuted by a homophobic colleague,

---

2 "The primary stage in preaching the resurrection [is] as an invitation to *recognize one's victim as one's hope*" (11; my italics).
3 Luke Bretherton, *Being Alive: A Primer in Christian Ethics*, p. 19 of typescript
4 Isaiah 11:6 actually says, "The wolf shall live with the lamb, the leopard shall lie down with the kid, the calf and the lion and the fatling together."

and I said, "I feel like the sheep, and I don't want to lie down with the lion." When I got back from dinner, she said, "I've been thinking about what you said. It's not a requirement; it's an intervention of grace." It's as strange as the resurrection. That's why it's an eschatological vision.

If you were writing reaction papers for me, I would not want to read that Jesus is the answer. This time, that's not the point. This time, the point is that your own victim—your mother or your ex or your sibling or your opponent—is the one in whom your salvation lies. This time, salvation is a horizontal concept; it's reconciliation breaking out among people.

This is a different and more difficult Easter, an Easter with a task. But it is also a more hopeful Easter, one that might make a difference on earth. It's not a ghostly resurrection but a thoroughly embodied one, one that goes to the neighbor face-to-face if possible—or in the time of virus, goes to the neighbor by FaceTime or Zoom.

21 Christians Talk as if Breaking the Wafer Opens the Trinity

> In the Eucharist, God's body joins believers to the life of the Trinity and creates a common feast for the forgiven.

Eucharist means "thanksgiving" in Greek. Add an accented *o* to the end, and pronounce the *u* as an *f*, and you have the Modern Greek word for "thank you," *eucharistó*, which is pronounced like the name of a lawyer, F. Harry Stowe. The Eucharist, the Great Thanksgiving, is also called Communion or the Lord's Supper. It's a good place to sum up.

God chooses. God chooses the human being. God chooses God's own self to be with the human being in Jesus. God's choice of God's self to be with the human being, to take the lost cause of the human being to be God's own cause, opens God up to suffering and death. God's choice to be with the human being takes the assertion of the Song of Songs 8:6—that "love is strong as death"—and poses it as a question. Is love as strong as death?

The Trinity tells us that God is love already in God's own self. God has otherness already within God so that there is one who loves, one who returns love, and one who witnesses, celebrates, and guarantees the love of two. So already in God, there is enough *distinction* for love.[1]

Otherness in God does not require creation. But it makes it possible. If God loves another already in God's own triune life, then God can also love another outside that life, and in creation, God actually creates additional, unnecessary, gratuitous others, who are not God, to share God's life.[2]

The difference between these creatures and God is space and time. They are different from God in that they are finite; they are made to change over time; they are made to grow. For them, space and time are created as a *means of love*. For us creatures, it does not show love to pass ghostlike through one another; we need spatial boundaries in order to develop in the womb, to nurse at the breast, to hug, to "make love," to do charity. We need finitude in space *in order* to love.

Similarly, we need succession in time in order to love. We need time to grow into love. We need time to talk or to sing. We fall in love not only by seeing and feeling the shape of one another's bodies; we fall in love also by hearing one

---

1 I owe the next six paragraphs, at closer or farther remove, to a lecture by David Yeago some twenty-five years ago.
2 Florensky, *Pillar and Ground*, 38.

another understand, respond, joke, and laugh, all of which take time and even timing.

The distinctions of space and time are not yet a fault. They are the appropriate conditions of creaturely intimacy.

Space and time also provide the impossible possibility that—unlike in God—love could fail. Distinction could become distance. Love could fail because of distance in space or from lack of time. Whether you think death would have come in the garden of Eden or only after sin, space and time first raise the question, Is love as strong as distance? And under conditions of sin, that question gains urgency: Is love as strong as death?

God becomes incarnate to return humans to the path of fellowship with God, to rebefriend the body and heal the soul. But we try to kill God. And in the death of Jesus, we succeed. The Trinity has come apart. It appears that death is stronger than love.

Under conditions of sin, a subplot opens.[3] Space can become separation, and time can lead to divorce. Can grace and gratitude survive in finitude? Here they have limits. Distinction can become distance, duration can become a burden, and death can cut life short. In "till death do us part," a promise becomes a threat.

"This is my body," Jesus says, "given for you" (Luke 22:19). God takes a body and lets death have it, lets hostility have its way with it. In the breaking of the bread, Jesus's body is also broken. Since Jesus's body is God's, we can also say that God's body is broken. In the death of Jesus, not only the body but the Trinitarian fellowship is broken, in that one of the Trinity dies for us, and the Son says to the Father, "My God, my God, why have you forsaken me?" (Matt 27:46).

Is love stronger than death? The story is not over, but God would complete what God began even or especially in the night in which Jesus was betrayed. On that night, human beings come to participate in the unconditional response to God's self-giving that the Son makes to the Father even unto death. A vain attempt, perhaps, a death-bed wedding.

Not only is the Trinity like a wedding feast. But Communion is like one also. These are not in conflict but a series of analogies. Communion is the wedding feast come down to earth, prepared as for the Psalmist "in the presence of my enemies" (Ps 23:5). For it is a marital remark: "This is my body, given for you." Communion as a deathbed wedding is most familiar in the words of this hymn:

> The Church's one foundation
> Is Jesus Christ her Lord;
> . . .
> From heaven he came and sought her

---

3 The reading for the course was Eugene F. Rogers Jr., *Sexuality and the Christian Body: Their Way into the Triune God* (Oxford: Blackwell, 1999), 249–56, 265–68. The following five paragraphs follow 249–50.

To be his holy bride;
With his own blood he bought her,
And for her life he died.[4]

And no one has put it more vividly than Jacob of Serugh:

The King's Son made a marriage feast in blood at Golgotha;
There the daughter of the day was betrothed to him, to be his,
And the royal ring was beaten out in the nails of his hands;
With his holy blood was this betrothal made. . . .
He led her into the Garden—the bridal chamber he had prepared for her.
At what wedding feast apart from this did they break
The body of the groom for the guests in place of other food?[5]

Under patriarchy, the woman suffers for the man. Jesus the bridegroom subverts
and atones for that pattern. Here one gendered male suffers for one gendered
female. That brings us back again to sacrifice, its abuses and reversals. I quote
Judith Butler:

To deconstruct [a binary] is not to negate or refuse either term. To deconstruct [the] terms means, rather, to continue to use them, to repeat them,
to repeat them subversively, and to displace them from contexts in which
they have been deployed as instruments of oppressive power. . . . [My]
options . . . are not exhausted by presuming [the terms of a binary], on the
one hand, and negating it, on the other. [I propose] to do precisely neither of these. . . . [My procedure] does not freeze, banish, render useless,
or deplete of meaning the usage of the term[s]; on the contrary, it [can]
mobilize the signifier[s for] an alternative production.[6]

Christianity's paradigm for that procedure is Jesus's announcement, "This is my
body, given for you."[7] Catholic eucharistic theology makes it a marital remark.[8] With
it, Jesus subverts and redeploys a structure of violent oppression—crucifixion—and
turns it into a peaceful feast. He reverses the movement of the fall, which counted

4 First widely published by Stanley J. Stone, *Hymns Ancient and Modern* (London: Samuel Clowes, 1868), no. 320.
5 Jacob of Serugh, *Homily on the Veil of Moses*, stanza 11, in Sebastian Brock, *Studies in Syriac Spiri-tuality*, Syrian Churches Series, vol. 13 (Poonah, India: Anita Printers, 1988), 95.
6 Judith Butler, "Contingent Foundations," in Seyla Benhabib et al., *Feminist Contentions: A Philo-sophical Exchange* (London: Routledge, 1995), 35–57; here, 51–52, paragraph boundary elided.
7 This paragraph is quoted with small changes from Eugene F. Rogers Jr., "Marriage as an Ascetic Practice," INTAMS *Review: Journal of the International Academy of Marital Spirituality* 11 (2005): 28–36.
8 John Paul II's eucharistic theology, Bernard Cooke's sacramentology. For a similar usage, see David Matzko McCarthy, "The Relationship of Bodies: The Nuptial Hermeneutics of Same-Sex Unions," *Theology and Sexuality* 8 (1998): 96–112.

divinity a thing to be grasped. Jesus rebefriends the body and creates the bread of heaven by counting divinity *not* a thing to be grasped. At the Last Supper, he performs a deathbed wedding, as if he said, "You can't violate my body; here, I give it to you."[9] He becomes a bridegroom of blood: you can't exsanguinate me; drink this, all of you. Gethsemane's bitterest cup becomes the toast at the wedding feast.

Communion like marriage interprets the atonement. In both cases, a body is given to another with all its precious fluids. In both cases, the gift begins in desire and ends in charity. Jesus died for his spouse not because his desire was faint but because his passion was great.[10] Jesus takes on the body to befriend it, to rescue it from scorn; he gives it in commitment to another. The atonement, like marriage, does not bypass the body but elevates it as gift.

In Romans 8:11, Paul identifies all three members of the Trinity by the resurrection of Jesus. There is the one who rises, Jesus, so full of the power of life that death cannot hold him. There is the Father who raises him. And there is "the Spirit of the One who raised Jesus from the dead" (modified), who spreads the life beyond death by indwelling other humans as a gift to the Son, the one who loved humans enough to share their mortal flesh.

Somehow the breaking of the body has become a breaking open. The preceding Psalm opens with the words, "My God, My God, why have you forsaken me" (Ps 22:1) and ends with the proclamation that "All the ends of the earth shall remember and turn to the Lord, and all the families of the nations shall worship before you" (Ps 22:27 ESV). In the breaking of the bread, too, the body of God opens up to let humans in, to admit them into the Trinitarian Communion at its point of greatest vulnerability, at its time of greatest risk. The Eucharist—the Great Thanksgiving—is the intra-Trinitarian exchange of gift and gratitude carried out in the face of death and shared with those who share it. At the Eucharist, as at the Last Supper, God takes the worst that humans can do—kill God—and does not take that for an answer but makes it an occasion to renew the invitation to the feast; the feast that God had planned from the beginning of the world, the wedding of the Lamb, for God would complete what God began.

---

9 For a longer version of this interpretation, see Rogers, *Sexuality and the Christian Body*, 249–68 and Eugene F. Rogers Jr., "Nature with Water and the Spirit: A Response to Rowan Williams," *Scottish Journal of Theology* 56 (2003): 89–100; here, 92–96.

10 Sebastian Moore, "The Crisis of an Ethics without Desire," in *Theology and Sexuality: Classic and Contemporary Readings*, ed. Eugene F. Rogers Jr. (Oxford: Blackwell, 2002), 157–69; here, 158.

Christians Talk about Human Bodies in Sex and Slavery

22 Williams Talks about God Desiring Humans as If They Were God

God can prepare a couple for life with God by binding them for life with each other.

This chapter is about consummation, or life with God, and one of its echoes in life with other human beings. Our interlocutory essay is about sex. It's in favor of same-sex relationships. Now, I know you're wondering, Rowan Williams is straight. He's married; he has two children; you can google image him. He looks like Gandalf: definitely straight. He's the one who wrote our interlocutory text about the resurrection. For ten years, as I wrote above, he was Archbishop of Canterbury (as was our friend Anselm nine hundred years earlier), leader of eighty-five million Anglicans. But the analysis he offers works for sexual attraction *as such* (gay, straight, bisexual, nonbinary)—whenever you wonder, Why is it so strong? Why does it seem to escape reason? Why does it happen so often in contexts removed from procreation? Why did God make it so difficult to control?

Because, Williams suggests, there's something alike about being with a *person* you can't control and being with a *God* you can't control—and even being with a God who craves, or chooses to crave, the love of *humans* whom God chooses not to control.

I will make just a few remarks here, because you really should read the essay yourself.[1] It's the best ten pages I know of about sex. When I was in grad school, Williams came to teach for a semester. Apropos of I don't know what, he remarked with some weariness in a faculty / grad student seminar that the whole business of sexuality had to be entirely rethought. It sounded as if he had an alternative view. He said he'd written something; I asked for a copy. When, months later, his essay fell into my hands, I sat on the steps outside the department in September sunlight to read it. The first time, I thought it was different from anything else I had ever read, but I didn't understand it. The second time, I thought it was changing my life, but I needed to read it again. The third time, I thought I was beginning to get it—and it was time to stand up.

---

1 Rowan Williams, "The Body's Grace," in *Theology and Sexuality*, 309–21. Further references will be by page number in the text. For further reading, I have written a lot on this topic. For the shortest version of my argument, see Eugene F. Rogers Jr., "Sanctified Unions," *Christian Century* 121, no. 12 (June 15, 2004): 26–29, 31. For the best version, see Good et al., "Theology of Marriage" and "Liberal Response," 51–87, 101–10. The same issue also features a conservative rival paper and responses to both from all over the Anglican Communion. For the fullest version, see Rogers, *Sexuality and the Christian Body*.

Around the same time, I thought I might like to take a course in spiritual direction. Spiritual direction is like therapy not with a psychologist but with a monk, nun, priest, or other wise person who meets you maybe once a month and tells you to reconcile with your neighbor, identify with Mary, or read the angry psalms. The woman who taught spiritual direction was austere. Her hair was pinned back until it hurt, and she wore a soutane. A soutane is a tight, straight-cut cassock that falls plumb from neck to ankles and closes with about a hundred buttons. Its color is sable. It is the severest robe a priest can wear. She opened the class with a pair of sentences. She said, "Most people come to spiritual direction seeking self-control. I teach them self-abandonment."

It was enough to keep me away. I never came back.

Williams thinks that good sex, like a good relationship with God, is marked by self-abandonment and that the attempt to exercise control ruins sex—and tends to rape—as it chases away God.

Williams thinks that celibates in the church—monks and nuns—teach us that desire is first about longing for God and only secondarily about longing for another human being. That doesn't mean that everybody has a vocation to the monastery—only people who, like Teresa of Ávila or John of the Cross, find their relationship with God better than sex.

Williams doesn't say so, but he seems to take a virtue approach to ethics. That is, he's asking not about the action but the person. He's not asking whether the *action* is "right" or "wrong." That's too punctiliar and impersonal for a virtue approach. Rather, he's asking whether the *habit* is one that leads to *growth* or *decline*. So he writes that there is no substitute for taking time and that relationships are most hopeful when sustained by lifelong, public commitments (he's describing—and avoiding—the word *marriage*). So he does not say that Sarah Layton's one-night stand is "wrong." He says that longer is likelier to lead to moral growth—to virtues of faith, hope, and charity. He's asking how God joins humans for life with another, to prepare them for life with God.

Why does he talk about this Sarah Layton, her one-night stand, her irregular pregnancy? He talks about her because he's giving a lecture—imagine this dense, peculiar text dedicated to rethinking what God wants with sex as an oral lecture!—and the whole audience (back in the late 1980s when whole audiences watched the same three channels of TV) has just watched a miniseries called *The Raj Quartet*. So this is a story that everybody knows. Students find fault with it because Sarah's story is not a "good" one.

Well, I wish Williams had used a biblical story instead, one that would have given him cover to say much the same things. The next couple of pages are a bit of a digression, but they serve the purpose of making Williams's argument biblical. Consider the four women that the Gospel of Matthew (chapter 1) inserts into the genealogy of Jesus. You remember how it goes. So-and-so begat so-and-so all the way back to Abraham, all men. It had to be all men, you know, because "begetting" refers to the male contribution to reproduction, like "siring" puppies. That makes it all the stranger that four women interrupt: Judah begat Perez and Zerah *by Tamar*, Salmon begat Boaz *by Rahab*, Boaz begat Obed *by Ruth*, and David begat Solomon *by the wife of Uriah*. The author expects the reader to remember their stories and draw the conclusion: each of the women is a sexual agent.

In Genesis, chapter 38, Tamar's husband dies, and according to the conventions of the time, her husband's nearest male relative is supposed to marry her to give her a home, an income, and sons. Well, Onan seems not to want to get her pregnant, which is his job, pulls out early, and falls dead. That's interesting. And it wasn't masturbation, as you may have been told as a teenager; it was coitus interruptus, and as the story goes, the problem was not the coitus but the interrupting. So the other male relatives became afraid of her, and she had no support.

Next in line is her father-in-law, Judah. He refuses outright. But Tamar is a wily woman. She knows his habits. She dresses as a prostitute and waits by the side of the road. He solicits her, has sex with her, and then lacks the money to pay. (You wonder why she wants him, except she's so much smarter than he is.) He gives her his ring and his staff with the promise that he'll pay up when she presents them. She is not interested in getting paid, so she keeps them until an appropriate time—three months later when a pregnancy begins to show and he threatens to put her to death. Bringing out the ring and the staff, she announces in public that the owner of those tokens is the father of the child.

In Joshua chapters 2 and 6, Rahab has the same middle name as Smokey the Bear: She's Rahab the Harlot. She has let Joshua's spies into Jericho; Salmon, the father, may have been one of the spies.

In the book of Ruth, the husband of Ruth has also died and left her without children. She pledges her troth to another woman, her mother-in-law, Naomi: "Entreat me not to leave you or to return from following you; for where you go I will go, and where you lodge I will lodge; your people shall be my people, and your God my God; where you die I will die, and there will I be buried. May the Lord do so to me and more also if even death parts me from you" (Ruth 1:16–17 RSV). If those words sound familiar, that's because they often ring out at weddings and give rise to the phrase "till death do us part." Ruth follows Naomi. Naomi has to advise Ruth how to catch a husband: get him drunk, uncover his "feet," "and he will tell you what to do" (Ruth 3:1–5). The joke, as every Hebrew student learns, is that "feet" (*regelim*) refers to all the members below the groin—feet, legs, genitals—and is a standard euphemism for the last. In short, Naomi has to coach Ruth, who had borne no children with her husband, on how to seduce a man. When the couple marries and Ruth bears a son, the book ends with this arch comment, "The women of the neighborhood gave him a name, saying, 'A son has been born to Na'omi'" (Ruth 4:17). To Naomi? But the mother is Ruth. What do the women of the neighborhood know about the relationship of Ruth and Naomi that they would say of Ruth's son that he was also Naomi's?

The author of Matthew does not call the final woman in the series by her own name. Matthew 1:6 says, "David was the father of Solomon by the wife of *Uriah*" (my italics). Uriah is the man whom David has sent to the front lines to be killed so that he can have Uriah's wife, Bathsheba (2 Sam 11).

What do all these women have in common? Their sex lives have been irregular: one seduced her father-in-law; one worked as a prostitute; one seduced her next of kin in order to get a baby whom the women of the neighborhood ascribed also to her primary emotional attachment, another woman; and one becomes the queen (her response is not recorded) after her lover sent her husband to death. Those women lead up to Joseph, whom another Gospel, Luke (1:34), takes pains to leave out of the parentage of Jesus so that, in effect, they lead up to Mary, who resembles those women as an unwed mother. They are all women with irregular sex lives whom God has used, according to Matthew, to bring redemption. If God can use them, God can use Sarah Layton. Or as a student of mine once said, "Now I know why Jesus used to hang out with prostitutes!"

"Why?" I asked.

She looked at me like I was an idiot and said, "Because it runs in the family!"

This is just what Williams is interested in when he talks about "the body's grace": *Can* God use the crazy sexual situations that people get themselves into? And if so, *how*? And I say "crazy" as a technical term to mean the set of improbable stories that Matthew's ancestors of Jesus pick out.

Williams makes profound and sweeping claims about what grace is, how God wants, what Christianity is for, what monks and nuns are for, and what marriage is for. In each case, see if you agree.

"Grace, for the Christian believer, is a transformation that involves knowing oneself to be seen in a certain way: as significant, as wanted" (311). Do you think that's true? In that way, Williams compares religious grace to the body's grace. He wants grace to really *transform the believer*, not just change God's attitude. Perhaps there you can see that the author of "Easter in Jerusalem" and the author of "The Body's Grace" are the same person. But the transformation depends on knowing yourself to be perceived in a certain way, as if the bumper sticker "Jesus loves you" or the cloverleaf game—"They love me / they love me not"—actually worked. Both the coupled life and the Christian life depend on allowing the loving, delighted perceptions of another, slowly or quickly, to transform you.

"The whole story of creation, incarnation, and our incorporation into the fellowship of Christ's body [church and Communion] tells us that God desires us, *as if we were God*, as if we were that unconditional response to God's giving that God's self makes in the life of the Trinity" (311): as if we were Christ responding to the love of the Father or the Spirit groaning in sighs too deep for words. Do you think that's true?

> We were created so that we may be caught up in this [the whole story in which God desires us as if we were Christ], so that we may grow into

the wholehearted love of God by learning that God loves us as God loves God. (312)

The life of the Christian community [the church] has as its rationale—if not invariably its practical reality—the task of teaching us so to order our relations that human beings may see themselves as desired, as the occasion of joy. (312)

If that is why we were created—for God's joy—then it comes not amiss if there were some echo of creation for joy also in human beings. That comes in two forms, Williams thinks, direct and indirect, monasticism and marriage. A few people find that the love of God is better than sex: they are called to experience joy, bodily joy, like Teresa of Ávila or John of the Cross, in celibate communities, in the monastery. That's why Williams writes,

the body's grace itself only makes human sense if we have a language of grace in the first place; this in turn depends on having a language of crea- tion and redemption. To be formed in our humanity by the loving delight of another is an experience whose contours we can identify most clearly and hopefully if we have also learned, or are learning, about being the object of the causeless, loving delight of God, being the object of God's love for God through incorporation into the community of God's Spirit [church] and the taking-on of the identity of God's Child [Christ]. It is because of our need to keep that perspective clear before us that the community needs some who are called beyond or aside from the ordinary patterns of sexual relation [monks and nuns] to put their identities directly into the hands of God in the single life. This is not an alternative to the body's grace. All those taking up the single vocation must know something about desiring or being desired if their single vocation is not to be sterile and evasive. Their decision (which is as risky as the commitment to sexual fidelity) is to see if they can find themselves, their bodily selves, in a life dependent simply upon trust in the generous delight of God. (317)

In short, Christians need monks and nuns to show them that sexuality is first of all for God. This means that Williams disagrees with the common psychological bromide that you "have to love yourself first." Under conditions of sin, humans can't manage that, not really. What Williams believes is that *God* loves us first, and it's part of the office of monks and nuns to bear witness to the priority of God's love. Only when we glimpse that *God* loves us first are we finally in position to undertake human relationships that make us as vulnerable as sexual ones.

Most people, on the other hand, find that they experience the echo of God's joy in the joy of another human being—they are called to marriage, which Williams describes like this:

When we bless sexual unions, we give them a life, a reality not dependent on the contingent thoughts and feelings of the people involved; but we do this so that they may have a certain freedom to 'take time' to mature and become as profoundly nurturing as they can. . . . The promise of faithfulness, the giving of unlimited time to each other, remains central for understanding the full 'resourcefulness' and grace of sexual union. I simply don't think we would grasp all that was involved in the mutual transformation of sexually linked persons without the reality of unconditional public commitments: more perilous, more demanding, more promising. (315)

In all those cases, Williams expects God to use the body's grace for our good, whether our decisions have been foolish or wise. That's because sexuality is not so much about right or wrong as about what good God can do with our vulnerability, with our self-abandonment, our giving up our titanic self-control. The body's grace opens us up to be formed by the perceptions of another, and that opens a school for virtue. Someone else can tell us the truth about ourselves, can discern our covered faults and believe in our untrusted talents. In relationship with someone of the *apposite* sex, not necessarily the opposite sex, we become open enough to the perceptions of another to undergo real change, moral growth. That's why same-sex and nonbinary relationships are so important: moral growth arises only from vulnerability, and if cross-sex relationships are the only template, other couples are cut off from sanctification. And no conservative has ever seriously argued (although Stanley Hauerwas has argued jocularly[2]) that same-sex or nonbinary couples need sanctification any *less* than cross-sex couples.[3]

With any other person, relationships are risky. But the avoidance of all risk simply reasserts our attempts at control. That's why Williams thinks the "causeless, loving delight of God" provides a more hopeful basis for risking the loving delight of another human being.

---

2 Stanley Hauerwas, "Why Gays (as a Group) Are Morally Superior to Christians (as a Group)," in *The Hauerwas Reader*, ed. John Berkman and Michael Cartwright (Durham, NC: Duke University Press, 2001), 519–21.

3 For the shortest version of this argument, see Rogers, "Sanctified Unions," 26–29, 31.

23 Stringfellow Talking about Slavery Shows How *Not* to Interpret the Bible

God's saving action includes empowering human words to do what they cannot do on their own—namely, reach God. Successful speech about God is already the work of the Holy Spirit, a participation in God's own speech about God in the triune life. In Christianity, the Word is God (John 1:1), but the Word that is God is Jesus, not the Bible. The Bible is witness to the Word (John 1:8). The test for scriptural interpretation is Trinitarian: it should arise from the Spirit of love, approach the Father of truth, and result in the likeness of Christ.

This is the last difficult topic of the book. What comes after that concludes the book: six views of salvation.

So on to the Bible.

It's unusual to put the Bible near the end of a course about how Christians talk. We have been seeing citations from the Bible since the beginning. I have begun many topics by saying, "Christology *or* atonement *or* Trinity *or* grace and free will is an attempt to go on talking about Jesus or God or freedom *in the way that the New Testament* talks." Many systematic theologies and many courses in seminary or divinity school start with a unit on Revelation, which means primarily God's self-revelation in Jesus and secondarily the witnesses gathered in the Bible to God's self-revelation in Jesus.

I have waited to introduce the Bible as an explicit topic for three reasons. First of all, this book arises from a religious studies course, not a seminary course, so we are interested in how Christians *use* the Bible. Second, Christians *disagree* about the Bible. Now, Christians disagree, as we have seen, about many things: but disagreements about the Bible can be particularly difficult because "the Bible" serves as a shield and screen for lots of other things. If we start with the Bible, we are unlikely to build up a body of shared language with which to approach it. The shared language we have built up is not necessarily one that we believe but one that we have learned how to use. That brings me to the third and most important reason I have saved the Bible for late. I wanted to have two specific topics in place before we approached the Bible: first, Christians' accounts of the body, which depend on having understood the body of God (that is, Jesus), and second, the Trinity—because later I will argue that *reading the Bible* can be an activity by which the Trinity draws humans into itself: Bible-reading works like prayer, resurrection, and doing good deeds in freedom by grace. It can be a means by which the Holy Spirit draws human beings to the Father so that Christlikeness happens.

You also know by now that sometimes I follow an evil plan according to which I assign a reading I expect you to hate. I do that again here. This time you are supposed to hate it because it's morally bad. I do that to inoculate you against the idea that if someone is smart, well educated, careful, sophisticated, supports the status quo, and quotes the Bible a lot, you should believe them.

But on the other hand—and here is the difficult part—many readers have a hard time identifying exactly what's wrong with our interlocutor, at *precisely* the same time that they know in their stomachs that it *is* wrong. What principles should we adopt to *roadblock*—to *prevent*—arguments like this? Note, I'm not advocating principles that will automatically generate a *good* biblical interpretation. On Christian grounds, that's up to the Holy Spirit and not under human control. I'm advocating something much more modest but still difficult: Are there any principles to *prevent bad* interpretations, or at least some of them?

Now stop reading this section and go read Thornton Stringfellow's biblical defense of slavery.[1] Stringfellow (1788–1869) was a Baptist minister in Culpepper, Virginia, who wrote three books defending slavery out of the Bible. Your job is to see and put into words *what's wrong with his exegesis* (his biblical interpretation). What principles might prevent it? With one exception: if you are descended from people who were enslaved in the United States and your stomach *really* doesn't want to read it or if you are descended from people who were enslaved and you start to read it and your stomach clenches up, you don't have to keep going. If you are *not* descended from slaves, like me, you *need* to read it because you need to see what kind of biblical interpretation people who benefit from enslaving others are capable of. Then come back to this section and see how your answer matches mine and how I describe what *good* biblical interpretation (exegesis) looks like.

•   •   •

Now, we're not in class together, so I can't tell what you'd say. From past experience, I'd guess there would be a debate about whether Stringfellow interpreted his passages with enough history or context. The trouble is, Stringfellow has already heard the objections that defenses of slavery are not historical or contextual enough, and so he claims to be historically aware and to interpret passages in context. Still, if

---

1 Thornton Stringfellow, "The Bible Argument: Or, Slavery in the Light of Divine Revelation," in *Cotton Is King and Pro-slavery Arguments*, ed. E. N. Elliott (Atlanta: Pritchard, Abbot & Loomis, 1860), 461–92. Multiple versions also exist online. For further reading, see Gregory of Nyssa, *Homily IV on Ecclesiastes*, in *Homilies on Ecclesiastes: An English Version with Supporting Studies*, ed. Stuart Hall (New York: De Gruyter, 1993), 73–78. This is the classic patristic argument that slavery dishonors the image of God. For further reading, see Victor Preller, "The Problem of Referring to God" and "The Material Moves of the Language of Faith," in *Divine Science and the Science of God* (Princeton, NJ: Princeton University Press, 1967), 4–22, 266–71.

you turned to history or context, those were good moves. You would probably still have to pursue them more radically than you might like to get around Stringfellow because he's prepared for you.

Or you may be sitting with your intuition that his argument is just wrong, plain evil, simply unjust. You may have experienced a primarily *moral* reaction. That too is useful, perhaps the most useful of all. But how do you turn it into a principle of interpretation?

If you want to take history more radically, you have to be able to say, We know some things are wrong now that some people didn't know (or culpably or innocently hid from themselves) then. So just because parts of the Bible think that polygamous marriage or slavery or homophobia or killing your children is right, doesn't mean it is.[2] That's a big principle. I'm in favor of it, but it may be too big for some people. The trouble is that you have to adopt *some* big principle, or you will be *unable to say what's wrong with Stringfellow*. And morally, we need to be able to identify one or more ways to stop him.

So if you're not going to buy history, try context. The trouble is that Stringfellow does seem to take care of *immediate* context, the context that interpreters of individual passages and even entire biblical books would require. You have to go big on context, too, if you want to stop him. You have to take the entire Bible as a whole. You even have to separate Jesus from Paul. After all, "Slaves, obey your earthly masters" (Eph 6:5; Col 3:22) comes from books attributed to Paul. We need to use all three critiques—historical, contextual, *and* moral—to get around those.

The context is Jesus. What did Jesus say that Stringfellow can't answer? As I said in passing, Jesus is himself the revelation; the Bible only testifies to that. Can we imagine Jesus as a slaveholder? No? But Stringfellow has an answer to that: Jesus referred to himself as a servant (slave).

The history is, Paul (and Jesus in Matt 24:34) expected the end of the world to come in his generation (1 Thess 4:16–17; 2 Thess 3:6–12). Paul often argued that people should not change their state—it was better to remain unmarried or under a master—because the world was ending soon. Logically, such passages fail to apply if you don't think the world is going to end before you have a chance to make it better.

The moral intuition turns out to be the same as the context of Jesus. I ask again, What did Jesus say that Stringfellow can't answer?

Before I tell you what I'm thinking of, let me tell you about Augustine's moral criterion for biblical interpretation.

Augustine famously said that the Bible must be interpreted to teach love in every part. Any interpretation of the Bible that did not teach love could *not* be a meaning

---

2 Note: the appeal to history is not meant to distinguish the New Testament from the Hebrew Bible. In the Hebrew Bible, God tells (or seems to tell) Abraham to kill his son and then intervenes to prevent it. In the New Testament, according to some atonement theories, God the Father plans to kill his son and goes right on through with it. For an argument that God does not really tell (or only sarcastically tells) Abraham to kill his son, see Eugene F. Rogers Jr., "Blood after Isaac: And God Said 'Na,'" in *Blood Theology*, 39–50.

of that verse. In the most famous example, Augustine considers Psalm 137:9, where the "little ones" who should have their heads smashed against the "rock" become the vices that should be destroyed by the sanctifying grace of Christ, the Rock.[3]

Notice that I said a reading that fails to teach love cannot be *a* meaning of the Bible. Augustine also had a lot more room than modern interpreters because he believed that the Holy Spirit—like even a human author—could design a passage to have more meanings than one. So he wrote that any reading of the text that saved the way words go (*salva litterae circumstantia*) *and* was true *just was* a meaning of sacred Scripture. And Aquinas took that over.[4] Their principle is wide open—but it has the criterion of truth. It's not true that slavery is loving. So the "good of slavery" meaning cannot be biblical. According to Augustine and Aquinas, those texts must mean something else.

But Stringfellow has an answer there too. He can even go so far as to claim that slavery *is* loving. That claim is particularly embarrassing to me. I loved my grandmother. She taught me to pray. She was born in 1894. She told lots of family stories, stories that always followed the female line, about her mother and her mother's mother all the way back. She loved her grandmother, her mother's mother. And her grandmother had owned slaves—had enslaved people. And my grandmother told me (maybe I asked about it; I was five or seven years old) that *her* grandmother had been "good to her slaves."

I loved my grandmother, but that's the weirdest thing she ever told me. At five or seven, I didn't know how weird it was. But that's why it's an even worse thing to tell a child—because the child may not be old enough to argue back. I wish I had asked her about it in adulthood. What could that possibly mean? It probably meant my grandmother's grandmother believed like Stringfellow. It makes me want to get up from the keyboard and wash my hands.

Well, the idea that slaveholding is compatible with love is horsefeathers. But how can we prove biblically that it's horsefeathers? I think there is just one saying of Jesus that will call it out—a saying he quotes from the Hebrew Bible (Lev 19:18): "You shall love your neighbor as yourself" (Mark 12:31; Matt 22:39; Luke 10:27). *If Stringfellow loved those he enslaved as he loved himself, he would have had to either go down into the fields and they all pick cotton together or let them live as he lived himself.*

Look out for preachers and politicians who will tell you that some form of bondage or misogyny is Christlike. They will tell you to take up your cross and follow

---

3 I owe the example and the wording to J. Warren Smith. See Augustine, *Expositions on the Psalms*, trans. J. E. Tweed, in *Nicene and Post-Nicene Fathers*, first series, vol. 8, rev. and ed. for New Advent by Kevin Knight, Psalm 136 [sic; the Latin numbering is different], para. 12, https://www.newadvent.org/fathers/1801137.htm.

4 Thomas Aquinas, *De potentia*, question 4, article 1, response, citing Augustine, *De Genesi ad litteram* 1 in *Quaestiones disputatae de potentia Dei*, trans. English Dominican Friars (Westminster, MD: Newman Press, 1952); online edition ed. Joseph Kenny at https://isidore.co/aquinas/QDdePotentia.htm. For discussion, see Bruce Marshall, "Absorbing the World," in *Theology and Dialogue: Essays in Conversation with George Lindbeck*, ed. Bruce Marshall (Notre Dame, IN: University of Notre Dame Press, 1990), 90–97.

Jesus. Ask them if they are willing to climb the cross with you. Ask them (as I said before) if they hold the hammer and the nails. Because if they are not willing to do it too, don't trust them.

Now, sometimes service is required. But it's freely chosen, and the people who require it must be in it with you. When Martin Luther King Jr. and Mahatma Gandhi went to their deaths, they, like Jesus, were leading their people for love's sake. No one who advised them to continue was not *with* them, and many who were with them urged them to quit for their own safety.

And note that this whole example—and other examples like it—has to do with the body. The Bible is often (mis)used to regulate bodies—the bodies of Black people during American slavery and the bodies of women and gay and trans people today. Over twenty-eight years of teaching theology, students have made many appointments to see me to talk about "the Bible." And every single time—*every single time*—the topic turned out to be what the Bible says *about sex and gender*—antigay passages, passages used to support or undermine women's leadership. And the only argument that combines history, context, Jesus, and love to flip those arguments is "Love your neighbor as yourself." Test every biblical reading that way. And "do not so confine the Bible to one meaning, as to expose the faith to ridicule" (Augustine and Aquinas)[5] but conform every reading to the command to love your neighbor as yourself. That's a big principle. Maybe too big for you. But I don't know what else will stop Stringfellow.

Now we're in a position to see what's Trinitarian about Bible interpretation. It works like (or is a kind of) prayer, in which the Holy Spirit (love) leads to the Father (truth), and what happens is Christlikeness. That's because the Spirit leads humans on the Way, which is Christ, or because the Spirit conforms them to him or because the Spirit overshadows Christians as it overshadows Mary, so that they bear Christ out of themselves. So an interpretation of the Bible that does not arise from love, lead to the truth, and result in the presence of Christ may be historically correct, but it is not theologically correct. Such an interpretation fails to join the interpreter to the life of the Trinity. Clearly, a biblical defense of slavery does none of those things.

Now, that also means several things at odds with theories of biblical interpretation popular in Protestant circles.

1. The Bible is not itself the self-revelation of God. Jesus is. The Word of God is first of all Jesus. John 1:1–4 says, "In the beginning was the Word, and the Word was with God, and the Word was God. He [Jesus, the Word] was in the beginning with God. All things came into being through him, and without him not one thing came into being. What has come into being in him was life, and the life was the light of all people."

---

5 Aquinas, *De potentia*, question 4, article 1.

2. Because the Word of God is primarily Jesus, the Bible is only *witness* to the Word. The prelude to the Gospel of John makes this explicit: "There was a man sent from God, whose name was John. He came as a witness to testify to the light, so that all might believe through him. He himself was not the light, but he came to testify to the light" (John 1:6–8).
3. The Bible can have more than one meaning.
4. It is wrong so to confine the Bible to one meaning, as to expose the faith to ridicule.
5. Any reading that respects the way the words go *and* is true is a meaning of the text.
6. This is a theory about the inspiration of the *reader*, not the inspiration of the text. The Holy Spirit inspires the *reader* with love and Christlikeness and leads the *reader* to the truth. The Holy Spirit does not inspire the *text* to love: texts can't love. The Holy Spirit does not inspire the *text* to Christlikeness: texts can't love. The Holy Spirit does not join the *text* to the Father: it is the Word that is Jesus with whom the Father is one, not the Bible. To treat the Bible the way you should treat Jesus is, on Christian terms, idolatry. To put it the most starkly, Jesus is the Word of God and *not* the Bible, which is the "witness to the Word" (the title of Barth's commentary on the Gospel of John).

What about inerrancy? Consider the example of Calvin. Calvin wrote that the Spirit of Christ "in some sense dictated" the biblical books to the human authors ("quodammodo dictante Christi Spiritu," *Inst.* IV.viii.8, 1155). But how did Calvin write the 1500 pages of the *Institutes* without a word processor? Without even a typewriter? Did he write it all out by his own hand? No, he had secretaries. Multiple secretaries. He *dictated* to them. And then he sent the secretaries' copies—whose shorthand maybe he couldn't even read—to the printer to be set in type. That is, the printer takes tiny individual metal letters and sets them by hand into grooves to make up a block to print a page. Then, using a press, the printer dipped the block in ink, pressed it onto paper to print the first page, and so on for the rest of the pages. Eventually, the printer could collate first copies—the proofs—to be proofread. (That's the origin of *proof*reading: to read the first copies, which are called the proofs.) That was the first time that Calvin would be able to read all together what he had dictated to multiple secretaries at once. Calvin complained in his letters that when he read proofs, they would be *riddled with errors*. Therefore, in the premodern period, metaphors of dictation were *perfectly compatible with human errors*. In Calvin's period and practice, metaphors of dictation *implied* human error.[6] Only in the modern period, with notions of scientific precision, would we come to mistake metaphors of dictation, which employ human agency and need to correct it, for metaphors of divine inerrancy.

---

6 I owe the story to Edward Dowey. For a compatible account, see John T. McNeill, "The Significance of the Word of God for Calvin," *Church History* 28 (1959): 131–46, esp. 139–45.

Christians Talk about
Salvation in Many Ways

24 Harvey and Tillich

Body or Soul?

> What do Christians think God has in store for human beings? Some say it
> takes a body to perceive and reflect the glory of God; others emphasize
> God's transformative forgiveness in the soul.

At last we come to six different views of salvation. Salvation, like our other topics, is
a site of Christian discussion and dispute. I arrange the views in pairs for contrast:
body or soul, faith or works, heaven or earth. And yet, like the contrasts of atonement
theories, they are finally compatible because a full picture will use aspects of them all.

Our first interlocutory text is about salvation in the body in Syriac Christianity.
Syriac Christianity is the Christianity that uses Syriac as a liturgical language—that
is, for the parts of the church service that stay the same from week to week or year
to year. Syriac Christianity ranges through Israel, Syria, Jordan, Turkey, and Iraq
with far-flung communities in South India. Syriac is a Semitic language, related to
Hebrew and Arabic, and even more closely to Aramaic, the language Jesus spoke.
Theology, poetry, and liturgy written in Syriac interest scholars of Christianity
because the fund of metaphors and images differs from those familiar in the West,
which tend to come from Latin or Greek.

In this article, Susan Harvey (b. 1953) argues that in Syriac Christianity, "God
created the body to be a means of knowing God and of being in God's presence."[1]
Harvey continues:

> Embodiment [is] the medium in which and by which the encounter between
> human and divine takes place. (5)

> For early Syriac writers, then, Christianity was located in the body because
> the body, in the most literal sense, was what God had fashioned in the
> beginning and where God had chosen to find us in our fallenness. This
> was why God acted through the incarnation. (9)

So the body is a means of knowing God first of all in the body of Jesus and second
in other human bodies as they see the world, hear the gospel, smell incense, taste
Communion, and take the hand of their neighbor. It is a means of being in God's

---

1 The reading for the course was Susan Harvey, "Embodiment in Time and Eternity," in *Theology and
Sexuality*, 3–22; here, 4. Further references will be by page number in the text.

presence in Christ and the neighbor, in worship or in doing good for others. How can humans worship God or serve their neighbor without bodies?

For the Syriac tradition, monasticism does not renounce the body but uses it to experience and manifest the glory of God. Take Symeon the Stylite, who practiced asceticism by living for forty years atop a pillar. Harvey writes, "His body imaged the defeat of Satan's wiles through his conquest of hunger, sickness, and despair in himself by means of his ascetic practices. As a result, in his presence the sick were healed, the hungry were fed, the weary received their rest." For Syriac Christians, she concludes, "The body is the place in which salvation happens and the instrument by which it is done" (10).

Christians say in the Apostles' Creed every Sunday that they believe in "the resurrection of the body." Many think then of the resurrection of Jesus. But that has already been covered earlier in the Creed. The sentence "I believe in the resurrection of the body" refers to the "general resurrection"—that is, the resurrection of other human beings at the end of time. At the last day, the departed get their bodies back.

Even in the West, medieval theologians wondered how the separated souls after death could see and hear without bodies. They decided that God must supply them with sense impressions until they got their bodies back, which we might now compare to a movie in Sensurround that God infused into a brain in a vat supplied with electrodes. For a contemporary Western vision of the resurrection of the body, see Stanley Spencer's *The Resurrection, Cookham* (figure 24.1).

Figure 24.1. Stanley Spencer (1891–1959), *The Resurrection, Cookham* (1927),
oil on canvas, Tate Modern, London. The general resurrection takes place
in the village where Spencer grew up.[2]

Syriac Christians cherish a more concrete vision of what that means. How will the blessed in heaven see or sing to God without bodies? "Ephrem spoke of the souls of the dead camped at the gates of paradise, awaiting their reunion with their bodies so that they might enter therein, together to praise their Savior. For Jacob of Serugh, the period of separation was rather more harrowing. He vividly describes the souls of the dead huddled around the eucharistic offering. . . . There they drink the 'fragrance of life' (*riha d-hayye*) emanating from the holy oblation for sustenance until the eschaton when they will be rejoined to their bodies for eternity" (13).

Another example comes from a tradition near Syria. In Egypt, Christians don't use Syriac as their liturgical language; they use Coptic. But their respect for the body is similar. The British journalist William Dalrymple wrote a marvelous travelogue of Christians in the Middle East called *From the Holy Mountain*, in which he tells an anecdote about the monks at St. Anthony's Monastery in Middle Egypt. St. Anthony was, according to our friend Athanasius, the first hermit. I saw his cave there and met the monk, Father Dioscuros, who told Dalrymple this story about the importance of the body:

> "You won't believe this"—here Fr. Dioscuros lowered his voice to a whisper. "You won't believe this, but we had some visitors from Europe two years ago—Christians, some sort of Protestants—who said they didn't believe in the power of relics!"
>
> The monk stroked his beard, wide-eyed with disbelief. "No," he continued. "I'm not joking. I had to take the Protestants aside and explain that we believe that St Anthony and all the fathers have not died, that they live with us, continually protecting us and looking after us. When they are needed—when we go to their graves and pray to their relics—they appear and sort out our problems."
>
> "Can the monks see them?"
>
> "Who? Protestants?"
>
> "No. These deceased fathers. . . ."
>
> "Well, take last week for instance. The Bedouin from the desert are always bringing their sick to us for healing. Normally it is something quite simple: we let them kiss a relic, give them an aspirin and send them on their way. But last week they brought us a small girl who was possessed by a devil. We took the girl into the church, and as it was time for vespers one of the fathers went off to ring the bell for prayers. When he saw this the devil inside the girl began to cry: 'Don't ring the bell! Please don't ring the bell!' We asked him why not. 'Because,' replied the devil, 'when you ring the bell it's not just the living monks who come into the church: all the holy souls of the fathers join with you too, as well as great multitudes of angels and archangels. How can I remain in the church when

that happens? I'm not staying in a place like that.' At that moment the bell began to ring, the girl shrieked and the devil left her!" Father Dioscuros clicked his fingers: "Just like that. So you see," he said. "That proves it."[3]

Proves what? That just as Jacob of Serugh wrote, the separated souls are hanging out around the altar because the consecrated bread and wine of the Eucharist—the postresurrection body of Christ—are the closest they can get, until the general resurrection, to getting their bodies back.

•   •   •

On the other end of the spectrum, we have Paul Tillich (1886–1965), an American theologian (born in Germany) who taught at Union Theological Seminary in New York, Harvard University, and the University of Chicago and appeared on the cover of *Time* magazine. Tillich was my favorite theologian in high school, and at the time, I thought the sermon "You Are Accepted" was the best sermon I had ever heard or read.[4]

Tillich is preaching on Romans 5:20: "Where sin abounded, grace did much more abound." He begins with the word *sin*. (You might object that this makes his theology depend on sin, "hamartiocentric." Or you might observe that he is simply following the order of the words in the verse.) Tillich says, "I should like to suggest another word to you, not as a substitute for the word 'sin,' but as a useful clue in the interpretation of the word 'sin': 'separation.' To be in the state of sin is to be in the state of separation"—among people, from oneself, and from the Ground of Being—"*Existence is separation!* Before sin is an act, it is a state" (154–55). (If you have ever wondered what "existentialism" might be, this is an example. For Tillich, sin is a contingent but universal characteristic of human existence, like language.) Grace, on the other hand, is, according to Tillich, not a state; it is an intervention, an incursion, a stroke. Tillich says, "Do we know what it means to be struck by grace? It does *not* mean that we suddenly believe that God exists, or that Jesus is the Saviour, or that the Bible contains the truth. To believe that something *is*, is almost contrary to the meaning of grace. Furthermore, grace does not mean simply that we are making progress in our moral self-control, in our fight against special faults, and in our relationships. . . . Moral progress may be a fruit of grace; but it is not grace itself, and it can even prevent us from receiving grace" (161).

Tillich is speaking from experience here. He was a notorious womanizer. I was told in the late 1980s by a woman who had been an undergrad at Sweet Briar, a women's college, in the 1950s that when the great man came to speak, the women

---

3   William Dalrymple, *From the Holy Mountain: A Journey among the Christians of the Middle East* (New York: Henry Holt, 1997), 406–7.
4   The text assigned was Paul Tillich, "You Are Accepted," in *The Shaking of the Foundations* (New York: Charles Scribner's Sons, 1948), 53–63. Further references are by page number in the text.

were called together before the lecture and warned that he would be making a pass at one or more of them and they should be prepared to make their escape. That, of course, is just hearsay. But Tillich's wife also wrote a book about their marriage that makes much of his affairs. Her title is *From Time to Time*,[5] but people called it "Time after Time."

Read this next paragraph to yourself out loud. It was meant to be spoken.

> For there is all too often a graceless acceptance of Christian doctrines and a graceless battle against the structures of evil in our personalities. Such a graceless relation to God may lead us by necessity either to arrogance or to despair. It would be better to refuse God and the Christ and the Bible than to accept Them without grace. For if we accept without grace, we do so in the state of separation, and can only succeed in deepening the separation. We cannot transform our lives, unless we allow them to be transformed by that stroke of grace. It happens, or it does not happen. And certainly it does *not* happen if we try to force it upon ourselves, just as it shall not happen so long as we think, in our self-complacency, that we have no need of it. Grace strikes us when we are in great pain and restlessness. It strikes us when we walk through the dark valley of a meaningless and empty life. It strikes us when we feel that our separation is deeper than usual, because we have violated another life, a life which we loved, or from which we were estranged. It strikes us when our disgust for our own being, our indifference, our weakness, our hostility, and our lack of direction and composure have become intolerable to us. It strikes us when, year after year, the longed-for perfection of life does not appear, when the old compulsions reign within us as they have for decades, when despair destroys all joy and courage. Sometimes at that a moment a wave of light breaks into our darkness, and it is as though a voice were saying, "You are accepted. *You are accepted*, accepted by that which is greater than you, and the name of which you do not know. Do not ask for the name now; perhaps you will find it later. Do not try to do anything now; perhaps later you will do much. Do not seek for anything; do not perform anything; do not intend anything. *Simply accept the fact that you are accepted!*" If that happens to us, we experience grace. After such an experience, we may not be better than before, and we may not believe more than before. But everything is transformed. In that moment, grace conquers sin, and reconciliation bridges the gulf of estrangement. And nothing is demanded of this experience, no religious or moral or intellectual presupposition, nothing but *acceptance*. (161–62)

---

5 Hannah Tillich, *From Time to Time* (New York: Stein and Day, 1973).

This is perhaps the most moving statement of the Lutheran doctrine of salvation by grace without works of the law. Even the acceptance is not a work but is carried by victorious grace. And yet—it took Barth for me to notice—Tillich does it almost Jesus-free.

Tillich's view is like that of those Protestants in whom Father Dioscuros could hardly believe even though he had seen them with his own eyes: Tillich does it all without the body.

The feminist theologian Carter Heyward put it this way: the trouble with Tillich was that his "Ground of Being" (one of his circumlocutions for "God") was so far removed from the ground of his being (earthy, bodily things like sex).[6]

---

6   Carter Heyward, "Heterosexist Theology: Being above It All," *Journal of Feminist Studies in Religion* 3 (1987): 29–38; here, 31–33.

25 Barth and Chrysostom

Faith or Works?

How does God lift human beings up to God? Barth emphasizes the gift
of the meeting of the human being and God; Chrysostom emphasizes
that it's not money or professional school that gets you into heaven.

We have just encountered one view of faith, Tillich's "You Are Accepted." Barth's is a
different one. As a freshman, I was offended to read Alasdair MacIntyre's assessment
that Tillich was such thin beer that his position amounted to the recommendation
to adopt a psychological attitude[1] ("*Simply accept the fact that you are accepted*").
Barth is able to make clear that in faith, *God* is doing something, because Barth has
such a robust language about Christ. Here, as often, everything you need to know
is packed into the thesis paragraph: "Christian faith is the *gift* of the *meeting* in
which human beings *become free* to hear the word of grace which God has spoken
in *Jesus Christ* in such a way that, in spite of all that contradicts it, they *may* [this
is the *may* of permission, not the *may* of uncertainty] once for all, exclusively and
entirely, hold to His promise and guidance."[2]

See how that differs from Tillich. Faith is a gift from another rather than a gift
you give yourself; it is a meeting rather than an attitude, and it involves another
person (Jesus) rather than your own psyche. Now, my contrast is a little unfair to
Tillich; he says that grace is a "stroke," and isn't that just as much an intervention
as a "gift"? Well, it exposes another contrast: Barth's gift makes something else
possible, a "holding" to the promise "once for all," which implies something that
lasts rather than something that only intervenes, a history rather than a point.
(There are other parts of Barth that are more "eventful," but this essay seems to
imagine something lasting.)

"Why a gift, and why a gift of freedom?" Barth asks. He explains,

What it means is that this meeting of which the Creed speaks does not
take place in vain. It rests not on a human possibility and human initia-
tive, nor on the [idea] that we [human beings] bear in us a capacity to
meet God, to hear [God's] Word. Were we to reckon up for ourselves what
we [human beings] are capable of, we [would] strive in vain to discover

---

1 Alasdair MacIntyre, "The Fate of Theism," in *The Religious Significance of Atheism* (New York:
  Columbia University Press, 1969), 26–28.
2 Karl Barth, "Faith as Trust," in *Dogmatics in Outline*, 15–21; here, 15, with my italics. Further references will be by page number in the text.

anything which might be termed a disposition towards the Word of God. Without any possibility on our side God's great possibility comes into view, making possible what is impossible from our side. . . . It is grace all over again if our eyes and ears are opened to this grace. (17)

That which I do I in believing is the only thing left to me, to which I have been invited, to which I have been made free by [the One] who can do what I can neither begin nor accomplish of myself. . . . I breathe, and now I breathe joyfully and freely in the freedom which I have not taken to myself, which I have not sought nor found by myself, but in which God has come to me and adopted me. (18)

"Faith" is not an act (or not an independent act): it is a *relationship*. It's like falling in love with someone you weren't looking for and hadn't anticipated. In fact, it has the character not of because, because, because, now therefore (20) but of "in spite of" (19) or nevertheless. For "we would rather not live by grace. Something within us energetically rebels against it. We do not wish to receive grace; at best we prefer to give ourselves grace" (20). Just in case you can't tell, the tone of this passage is sardonic. Barth does *not* mean that it would be good to give yourself grace.

● ● ●

The apparent opposite of this passage is Chrysostom's sermon on Lazarus and the Rich Man (Luke 16:19–31).[3] For Chrysostom (347–407), we are given goods in trust to share with others. We are not really rich until we give them away. But the passage in Luke is quite frightening enough without Chrysostom's sermon. I want you to read it three times. I have added comments in footnotes. The first time, just read it straight: don't look at the footnotes.

There was a rich[4] man who was dressed in purple and fine linen and who feasted sumptuously every day.[5] And at his gate lay a poor man named Lazarus, covered with sores, who longed to satisfy his hunger with what fell from the rich man's table; even the dogs would come and lick his sores.[6] The poor man died and was carried away by the angels to be with Abraham. The rich man also died and was buried.[7] In Hades, where he was being tormented, he looked up and saw Abraham far away with Lazarus

---

3 John Chrysostom, "2d Sermon on Lazarus and the Rich Man," in *John Chrysostom on Wealth and Poverty* (Crestwood, NY: St. Vladimir's Seminary Press, 1984), 39–41, 45–55.
4 Is there a way in which Jesus is "rich"?
5 Who in the Bible wears a purple robe? (Check Mark 15:17 and John 19:2.) Who wears linen? (Check Luke 23:53 and John 19:40.)
6 Where do dogs receive crumbs that fall from a table? (Check Mark 7:28.)
7 Who else "died and was buried" in those words? (Check the Apostles' Creed.)

by his side. He called out, "Father Abraham, have mercy on me, and send Lazarus to dip the tip of his finger in water and cool my tongue; for I am in agony in these flames."[8] But Abraham said, "Child, remember that during your lifetime you received your good things, and Lazarus in like manner evil things; but now he is comforted here, and you are in agony. Besides all this, between you and us a great chasm has been fixed, so that those who might want to pass from here to you cannot do so, and no one can cross from there to us." He said, "Then, father, I beg you to send him to my father's house[9]—for I have five brothers—that he may warn them, so that they will not also come into this place of torment." Abraham replied, "They have Moses and the prophets; they should listen to them." He said, "No, father Abraham; but if someone goes to them from the dead, they will repent."[10] He said to him, "If they do not listen to Moses and the prophets, neither will they be convinced even if someone rises from the dead." (Luke 16:19–31)

The second time, read it so that Lazarus is a Jesus figure. Still do not look at the footnotes. Now, that's easy, right?—because there's another figure in the New Testament, whose name is also Lazarus, who *does* rise from the dead (Luke 7:12–17). The figures are not the same, but the author of Luke has clearly related them and wants to show you a similarity. It is often the case, in the parables of Jesus, that one of the characters is a Jesus figure.

Now I want you to read it a third time. Some interpreters try, as a spiritual exercise, to see Jesus in *every* character in a parable. For instance, Jesus can be the prodigal son *and* his father *and* the fatted calf. Can you see Jesus as *the rich man*?

This is an important exercise because *from the perspective of poorer parts of the world*, all of us "first world" English speakers, especially those who buy books or even go to universities, count as *rich*. If there is no hope for the rich man, how can there be any hope for us? This time when you read the story, try to do the contrary thing and imagine the rich man as a Jesus figure. Of course, the moral features don't fit. But it's surprising how much does.

If you're not reading it yet, go back and read it with the footnotes. If you don't read it with the footnotes, you won't get the point.

Can Jesus be a rich man *who aligns himself with the poor*? That's not this rich man, but it *could* be a rich man, the kind of rich man who is God and who dies for the poor. So Jesus can be that *other* rich man, the one who identified with the poor. Perhaps the author of Luke—or the Holy Spirit—hints at that possibility in the tiniest details.

---

8 Who else is "in agony"? (Check Luke 22:44 and Acts 2:24.) Flames? (Check full versions of the Apostles' Creed, which include the statement "He descended into hell," as well as 1 Peter 4:6 and Ephesians 4:9.)

9 Who else refers to his "father's house"? (Check Luke 2:49 and John 14:2.)

10 Who else—besides the other Lazarus!—rises from the dead? (Check Luke 24:1–12.)

26 Cone and Schmemann

Heaven or Earth?

> Black spirituals offer the richest vision of heaven. Eastern Orthodoxy
> thinks of salvation as a sharing in God's own triune life beginning in this
> life at the Eucharist.

The next two interlocutors contrast as heaven and earth, although both of them
tend to see heaven *on* earth. In James Cone's (1938–2018) "Heaven in the Black
Spirituals," for Black people enslaved in the American South, "heaven" is code for
the North, Ohio, Canada. In Alexander Schmemann's *For the Sake of the World*,
heaven takes place (perhaps implausibly!) in church at Communion.

It's not that I want to reduce heaven to earth. It's just that when I look for texts
about an otherworldly heaven, they are either abstract or boring or both. Descriptions of the vision of God are over in two lines. Descriptions of crystal palaces
and streets paved with gold are cloying. The mystical tradition is interesting, but
what you will find in Schmemann is mysticism about the liturgy, which is concrete,
accessible, and as earthy as bread and wine.

First, consider this spiritual:

> O Canaan, sweet Canaan,
> I am bound for the land of Canaan.[1]

In Cone's "Heaven and the Black Spirituals," "Canaan" was code for "Canada,"
and the "promised land over the Jordan" were the free states over the Ohio River.
Heaven was "not just a transcendent reality. It was the North . . ." (88–89).

"Swing low, sweet chariot" referred to the Underground Railroad. The text of the
hymn was not written to serve as code but was certainly used as code: "I looked
over Jordan [Ohio River] and what did I see, Coming for to carry me home" (90).

So "heaven" was first of all a concrete earthly reality of freedom and justice
north of the slave states.

Heaven had other meanings too. Even if you couldn't escape, Cone thinks the
spirituals could help slaves "not passively [wait] for the future; they were actively
living as if the future were already present in their community" (92).

---

1 The reading for the course was James Cone, "The Meaning of Heaven in the Black Spirituals," in *The
Spirituals and the Blues* (New York: Seabury Press, 1972), 86–107; here, 88. Further references will
be by page number in the text.

One day when I was walkin' alone, Oh yes, Lord,
De element opened, an' de Love came down, Oh, yes, Lord. (92)

Cone comments, "These songs make clear that the future . . . is a reality that has already happened in Jesus' resurrection, and is present now in the midst of the black struggle for liberation" (89). This gave enslaved people a different perspective on oppression and violence: in the sight of God, they were a chosen people, a people of dignity and worth, whom God would liberate someday.

But heaven was not *only* an earthly reality of justice in a different place, like Canada, or in a different time, like the future. It was also the promise of justice in the next world, of rest and reward for the formerly enslaved, and of punishment for the enslaver. The best example of this is a piece of slave exegesis that Cone did not know when he wrote.[2] Two verses of Revelation describe the physical appearance of Jesus when he comes back to judge the living and the dead. The King James Version that enslaved and enslavers both used says, "His head and *his* hairs *were* white like wool, as white as snow; and his eyes *were* as a flame of fire; And his feet like unto fine brass, as if they burned in a furnace; and his voice as the sound of many waters" (Rev 1:14–15).

Two of those details—hair like wool and skin as if burned in a furnace—made clear to enslaved Black people that when Jesus came back, *he would be Black.* It would be as one of them that Jesus returned to judge the quick and the dead. And *that* was the way in which "many who are first will be last, and the last will be first" (Matt 19:30 and parallels).

In all three ways—in place, in time, or in the beyond—heaven represented a radical change in the way things were, a change for dignity and justice for the enslaved. That's what heaven usually is: a radically different perspective on the here and now that functions to reimagine society.

•   •   •

Alexander Schmemann (1921–83) locates that change in perspective in the liturgy, in the transfiguration that Communion works in the life of believers.[3] The writing is irreplaceable. To end this book, therefore, I can do no better than to quote it at length. "Human beings are what they eat," Schmemann begins.[4] "With this statement the German materialistic philosopher Feuerbach [1804–72] thought he had put an end to all 'idealistic' speculations about human nature"—reducing the human being to unspiritual matter. Schmemann continues:

---

2   I associate this piece of exegesis with Albert Raboteau, *Slave Religion* (New York: Oxford University Press, 1978), but I have not been able to find it there.

3   Although its identification of "us" and "them" worked characteristic damage in the lives of medieval Jews: Lauren Winner, *The Dangers of Christian Practice* (New Haven: Yale, 2018), 19–56.

4   The text assigned was Alexander Schmemann, *For the Life of the World* (Crestwood, NY: St. Vladimir's Seminary Press, 1998), 11–22; here, 11. Further references appear as page numbers in the text. Schmemann quotes from Feuerbach a German pun: *Der Mensch ist, was er isst.*

In fact, however, he was expressing, without knowing it, the most religious idea of the human being. For long before Feuerbach the same definition of the human being was given by the Bible. In the biblical story of creation human beings are presented, first of all, as hungry beings, and the whole world as their food. Second only to the direction to propagate and have dominion over the earth, according to the author of the first chapter of Genesis, is God's instruction to human beings to eat of the earth: "Behold I have given you every herb bearing seed . . . and every tree, which is the fruit of a tree yielding see; to you it shall be for meat. . . ." [Gen 1:29]. Human beings must eat in order to live; they must take the world into their bodies and transform it into themselves, into flesh and blood. Human beings are indeed that which they eat, and the whole world is presented as one all-embracing banquet table for the human being. And this image of the banquet remains, throughout the Bible, the central image of life. It is the image of life at its creation and also the image of life at its end and fulfillment: ". . . that you eat and drink at my table in my kingdom." (11; modified for inclusive language, quoting Luke 22:30)

"Human beings are what they eat," Schmemann repeats. "But what do they eat and why?" Schmemann's questions seemed irrelevant to both Feuerbach and his opponents, because, according to Schmemann, they agreed to get it wrong.

To them, as to him, eating was a material function, and the only important question was whether in addition to it the human being possessed a spiritual "superstructure." Religion said yes. Feuerbach said no. But both answers were given within the same fundamental opposition of the spiritual to the material. "Spiritual" *versus* "material," "sacred" *versus* "profane," "supernatural" *versus* "natural"—such were for centuries the only accepted, the only understandable moulds and categories of religious thought and experience. . . .

But the Bible, we have seen, also begins with the human as a hungry being, with humans who are that which they eat. The perspective, however, is wholly different, for nowhere in the Bible do we find the dichotomies which for us are the self-evident framework of all approaches to religion. In the Bible the food that we eat, the world of which we must partake in order to live, is given to us by God, and it is given as *communion with God*. The world as human food is not something "material" and limited to material functions, thus different from, and opposed to, the specifically "spiritual" functions by which the human being is related to God. All that exists is God's gift to the human being, and it all exists to make God known to the human being, to make human life communion with God. It is divine love made food, made life for the human being. . . . "O taste and see that the Lord is good" [Ps 34:8; often used as an invitation to Communion].

Humans are hungry beings. But we are hungry for God. Behind all the hunger of our life is God. All desire is finally a desire for God. To be sure, the human is not the only hungry being. All that exists lives by "eating." The whole creation depends on food. But the unique position of human beings in the universe is that we alone are to *bless* God for the food and the life we receive from God. We alone are to respond to God's blessing with our blessing. . . .

In the Bible to bless God is not a "religious" or a "cultic" act, but the very *way of life*. God blessed the world, blessed the human being, blessed the seventh day (that is, time), and this means that God filled all that exists with God's love and goodness, made all this "very good." So the only *natural* (and not "supernatural") reaction of the human being, to whom God gave this blessed and sanctified world, is to bless God in return, to thank God, to *see* the world as God sees it and—in this act of gratitude and adoration—to know, name, and possess the world. All rational, spiritual, and other qualities of the human . . . have their focus and ultimate fulfill-ment in this capacity to bless God, to know, so to speak, the meaning of the thirst and hunger that constitutes their life. "*Homo sapiens*," "*homo faber*" [the wise human, the maker] . . . yes, but, first of all, "*homo adorans*" [the worshiper]. The first, the basic definition of human beings is that we are *priests*. (14–15; modified for inclusive language)

The basic difference between the Protestant "minister" and the Catholic or Orthodox "priest" is that a minister is to *serve* something (at Communion in the sense of a meal), whereas a priest is to *offer* (at Communion in the sense of an offering, often a sacrifice). Schmemann says, "Humans stand in the center of the world and unify it in their act of blessing God, of both receiving the world from God and offering it to God—and by filling the world with this Eucharist [Com-munion as thanksgiving] we transform our life, the life we receive from the world, into life with God, communion with God. The world was created as the 'matter,' the material of one all-embracing eucharist, and the human being was created as the priest of this cosmic sacrament" (14–15; modified for inclusive language).

Here endeth the reading from Schmemann. At the back of the book you will find a "Syllabus in Theses with Readings." The theses are italicized sentences or paragraphs that encapsulate the point of each chapter or section. See if you can skip from one italicized portion to the next to read the italicized portions as if they were dense but continuous exposition.

Appendix

Objections to the Cultural-Linguistic Approach

If a religion is like a language, you have to practice religious language and ritual to get it. In this, religious studies resembles secular anthropology. This raises objections to my approach from both anthropology and Christianity.[1]

A religion is a set of community practices. Some practices are physical, like crossing oneself, taking the Eucharist, and offering sanctuary to fugitives . . . even those from faculty meetings. Some practices are also intellectual—which is *not* to say nonphysical—like giving rationales for other practices to those who ask, encouraging lines of further questioning, carrying on conversation with others. The only excuse for distinguishing intellectual from nonintellectual practices is the medieval axiom "distinguish to unite." We distinguish intellectual from physical practices only to bind them more closely together. Many religious communities have well-developed, indigenous, higher-order metapractices, Christianity among them. As an anthropologist, you're interested in higher-order, critical, native models. You may find such models helpful or misleading, but the account that a community gives of itself belongs to your data. It's part of what you receive from a good informant, one with skills of knowledge, judgment, observation, and relative distance.

Native is Geertz's term. In religious studies, we're right to suspect it. Sometimes good informants are native, more often hybrid. You value their skills, not their parentage. I'll speak not of "native" models but of "socialized" or "naturalized" ones, since ideas are never autochthonous and often nomadic. What does "naturalized" mean? A variety of things, but one kind of naturalization paper is a PhD. Peer review of books and articles habituates that naturalization. Dual or multiple naturalization is encouraged and often required.

Christianity is a religion with highly developed practices of teaching, evaluation, self-criticism, and reform. Self-reflection is naturalized enough to have a name, as do its naturalized practitioners. Critical models naturalized in Christianity are called theologies, their teachers theologians—those are the naturalized terms. A student of religion needs to know about such naturalized models (many rooted elsewhere) and talk to those informants. In modern Christian theology, the practice is so highly developed and self-critical that we find it in seminaries and university divinity schools with high proportions of PhDs and great familiarity with secular

---

1 This section comes from Eugene F. Rogers Jr., "Theology in the Curriculum of a Secular Religious Studies Department," *Crosscurrents* 56 (2006): 364–74; here, 366–74.

disciplines. Our informants do not track popular religion so much as they track academic theology. The best informants, like the best anthropologists, have skills at crossing boundaries and assimilating other skills to those already habituated. Informants and ethnographers share skills.

Self-critical practices are constructed differently in other religions and go under different names. The term *theology*, for example, is naturalized from Greek religion, where it referred to the exegesis of Homer.

Consider Peter Metcalf's lovely book about former headhunters: A *Borneo Journey into Death: Berawan Eschatology from Its Rituals.*[2] When one of their own has died, the Berawan need to create immediate community for the departed—or did until the British stopped them. To render their former practice intelligible, Metcalf explicates second burial after the bones are clean, in naturalized Berawan terms, of the tales they sing, the genealogies they rehearse. Some informants excel at articulating their practices. It's those people he finds most helpful. He might have found them most obscurantist. But there's no avoiding them. They occupy too prominent a place in the culture's functioning.

In a way, they seek the same thing he does: *they seek to understand.* Both the anthropology professor and the Berawan teacher start with some practices and explicate them in terms of others. The naturalized Christian understanding of what the Berawan and the anthropologist seek is thoroughly Anselmian. Both engage in a project of "faith" seeking understanding. That does not mean that the anthropologist or the Berawan "has" faith in the vulgar Protestant sense. It means they practice certain skills in order to understand; as Anselm wrote, "Credo ut intelligam" (I believe in order to understand). This approach says little about their commitment, except that they each have enough to seek understanding. It's logically possible that either or both of them might use their understanding to undermine the community. Berawans, for example, come under pressure to stop telling the old tales not from the anthropologist but from evangelical Berawan groups naturalized near the coasts. The anthropologist has done more than any living Berawan to preserve the stories told him.[3] I liked *Borneo Journey into Death*—in praise the author might be displeased to receive—because it was theologically musical, it had *Fingerspitzengefühl.*

On this model, religious studies has not only a place for theology—among other disciplines—but a need for it. The boundary between already and not yet naturalized opens and shifts; the skills of anthropologist and theologian overlap. What you *call* this in religious studies matters pragmatically rather than ideologically. "Theology" gains from being the naturalized term, signaling that UVA competes for PhD students with other programs that use it. "Modern religious thought" gains by

---

2   Peter Metcalf, A *Borneo Journey into Death: Berawan Eschatology from Its Rituals* (Philadelphia: University of Pennsylvania Press, 1982; and Kuala Lumpur, Malaysia: Abdul Majeed, 1991).

3   In a second book, Peter Metcalf, *Where Are You, Spirits: Style and Theme in Berawan Prayer* (Washington, DC: Smithsonian, 1989).

signaling that not yet naturalized speakers are needed, like Conrad and Jespersen. "Theology" suffers in recalling more oppressive uses of the term and attracting legal scrutiny, while "modern religious thought" suffers in divorcing thought from practice, or modernity from its roots, putting Descartes before the source. But how Christians evaluate, criticize, and seek to extend their practices matters to all students of the humanities, from English to politics, history to anthropology.

Objections to this account arise from both religious studies and theology.

The objection from religious studies has to do at bottom with power relations and patterns of familiarity. Teaching the rationales naturalized in Christianity and those naturalized in Berawan religion differs tremendously. The differences are not really methodological but contingent, political, historical. Christianity has dominated Western culture for two thousand years. Even today—however much certain Christians may claim for themselves the status of martyrs and cultivate the politics of resentment—there are few political programs Christian groups could not put through, if only they agreed among themselves. Fortunately, Christians agree among themselves no more than other groups. But the danger of hegemony persists. No one is putting the moral code of the Berawan in granite before an Alabama courthouse. Jobseekers in theology who fail to see the enormous power in the study of Christianity show willful naivete and thus bad faith. That the nineteenth-century study of religion is largely a critique of Christianity and that it gave rise to the collection of books that students of religion form themselves upon cannot be said about other religions (although postcolonial studies is modifying that generalization). Religious studies is right to fear theology because theology remains the most politically powerful subfield in the English-speaking academy where religious studies prevails. When religious studies exercises suspicion of the naturalized rationales of the Christian community, it merely sticks to its last. These were the traditions that the hermeneutics of suspicion was trained on. These were the traditions that the hermeneutics of suspicion was invented to suspect. How indeed could it be otherwise?

Religious studies cannot give up its critique of Christian power unless Christianity becomes powerless. But this critique is, for that reason, always pragmatic rather than ideological. The greater the Christian power, the more students of humanities need to know how Christians think and act. The danger persists that students of Christianity will use their power badly: but to banish the study of Christian rational practices from the study of religion gains only temporary advantage. Now that religious studies departments have distinguished themselves from divinity schools, they can no longer afford to abandon the study of Christian intellectual and liturgical practice to the latter.

Since theology is a practice, there is no better way of learning it than by practice. That goes especially for graduate programs. In other departments of a university, such a practice is called "composition." Music appreciation and Greek for reading knowledge are for undergrads. Professors must know how to practice what they teach. In graduate school, music professors took courses in musical composition, even if they are not now composers. Classics professors took courses in Greek composition, even if they do not now compose Greek—or *because* they now teach grammar, edit texts, or comment on Homer. (Indeed, if they write about Homer, they're entitled to call themselves theologians in the Attic sense of the term.) Can a classics department with a graduate program really hire someone to teach Greek who has never composed a Greek sentence? Can a music department really hire someone to teach music history who has never written counterpoint? Religious studies cannot finally dispense with theology.

There is of course a mirror image worry on the part of Christian theology. Is not the anthropological study of religion a Trojan horse? It claims to study God only as constructed by human groups. The account of theology offered above insists that it can be practiced by anthropologists rather than believers—or that anthropologists and believers hold theological practices in common. Theology is a skill that can be taught, gained by practice rather than conversion. Well, we could do worse than to turn to Aquinas here.

The first question of the *Summa* distinguishes two kinds of theology, the one that belongs to human disciplines and the one that belongs to sacred teaching, which is a practice or discipline habituated by God. Jesus Christ is the real form of the teaching that has its inseparable mental aspect in the human heart of the believer that Christ indwells or habituates. Aquinas devotes the *Summa* to sacred teaching as God's discipline. So the question arises early in the *Summa* of what kind of skill one needs to practice sacred teaching. It would seem, Aquinas begins, that to practice the discipline of God, one needs the wisdom of the Spirit. But that is the false seeming of an objection Aquinas rejects:

> There are two modes of . . . wisdom. For how someone judges depends, in one way, on . . . inclination, as when she has the habit of virtue, she judges rightly about things to be done according to that virtue, to the extent that she is inclined to them. . . . In another way, it depends on . . . knowledge: as when one instructed in a moral science is able to judge about acts of a virtue, even if she does not have the virtue. . . . The first way of judging . . . pertains to the wisdom called the gift of the Spirit. . . . But the second way of judging pertains to this teaching, since it is had by study, granted that its principles are had from revelation. (I.1.6 *ad* 3)

The *existence* of sacred doctrine depends on revelation. But not teaching it. Similarly, the existence of anthropology depends on communities but not its classroom study. To teach sacred doctrine or anthropology, you need the wisdom gained by study. You do not need native identity.

For Aquinas, Aristotelian first principles are all undeduced sources of light from things, birds, frogs, drama, politics. First principles are, in a word, small-*r revelations*, sources of light and wonder. Learning from Christian revelation is not different in kind from learning from biological revelations: both proceed by observation through the senses. Sacred doctrine does not differ from those other disciplines, according to Aquinas, in preceding from a revelation. Rather, revelation with a capital R makes it science par excellence (ST I.1.2). It *cannot* require a teacher to be in a state of grace (I.1.6 *ad* 3)—Aquinas denies that one could have certainty about that (I–II.112.5). But it does require practice.

Even if one *had* a personal revelation, Aquinas—like students of mysticism elsewhere—would be suspicious of it. His article on rapture, *De raptu*, finds that revelations taking a human being out of the body produce nothing stably linguistic enough to communicate or deny (II-II.175.4 esp. *ad* 3). So personal revelations don't function in sacred doctrine; it has its disciplined character simply by proceeding from first principles, like ornithology (I.1.2).

Sacred doctrine does have a privileged character, in that its principles descend from God. But its practitioners are *denied* that privilege in this life. Sacred doctrine in this life is a language lacking native speakers, because those who *possess* its first principles as their own are only God and the blessed in heaven.[4] Like a headhunter, God has to kill them for that. Like anthropologists, they work only as outsiders being naturalized into that other community, a practice maintained only by a "few" and always with "an admixture of many errors" (I.1.1). They study sacred doctrine in just the way that they would study *other* religious practices—with respect and humility; with virtues, that is, of faith, hope, and charity; and with justice and prudence, forbearance, temperance, and courage. They study it with interpreters' virtues.[5] But these do not distinguish their study of this religion from others. If an interpreter received from the Holy Spirit a supernatural infusion of charity, that would tend to increase the justice of her interpretations of Buddhism too.

In the final analysis, Christian theology cannot dispense with religious studies because it holds that God became a human being and practiced religion. The trouble is that it also sometimes held that God became a human being to launch a critique of religion universal in extent but fratricidal in intent.

A final complaint therefore joins theology with religious studies, this time from colonial studies. Religious studies is not alone in criticizing religion. It first learned its critique from an earlier critique of religion *within* Christian theology. Several chapters in Mary Douglas's *Purity and Danger* show, in passing or in detail, that Scots Calvinist anthropologists regularly continued anti-Catholic theological arguments by anthropological means.[6] Magic was bad because it reminded them

---

4   Eugene F. Rogers Jr., *Thomas Aquinas and Karl Barth* (South Bend, IN: Notre Dame University Press, 1995), 17–70.

5   Eugene F. Rogers Jr., "How Aquinas Reads Scripture," in *Aquinas and the Supreme Court: Race, Gender, and the Failure of Natural Law in Thomas's Biblical Commentaries* (Oxford: Wiley-Blackwell, 2013), 97–117.

6   Mary Douglas, "Magic and Miracle," in *Purity and Danger: An Analysis of the Concepts of Pollution and Taboo* (London: Routledge, 1966), 58–72.

of Catholic sacramentalism; texts were good because they reminded them of Protestant scripturalism. Jay Carter's book *Race: A Theological Account*[7] reminds us that the German Lutheran who wrote *Religion within the Bounds* also wrote a racist *Anthropology*, so Kant's theory of religion went hand in hand with Christian anti-Judaism. Both Christian theology and religious studies pursue critiques of religion that arose in part out of anti-Judaism or out of anti-Catholicism on the pattern of anti-Judaism. Both Christian theology and religious studies have anti-Judaism in their past. Both have significant resources for self-criticism in their ideals. Does either have repentance in its future?

In 1996, David Chidester's *Savage Systems: Colonialism and Comparative Religion in Southern Africa* appeared, significantly no doubt, from the University Press of Virginia. Briefly, indigenous people over the frontier of British control were said to have no religion. Once the frontier moved inland, the same people were discovered to have religion after all. Those who had no religion were not quite human and could thus be conquered. Those who had religion were credulous and could thus be governed. The study of religion in southern Africa emerged as a managerial, bureaucratic device for social control. Theology and religious studies have that too in common. They both have colonialism/Constantinianism in their past. They both have self-criticism among their ideals. Does either have empire—again—in its future?

Let me mention a research program to give religious studies and theology something more profitable to do than defer hiring and deny graduate students effective instruction (and here I don't mean UVA). In the Scottish Enlightenment, *two* disciplines succeeded Protestant theological critique of Catholics. An impulse to purify the study of religion of everything that was a people or a church, that took up space in the world, led to the philosophy of religion, as in David Hume. A corresponding impulse to explain away certain concrete features of religious community led to a sociology of religion in Robertson Smith. Both sides would have agreed that there is no church of theism, whether because theism could do without community or because community explains theism away. For its own integrity, religious studies must seek the divide between thought and practice in the ambivalence of Protestantism toward alternative strategies of purification and explanation. For its own integrity, Christian theology must acknowledge religious studies as not a rival but a development of its own critical faculties. Christian theology and religious studies have undergone sibling differentiation. Such differentiation centers research into Late Antiquity on Jews and Christians; why not also in modernity?

These possibilities do not call for more method. They call for more formation and tact, for scholarly virtues. What to practice in the classroom, for example, depends on circumstance and tact. (As Jeffrey Stout has quoted Camus, *Quand on n'a pas de caractère, il faut se donner une méthode.*)[8] I don't mean to sound

---

7 J. Kameron Carter, *Race: A Theological Account* (Oxford: Oxford University Press, 2008).
8 Jeffrey Stout, *Ethics after Babel: The Languages of Morals and their Discontents* (Princeton, NJ: Princeton University Press, 2001), 296.

pious. I mean to identify good practices of scholarship—which fortunately coincide rather than conflict. If we were asking about *rival* commitments, we could justify a politics of struggle. But we're asking about common commitments to humility. Both theologians, on christological grounds, and anthropologists, on grounds of method, are committed to practice not self-importance but humility, certainly not the narcissism of their differences. Theologians should count divinity not a thing to be grasped, but take the form of a (civil) servant. Anthropologists seek to understand as if from within. Sometimes theology will need to speak up for itself, or bureaucratic students of religion will want to outlaw the taking of heads. But neither will succeed without humility before the communities they study. In this practice, they coincide in the virtue to repair their common vice.

Humility means that students of religion ought to avoid universal claims not only because they are a power play of colonialism but also because they perpetuate a bad form of Christian theology, one that ignores or seeks to eradicate the particular, which it identified with Jews, in favor of a universal that emerged only as they abstracted and expropriated a particular god, the God of *Israel*. In becoming anthropologists, Christian theologians ought to imitate the God who in the Logos, they claim, became anthropos. For that reason, Gregory of Nazianzus denies, as too static, that this God's deity requires infinity in *extent*. Unlike a British colonialist, Gregory's God does not push out or erase a frontier but *crosses* it (Fifth Theological Oration). That God crosses a frontier to learn as a human being, to become naturalized as one of the others. Likewise, that God promises Abraham that by him, all the nations will be blessings *to one another*. Christian theologians, therefore, if they imitate God's anthropology, ought to reject theories universal in extent in favor of practices dynamic in crossing frontiers for naturalization among others. Anthropologists, unless they hope to perpetuate a theological mistake, ought to do the same thing.

A Syllabus in Theses with Readings

Christianity Is a Language in Which to Disagree

1. *Jefferson and Lewis disagree on the elements of Christian thought. Two thinkers beloved of laypeople and undergraduate students of religion, Thomas Jefferson and C. S. Lewis, disagree on what the elements of Christian thought might be. We will be investigating, as a cultural anthropologist might, reasons many Christians consider central the very beliefs Jefferson found dispensable. Our native informants are called theologians.*

   - Thomas Jefferson, Syllabus of Christianity in *Jefferson's Extracts from the Gospels: "The Philosophy of Jesus" and "The Life and Morals of Jesus,"* ed. Dickinson W. Adams and Ruth W. Lester, The Papers of Thomas Jefferson (Princeton, NJ: Princeton University Press, 1983), 401–2, 405–6, 391n3.
   - C. S. Lewis, "What Are We to Make of Jesus Christ?," in *The Joyful Christian: 127 Readings from C. S. Lewis* (New York: Macmillan, 1977), 72–74.

2. *The study of religion is like the study of a language. Native speakers can speak it badly, and non-native speakers can speak it well. In this book, we will be quoting and engaging well-formed samples of Christian-speak. The insights of both "insiders" and "outsiders" are necessary for us to hear what's going on in Christian-speak. In the late twentieth and early twenty-first centuries, there have been five ways of relating Christian-speak to common language.*

   - Jeffrey Stout, "Five Types of Christian Theology," a section in "Hans Frei and Anselmian Theology," in *Ten Year Commemoration to Hans Frei*, ed. Giorgy Olegovich (New York: Semenenko Foundation, 1999), 30–32.
   - For further reading, see George Lindbeck, *Nature of Doctrine* (London: SPCK, 1984), 30–42, 73–88.
   - For further reading, see Clifford Geertz, "Thick Description," "Religion as a Cultural System," and "Ethos and Worldview," in *The Interpretation of Cultures* (New York: Basic Books, 1973), 3–30, 87–141. Note esp. 14n1 and 15n2, where theology can be regarded as a higher-order native model.

Christians Talk about Election, or How God Chooses

3. *The "language" that Christians speak (as well as the language of the rabbis) developed out of one first spoken by Jews. Central to this Jewish "language" is the concept of chosenness, or election. Christians (and Jews and Muslims) speak of a God who makes particular choices. Michael Wyschogrod talks about God's love in terms of the people Israel.*

- Here, Michael Wyschogrod, "Israel, the Church, and Election," in *Brothers in Hope*, ed. John M. Oesterreicher (New York: Herder and Herder, 1970), 79–87; more recently in Michael Wyschogrod, *Abraham's Promise*, ed. Kendall Soulen (Grand Rapids, MI: William B. Eerdmans, 2004), 179–87.
- For further reading, Michael Wyschogrod, "Incarnation," *Pro Ecclesia* 2 (1993): 208–15.
- For further reading, Michael Wyschogrod, *The Body of Faith: Judaism as Corporeal Election* (New York: Seabury, 1983), also with different subtitles from different presses: the text is always the same.

4. *John Calvin talks God choosing individuals for God's purpose. Against his intention, succeeding generations came to regard Calvin's God as a giant sorting mechanism.*

- John Calvin, *Institutes of the Christian Religion*, trans. Ford Lewis Battles (Philadelphia: Westminster Press, 1960), 2:920–36, 970–71 (III.xxi–xxii.3, xxiv.5).
- For further reading, the most charitable reading of Calvin's doctrine of election (which makes him sound like Barth) is Wilhelm Niesel, *The Theology of Calvin*, trans. Harold Knight (Philadelphia: Westminster Press, 1956), 159–81.

5. *Karl Barth talks about God choosing humanity in Jesus. In Jesus, God chooses God's own self to be for the sinful human being and the human being to share God's glory.*

- Karl Barth, "The Election of Jesus Christ," in *Church Dogmatics*, 4 vols. in 13 part-volumes (Edinburgh: T&T Clark, 1957), vol. II/2, 3, 94–179, large print only. This volume is printed in two sizes of print, large and small. Small print can run for pages. The large print runs only thirty-nine pages. The relevant large print appears on pages 3, 94–95, 99–102, 103–6, 115–17, 118, 120–27, 145, 161–65, 166–68, 168–74. Pay special attention to the boldface thesis paragraphs on 3 and 94.
- For further reading, see 449–506 in the same volume on Judas.

Christians Talk about Incarnation, or God Chooses Humanity

6. *Christians speak of a God who chooses to become a human being. Biblical narratives require two ways of describing the unitary character of Jesus, human and divine. Doctrine calls the two ways of talking two natures in one person, or two whats in one who. The two ways of talking describe one character who does divine things by human means and human things with divine result.*

   - Athanasius, *Orations against the Arians*, in *The Christological Controversy*, ed. and trans. Richard A. Norris Jr. (Philadelphia: Fortress Press, 1980), 83–101.

7. *Tanner refuses to talk about divine and human as rivals because the Person of the Word is elevating (saving) human nature.*

   - Cyril of Alexandria, *2d Letter to Nestorius*, in *Christological Controversy*, 131–35.
   - Kathryn Tanner, "Who Is Jesus?," in *Jesus, Humanity and the Trinity* (Minneapolis: Fortress Press, 2001), 1–34.

Christians Talk about Atonement, or God Chooses the Lost

If God becomes human, is God subject to death? How can human beings join the Trinitarian feast if the community is sundered by death? Christians offer various accounts of why God became a human being. Did God become human to die for sin or to exemplify love? Did God become human to descend into hell and lead captives to heaven?

8. *Athanasius talks about God becoming human to make humans divine.*

   - Athanasius, *Orations against the Arians*, as above.

9. *Anselm talks about Christ paying a debt of honor. Anselm originates the most popular atonement theory, that Christ pays a debt for our sins. But "debt" doesn't mean money, and you don't accept the payment with your mind. You accept it into your mouth.*

   - Anselm of Canterbury, *Meditation on Human Redemption*, in *Prayers and Meditations of Saint Anselm*, ed. and trans. Benedicta Ward (New York: Penguin, 1973), 230–37.

10. *Abelard talks about Christ teaching love by word and example. He abhors the idea of the Father sacrificing or punishing his Son. Abelard never uses Anselm's name. Is he criticizing Anselm or helping us to understand him properly?*

- Peter Abelard, *Commentary on Romans*, in A *Scholastic Miscellany: Anselm to Ockham*, ed. and trans. Eugene Fairweather, Library of Christian Classics (Philadelphia: Westminster Press, 1956), 10: 280–84.

11. *Excursus: Protestants talk about Anselm and Abelard to debate punishment.*

- For further reading, see John Calvin, *Institutes*, 2 vols., trans. Ford Lewis Battles (Philadelphia: Westminster, 1960) II.xii.2–3, vol. 1, 465–67. Note that these passages are very short and compete with other metaphors that carry more weight.
- For further reading, see Jonathan Edwards, "Concerning the Necessity and Reasonableness of the Christian Doctrine of Satisfaction for Sin," §9, in *Works of Jonathan Edwards*, vol. 2, at https://tinyurl.com/y28j5bha.
- For further reading, Martin Luther, *Lectures on Galatians 1–4*, 1535, vol. 26, *Luther's Works* (Saint Louis: Concordia, 1963), 276–91, talks about "the Law" as a sinner's perception of God accusing the conscience and administering punishment. Luther treats "the Law" and grace as one piece, one reversal of a comprehensive, Athanasian blessed exchange. Although Luther's theory includes wrath and punishment, its emphasis on the blessed exchange brings it closer to Athanasius than Anselm. And although Luther's theory is infected with anti-Semitic tropes and supersessionism, what Luther means by "the Law" is entirely different from what Jews mean by Torah (which is more of a structure that liberates and closer to what Luther means by "command").
- For more about penal substitution, see Stephen Holmes, "Penal Substitution," in *T&T Clark Companion to Atonement*, ed. Adam J. Johnson (London: Bloomsbury T&T Clark, 2017), 295–314.
- For a defense of Anselm as Athanasian, see D. Bentley Hart, "A Gift Exceeding Every Debt: An Eastern Orthodox Appreciation of Anselm's *Cur Deus Homo*," *Pro Ecclesia* 7 (1998): 333–49.

12. *The Spirit, the Giver of Life, gathers a new community (the church) around the martyred body of Jesus. Stephen Ray sees Jesus's Spirit gathering a new community (Black Lives Matter) around the martyred body of Michael Brown Jr. To explain life from the dead, Ray revives the trickster atonement theory of the early church.*

- Stephen G. Ray Jr., "Black Lives Matter as Enfleshed Theology," in *Enfleshing Theology: Embodiment, Discipleship, and Politics in the Work of M. Shawn*

Copeland, ed. Robert J. Rivera and Michele Saracino (Minneapolis: Fortress Press, 2018), 83–93, esp. 91–92.

13. *Julian of Norwich talks about sin as a wound. She proposes a no-blame (if not no-fault) theory of sin and explains it with a vision of a servant in whom Christ and Adam coincide.*

   - Julian of Norwich, *Showings*, trans. into modern English by Edmund Colledge and James Walsh (New York: Paulist Press, 1978), the Long Text, chs. 36–39 and 50–52 = pp. 238–45 and 267–82. Other translations are available as well as the Middle English in Julian of Norwich, *Showings: Authoritative Text, Contexts, Criticism*, ed. Denise N. Baker (New York: W. W. Norton, 2005).

14. *Balthasar talks about Christ emptying hell. Barth suggested an empty hell because of God's choice of Godself to bear the sin of the human being; Balthasar hoped for an empty hell because of Christ's descent to the dead.*

   - John Saward, "The Incarnation, the Descent into Hell and the Resurrection," in *The Mysteries of March* (Washington, DC: Catholic University of America Press, 1990), 105–43.
   - For further reading, Hans Urs von Balthasar, *Mysterium Paschale*, with an introduction by Aidan Nichols (Edinburgh: T&T Clarke, 1990; Grand Rapids, MI: William B. Eerdmans, 1993).
   - For further reading, Hans Urs von Balthasar, *Dare We Hope "That All Men Be Saved," with a Short Discourse on Hell* (San Francisco: Ignatius, 1988).
   - For further reading, Hans Urs von Balthasar, *First Glance at Adrienne von Speyr* (San Francisco: Ignatius, 1981).
   - If you can get hold of it, Adrienne von Speyr, *Kreuz und Hölle*, vols. 3–4, *Nachlasswerke* (Einsiedeln, Switzerland: Johannes Verlag, 1966).

Christians Talk about the Trinity, or Love Stronger Than Death

15. *The doctrine of the Trinity is a set of rules to enable Christians to go on talking the way the New Testament talks about the Three who are God. Jesus's relations with those he calls "Father" and "Spirit" presuppose that God is a community interacting among themselves and sharing one activity beyond themselves, or towards creatures. The Three seek always and in everything to join us to their fellowship; the New Testament makes analogies to prayer and feasting.*

   - The "Athanasian" Creed, widely available online.

- Richard Norris, "Trinity," in *The Holy Spirit: Classic and Contemporary Readings*, ed. Eugene F. Rogers Jr. (Oxford: Blackwell, 2002), 19–43.
- For further reading, Eugene F. Rogers Jr., *Sexuality and the Christian Body: Their Way into the Triune God* (Oxford: Blackwell, 1999), 195–204.
- For further reading, Sarah Coakley, "Living into the Mystery of the Holy Trinity: Trinity, Prayer, and Sexuality," in *Holy Spirit*, 44–52.
- For further reading, R. Kendall Soulen, "The Name of the Holy Trinity," *Theology Today* 59 (2002): 244–61.

Christians Talk about God Enabling Difference in Creation and Freedom

16. *Barth talks about the Trinity enabling creation, or difference within God allowing difference from God. Because God loves others already in the life of the Trinity, God can love others also outside the Trinity, in the world.*

- Karl Barth, "God the Creator," in *Dogmatics in Outline*, trans. G. T. Thompson (London: SCM Press, 1949), 50–58.

17. *Augustine talks about grace and free will in such a way that God's freedom empowers human freedom. After God becomes human, does God leave other human beings to their own devices, or do they participate in the humanity of God? In other words, are God's freedom and human freedom in competition?*

- Augustine, *On Grace and Free Will*, in *Anti-Pelagian Writings*, trans. Peter Holmes and Robert Ernest Wallis, Nicene and Post-Nicene Fathers (Grand Rapids, MI: William B. Eerdmans, 1971), 5:436–65. Multiple versions also exist online.
- Kathryn Tanner, *God and Creation: Tyranny or Empowerment?* (Minneapolis: Fortress Press, 2004), 46–48.
- For further reading, the Council of Orange (529) shows where later bishops drew the heresy line between double and single predestination. See "The Council of Orange," sourcebooks.fordham.edu, March 15, 1994, https://sourcebooks.fordham.edu/basis/orange.txt.
- Aquinas, *Summa Theologiae*, I.105.4, I.22.4, I.23.6, puts the matter very simply. Grace is eminently resistible, but God's will is nevertheless infallible. God wills what will happen *with its mode* so that what God wills to happen necessarily happens with necessity, what God wills to happen contingently happens contingently, and what God wills to happen freely happens freely. Unlike Calvin, this does not mean that God "controls" the free actor in such a way as to bind their freedom. Rather, God *inspires* the free actor to act

most freely. The most useful is the "Benzinger" or "American" edition, published in multiple editions in three to five volumes from 1911, translated by the Fathers of the English Dominican Province (Laurence Shapcote), New York: Benzinger Brothers, 1948; and Allen, TX: Christian Classics, 1981; and online at www.newadvent.org.

Christians Talk about God's Body Absorbing Evil

18. *If God is good and all-powerful, why is there evil? Theologians answer that evil has no reality of its own, but suffering is real. G. K. Chesterton suggests that in Christ, God drinks the cup of suffering with creatures.*

   - G. K. Chesterton, The Man Who Was Thursday (London: Penguin, 1986). Multiple versions also exist online.

19. *Human sin renews the question of where God is in the presence of evil. Phyllis Trible parallels the story of the concubine in Judges 19 to the story of Jesus to suggest that God is in the victim.*

   - Phyllis Trible, "An Unnamed Woman: The Extravagance of Violence," in Texts of Terror (Philadelphia: Fortress Press, 1984), 65–92.

Christians Talk about God's Body in Resurrection and Eucharist

20. *Those responses to evil suggest that God shares suffering. But how does God overcome it? Rowan Williams's account of the resurrection suggests how reconciliation could break out among sinful people with the principle "In your victim lies your hope."*

   - Rowan Williams, "The Judgement of Judgement: Easter in Jerusalem," in Resurrection: Interpreting the Easter Gospel (Harrisburg, PA: Morehouse, 1994), 7–28.
   - For further reading, Hans Frei, The Identity of Jesus Christ (Philadelphia: Fortress Press, 1975).

21. *In the Eucharist, God's body joins believers to the life of the Trinity and creates a common feast for the forgiven.*

   - Rogers, Sexuality and the Christian Body, 249–56, 265–68.

Christians Talk about Human Bodies in Sex and Slavery

22. *Bodies can remind Christians that God desires human beings as if they were God, or consummation. God can prepare a couple for life with God by binding them for life with each other.*

   • Rowan Williams, "The Body's Grace," in Rogers, *Theology and Sexuality: Classic and Contemporary Readings* (Oxford: Blackwell, 2002), 309–21.

23. *Pro-slavery arguments show how not to interpret the Bible. God's saving action includes empowering human words to do what they cannot do on their own— namely, reach God. Successful speech about God is already the work of the Holy Spirit, a participation in God's own speech about God in the triune life. In Christianity, the Word is God (John 1:1), but the Word that is God is Jesus, not the Bible. The Bible only witnesses to the Word (John 1:8). The test for scriptural interpretation is Trinitarian: it should arise from the Spirit of love, approach the Father of truth, and result in the likeness of Christ.*

   • Thornton Stringfellow, "The Bible Argument: Or, Slavery in the Light of Divine Revelation," in *Cotton Is King and Pro-slavery Arguments*, ed. E. N. Elliott (Atlanta: Pritchard, Abbot & Loomis, 1860), 461–92. Multiple versions also exist online.
   • For further reading, see Gregory of Nyssa, *Homily IV on Ecclesiastes*, in Gregory of Nyssa, *Homilies on Ecclesiastes: An English Version with Supporting Studies*, ed. Stuart Hall (New York: De Gruyter, 1993), 73–78. This is the classic patristic argument that slavery dishonors the image of God.
   • For further reading, see Victor Preller, "The Problem of Referring to God" and "The Material Moves of the Language of Faith," in *Divine Science and the Science of God* (Princeton, NJ: Princeton University Press, 1967), 4–22, 266–71.

Christians Talk about Salvation in Many Ways

24. *Body or soul? What do Christians think God has in store for human beings? Some say it takes a body to perceive and reflect the glory of God; others emphasize God's transformative forgiveness.*

   • Susan Harvey, "Embodiment in Time and Eternity," in *Theology and Sexuality*, 3–22.
   • Paul Tillich, "You Are Accepted," in *The Shaking of the Foundations* (New York: Charles Scribner's Sons, 1948), 53–63.

25. *Faith or works? How does God lift human beings up to God? Barth emphasizes the gift of the meeting of the human being and God; Chrysostom emphasizes that it's not money or professional school that gets you into heaven.*

- Karl Barth, "Faith as Trust," in *Dogmatics in Outline*, 15–21.
- John Chrysostom, "2d Sermon on Lazarus and the Rich Man," in *John Chrysostom on Wealth and Poverty* (Crestwood, NY: St. Vladimir's Seminary Press, 1984), 39–41, 45–55.

26. *Heaven or earth? African American spirituals offer the richest vision of heaven. Eastern Orthodoxy thinks of salvation as a sharing in God's own triune life beginning at the Eucharist.*

- James Cone, "The Meaning of Heaven in the Black Spirituals," in *The Spirituals and the Blues* (New York: Seabury Press, 1972), 86–107.
- Alexander Schmemann, *For the Life of the World* (Crestwood, NY: St. Vladimir's Seminary Press, 1998), 11–22.

General Index

Abailard. See Abelard, Peter
Abel, 39
Abelard, Peter, 61, 65–85, 149, 157, 206
Abraham, 19, 20, 21, 99, 114, 168, 175, 188–189, 201
Adam, 21, 38, 59, 69, 87, 90, 92, 97–99, 143
agency. See freedom/free will
anastasis. See resurrection (of Jesus)
Anglicanism, 156, 167
Annunciation, 93, 96–97
Anselm/Anselmian, xviii, 11–13, 57
Anthony, 62, 183
anthropology, 3, 79, 83, 90, 195–201, 203
apologetics, 9, 12–13
Apostles' Creed, 95–96, 182, 188, 189
Aquinas. See Thomas Aquinas
Arius/Arians, 35–36, 45–46
assurance, problem of, 28–29
Athanasian Creed, 110
Athanasius, 4, 5, 6, 35–36, 45–51, 57–63, 68, 72, 81, 183
atonement, xviii, 13, 37–38, 55–105, 156–157, 164, 173, 175, 181
Augustine, 40, 111, 113–114, 117, 127–139, 143–145, 175–177

Balthasar, Hans Urs von, 36, 53, 93, 95–105, 114
banks, 64
baptism, 20, 50, 111–112, 118, 127–128
Barnabas, Epistle of, 143
Barth Karl, 12–13, 23, 24, 31–41, 45, 49, 51, 65, 78, 87, 95, 98, 101, 102, 123–125, 178, 186–188, 199
Bathsheba, 170
Berawan, 196
Beza, Theodore, 26–28, 33, 36

Black Lives Matter, 78, 83–85
blessed exchange, 49–50, 78, 81
blood, 66, 70, 79–80, 146–147, 163–164, 175, 193
Boaz, 169
Bradford, Aminah, 59
Bretherton, Luke, 159
Brown, Michael, Jr., 83–84
Butler, Judith, 163

Cain, 139
Calvin, John, 4, 5, 6, 23–26, 28–29, 31–37, 41, 45, 52, 72, 76, 80, 99, 137, 138, 178, 199
Carter, J. Kameron, 200
Chesterton, G. K., 143–148, 149, 150, 151
Chidester, David, 200
choosing/chosenness, 15–21, 23–24, 28, 31, 34, 36–37, 44–45, 55, 78, 79, 85, 95, 124, 129, 138, 161, 167, 181, 192
Christianity (as a language), xi, xvii, xviii, 1, 6–7, 9–13, 17, 19, 45, 47, 53–54, 64, 66, 76–79, 110–112, 115–118, 124, 131, 139, 171, 173, 174, 184, 187, 193, 194, 195, 199, 200
Christianity (as a practice), xviii, 11, 13, 51, 68, 78, 93, 118–119, 127, 130–131, 159, 163, 178, 182, 195–201
Christmas, 32, 61, 93, 96
Chrysostom. See John Chrysostom
church, xvi, xviii, 11, 17, 18, 20, 33, 38, 57, 66, 67, 73, 79, 83–85, 87, 91, 92, 95, 96, 97, 100, 102, 103, 105, 110, 114, 118, 137, 156, 162, 168, 170, 171, 181, 183, 191, 200
Coakley, Sarah, 115
communicatio idiomatum. See blessed exchange

communion, 53, 66, 68, 74, 79, 92, 100, 105, 125, 148, 150–151, 157, 161–164, 170, 181, 183–184, 191, 192–194, 195
Cone, James, 191–192
Confucius, 6
coronavirus. See COVID-19
corruptibility, 59–61, 63
covenant, 21, 114, 147
COVID-19, xvii, 58, 87, 135, 137
creation, 23, 34, 46, 50, 59, 60, 67, 77, 84, 97, 111, 123–125, 130, 137, 161, 170, 171, 193, 194
cross. See crucifixion
crucifixion, 21, 36, 39, 46, 48, 61, 63, 75–76, 78–79, 83, 98, 100–102, 105, 163, 176–177
cultural-linguistic approach to religion, 10, 195–201
Cyril of Alexandria, 48, 52–53

Dalrymple, William, 183
damnation. See hell; rejection
David, 39, 169–170
death, xv, 21, 23, 24, 36, 38, 48, 49, 52, 53, 57–59, 61, 63, 69–71, 75–77, 79–80, 83, 84, 85, 87, 88, 92, 95–97, 100, 105, 107, 114, 116, 125, 127, 137, 150, 156, 161–162, 164, 169, 170, 177, 182, 196
debt, xv, 57, 63–65, 68, 70, 76, 78, 81, 87, 105
decay, 58–59
descent into hell. See hell
devil, xv, 13, 69–70, 76, 80, 83–85, 98, 105, 125, 182–184
dictation, 178
dignity/dignify, 70, 75, 87, 137, 192
divinization/deification, 49, 57, 59, 62–63, 109, 113–115, 124, 161, 168
Donne, John
Douglas, Mary, 83–84, 199
Dowey, Edward, 178
Durkheim, Émile, 79

Easter, 61, 96, 98, 156–160
Eastern Orthodoxy. See Orthodoxy (Eastern)
ecclesiology. See church
Eden, 58, 60, 92, 162
Edwards, Jonathan, 80
election, xviii, 15–41, 78, 99, 124
enhypostatic, 51
environment, 59, 130
eros/eroticism, 66–67, 116, 186
Esau, 20, 23, 39
Esperanto, 12
Eucharist. See communion
evil, 13, 59, 85, 87–90, 124–125, 129, 135–139, 143–151, 155–156, 174–175, 185, 189
example/exemplar, 69–71, 75, 79, 91
experiential-expressivism, 9–10, 12

fall/fallenness, 25, 58, 60–61, 75, 87–88, 90–91, 93, 125, 128, 163, 181
Father, xv, 12, 20–21, 28, 33–34, 36–38, 47–48, 50, 52–53, 65, 67–69, 75, 77–78, 80, 92, 100–101, 105, 109–112, 114–118, 123, 144, 147, 156, 162, 164, 170, 173–174, 175, 177–178, 189
Feuerbach, Ludwig, 192–193
flesh, 20, 32, 35, 38, 47, 51–53, 58–59, 62, 73, 75, 78, 84–85, 88, 114, 116, 117, 164, 193
Florensky, Pavel, 124, 161
Fredriksen, Paula, 19
freedom/free will, 4, 5, 13, 17, 24, 32–34, 65–66, 77, 100, 117, 124–125, 127–139, 143, 150, 172, 173, 174, 187–188, 191
Frei, Hans, 11–12, 156
Freud, Sigmund, 35, 102

Gandhi, Mohandas K., 75, 77, 177
garden, 58–59, 92, 162–164
Geertz, Clifford, 3, 195
Gehenna. See hell

gender, 19, 32, 35, 67, 110, 115–118, 124, 137, 163, 177, 199

gentiles, 18–21, 23

Gethsemane, 92, 164

God-language, 32, 124. See also gender; Trinity

Golden Rule, 71, 105, 138, 176–177

Good Friday, 68, 85, 96–97, 101, 105

Gospel of Thomas. See Infancy Gospel of Thomas

grace, 13, 17, 25–26, 28, 31, 32, 35–38, 59, 61, 62, 70, 71, 81, 88, 105, 114, 123, 127–129, 132–139, 143, 160, 162, 167, 170–174, 176, 184–188, 199

grammar (as a metaphor for doctrine), 10–11, 13, 34, 40, 105, 109–111, 137, 198

Gregory of Nazianzus, 201

Gregory of Nyssa, 174

Gwenallt. See Jones, David Gwenallt

Hades. See hell

Hart, David Bentley, 81

Harvey, Susan, 181–184

hell, xv, 19, 25, 36, 57, 60, 65, 88, 92–93, 95–105, 125, 189

Heloise, 72

Holmes, Stephen, 81

Holy Saturday, 96, 104, 105

Holy Spirit, 6, 12, 17, 28, 29, 34, 36, 37, 50, 52, 59, 61, 67, 83–85, 87, 88, 92, 100, 105, 109–112, 114–118, 132, 164, 170, 171, 173–174, 176–178, 189, 198–199

homosexuality. See sexuality

honor, 63–65, 73–77, 87–90, 93, 146–148, 174

human being, xv, 31–37, 47, 49, 51–52, 58–62, 64, 65, 69, 75–77, 87, 95, 100, 124, 128, 130–132, 137, 143, 155, 161, 187, 192–194

humanity. See human being

Hume, David, 200

hypostasis. See Person (of Christ)

inerrancy, 178

Infancy Gospel of Thomas, 51

Isaac, 19, 39, 41, 175

Ishmael, 20, 39

Jacob, 21, 23, 39

Jacob of Serugh, 163, 183, 184

Jefferson, Thomas, xvii, 3–6

Jenson, Robert, 53, 115

Jesus. See atonement; natures (of Christ); Person (of Christ)

Jesus, face of, xvii, 6

Jews/Judaism, xviii, 4, 10, 12, 13, 17–21, 33, 38, 45, 66, 81, 109, 111, 118–119, 137, 150, 156, 158–159, 200, 201

Job, 84

John Chrysostom, 187–188

John of the Cross, 100, 168, 171

Jonah, 83

Jones, David Gwenallt, 80

Judas, 32, 39–40, 76, 98

Julian of Norwich, 87–93, 101, 102, 146

Jung, Carl, 102

justification, xvii, 69–70, 79, 92, 184–187

Kant, Immanuel, 11, 12, 200

Kaufmann, Gordon, 12

King, Martin Luther, Jr., 75, 77, 177

Lady Day. See Annunciation

language. See Christianity (as a language)

Last Supper. See communion

Lazarus (and the rich man), 188–189

Lazarus (resurrected by Jesus), 46, 48, 189

Leah, 39

Lewis, C. S., 3, 5–7

Lindbeck, George, 9–10, 13, 176

Logos, 12, 47, 50–53, 57–58, 74, 83, 130, 201

love, xv, 4–5, 12, 17, 20–21, 23, 28–29, 32–34, 37, 46, 53, 57, 58, 59, 62, 66–67,

love (*continued*)
    69–72, 74–75, 77–80, 85, 88–93, 100,
    105, 111, 113–114, 123–124, 132–134,
    143–145, 150, 157, 161–164, 167, 170–171,
    173, 175–178, 185, 188, 192–194
Luther, Martin/Lutheran, 24, 35, 52–53,
    81, 110, 128, 186, 200

MacIntyre, Alasdair, 187
man. *See* human being
Mangina, Joseph, xix, 73, 78
marriage, 72, 113, 114, 116, 128, 163, 164,
    167–168, 170–171, 175, 185
martyr, 72, 75–76, 79–80, 83, 85, 89, 114,
    159, 197
Mary, 47, 83, 96, 168, 170, 177
Mary Magdalene, 92
Metcalf, Peter, 196
monastery/monks/nuns, 61–62, 66–67,
    72, 99, 105, 117, 168, 170–171, 183
Moses, 25, 39, 139, 163, 189

Naomi, 169
natures (of Christ), 13, 45–53, 58, 65–66,
    70, 97
Norris, Richard, 47, 53–54

obedience (of Christ), 28, 73, 75, 77
Orthodoxy (Eastern), xviii, 59, 73, 81, 96,
    98, 111, 118, 143, 156, 191–194. *See also*
    Athanasius; Cyril of Alexandria

parable of the servant. *See* Julian of
    Norwich
payment. *See* penal substitution; sin as
    a debt
Pelagius, 127–128, 129, 131
penal substitution, 73–74, 76–81
Person (of Christ), 34, 38, 45, 47–49,
    51–52, 59, 92, 97, 118, 130, 187
Persons of the Trinity. *See* Trinity
Peter, 25, 48, 76, 98, 146, 147, 159

Pharaoh, 39, 138–139, 143
Phillips, D. Z., 12
pneumatology. *See* Holy Spirit
prayer, 17, 40, 109, 110, 114–116, 173, 177,
    183, 196
predestination, 24–28, 31–32, 39, 128. *See*
    also election; rejection
propositionalism, 9
psychological analogy for the Trinity,
    113
punishment. *See* penal substitution
purgatory, 99, 104–105

Rachel, 39
Rahab, 169
Ray, Stephen, 72, 80, 83–85, 100
reason. *See also* Logos
rejection, 19, 20, 23, 24, 36–37, 39, 99
religion, xi, xv, xviii, 3–5, 9–13, 32, 50, 97,
    193, 195–201
resurrection (of Jesus), 33, 46, 48, 95, 96,
    98, 100, 105, 115–116, 155–160, 164, 167,
    184, 192
resurrection of other people, xv, 33, 46,
    66, 114, 115–116, 173, 182, 184
Richard of St. Victor, 113–114
Robertson Smith, William, 200

salvation, xi, xv, xviii, 19, 23, 25–26, 28,
    31, 40, 59–61, 66, 75, 79, 80, 91, 98,
    113, 115–116, 124, 128–129, 159–160, 173,
    181–194
Satan. *See* devil
satisfaction, 39, 63, 65, 68, 73–80
Saul, 39
Schmemann, Alexander, 192–194
Scots Confession, 37–38
sexuality, 62, 66–67, 113–114, 116, 157,
    162–164, 167–172, 175, 186
Sheol. *See* hell
sin as a debt. *See* debt
sin as a wound, 29, 87–90

slavery, 137, 173–178
Smith, J. Warren, 52, 176
Soulen, Kendall, xix, 20, 33, 59, 73, 75
Spencer, Stanley, 182
Speyr, Adrienne von, 95, 100–105
Spirit. *See* Holy Spirit
spiritual direction, 101, 168
Stout, Jeffrey, 11–12, 200
Stowers, Stanley, 19
Stringfellow, Thornton, 173–177
suffering, 21, 34, 36, 38–39, 41, 48, 52, 57,
    61, 65, 70, 75, 78–79, 88, 91, 95–96, 100,
    102–105, 143, 146–148, 150–151, 155–156,
    161, 163, 197
syllabus, xvii–xviii, 3–5, 194, 203–211
Symeon the Stylite, 182
Syriac Christianity, 117, 156, 163,
    181–183

Tamar, 169
Tanner, Kathryn, 13, 49–50, 53, 128,
    131
Teresa of Àvila, 100, 168, 171
theology (as a discipline), xviii, 3, 9, 11–12,
    50–51, 67, 71, 83, 102, 103, 144, 173, 184,
    186, 195–201
Thomas Aquinas, 47, 128, 176–177,
    198–199
Tillich, Hannah, 185
Tillich, Paul, xviii, 12, 184–187
Toledo, Synod of, 116–117
Trible, Phyllis, 149–151
trickster figure, 83, 85

Trinity, xv, 13, 26, 28, 32, 33–34, 38, 48,
    52, 53, 65, 74, 75, 78, 92, 100, 103, 105,
    109–119, 123–124, 161–164, 170, 173, 177
tropos hyparxeos, 51

Unitarian, 5
universalism, 37, 95, 98

Vatican II, 9, 18
victim, 61, 69–70, 80, 83, 149–151, 155–160
victor/victory, 38, 61, 84, 89, 138–139, 150
virgin birth, 32, 35
Vult, Quicunque, 110

wedding analogy for the Trinity, 113–114,
    162–164, 169
Westminster Confession, 23, 28–29
what. *See* natures (of Christ)
who. *See* Person (of Christ)
wife of Uriah. *See* Bathsheba
Winner, Lauren, 192
witness, 17, 20–21, 28, 34, 40, 84, 97,
    113–114, 123, 161, 171, 173, 178
Wittgenstein, Ludwig, 12
Word (as a name for Jesus), xv, 35–36,
    46–53, 59–60, 97, 100, 118, 173, 177–178,
    188. *See also* Logos
Wyschogrod, Michael, 17–21, 23, 24, 26,
    33, 38, 99, 119

Yeago, David, 76, 78, 123, 161

zero, 41, 144–145

Scripture Index

Genesis   47, 144
1:2   111
1:26–28   137
1:29   193
3:19   92
18   114
38   169

Exodus   138–139
8:32   138
15:21   139
33:20–23   146

Leviticus   157
19:18   138, 176

Joshua
2–6   169

Judges
19   149–151

Ruth
1:16–17   169
3:1–5   169
4:17   169

2 Samuel
11   170

Psalms   66, 101
22:1   164
22:27   164
23:5   114, 147, 162
34:8   66, 193
82:6   59
110:3   117
137:9   176

Proverbs
8:22   35

Song of Songs/Solomon/
Canticles   66–67
8:6   53, 59, 100, 107, 161–162

Isaiah
11:6   159
53:5   78

Amos
4:11   24

Zechariah
3:2   24

Matthew
1:6   168, 170
5:23–24   157
5:24   157
7:12   138
8:14–17   78
19:30   192
22:2   114
22:39   176
24:34   175
25:40   151
26:27–29   147
26:39   147
26:42   147
27:46   162
28:19   118

Mark
1:1–11   50
7:28   188
10:35   147

Mark (*continued*)

10:37–38	147
10:45	147
12:31	176
14:26–42	149
14:41	149
15:17	188

Luke

1:34	170
2:49	189
6:31	138
7:12–17	189
10:27	176
16:19–31	188–189
22:19	162
22:30	193
22:44	189
23:53	188
24:1–12	189

John 144

1:1–4	27, 35, 36, 47, 50, 111, 173, 177
1:6–8	173, 178
3:17	98
3:18	117
6:53	68
9:6	48
10:1	5
14:2	189
15:13	71, 149–150
15:26	114
18:11	147
19:2	188
19:40	188
20:28	47

Acts

2:24	189
4:12	159
15:8	114

Romans

1:13	19
3:25	69
8:11	100, 113, 115, 164
8:11–29	115
8:15	115
8:16	114
8:22–27	117
8:23	115
8:26	115
8:28	138
9:1	114
9:3	100
9:3–5	19
9:13	23
10:1–2	19
11:13	19
11:23	19
11:23–24	25
11:28	19
11:31	19
11:33	27
15:15	19
16:4	19

1 Corinthians

10:16	147

Galatians

4:6	115
4:7	115

Ephesians

1:4	23
4:9	96, 189
6:5	175

Colossians

3:22	175

1 Thessalonians
    4:16–17   175

2 Thessalonians
    3:6–12   175

1 Timothy
    2:4   98

Hebrews
    2:4   114
    10:15   114

1 Peter
    4:6   96–97, 189

2 Peter
    1:4   59

1 John
    5:7   114

Revelation   144
    1:14–15   192